Concepts in geography
Analytical human geography

Concepts in geography

Concepts in geography

2 Analytical human geography

collection and interpretation of some recent work

edited by **P J Ambrose** Lecturer in Geography, University of Sussex

Longman

Longman Group Limited
London
Associated companies, branches and representatives throughout the world

© *Longman Group Ltd (formerly Longmans, Green & Co Ltd) 1969*

First published 1969
Third impression 1972
ISBN 0 582 31014 8

Made and printed in Great Britain by
William Clowes & Sons, Limited, London, Beccles and Colchester

Contents

To my students

In grateful recognition that the flow of wisdom has not been one way

'... my own experience suggests that students are often more ready to receive new ideas than we are ready to teach them ...'

Peter Haggett, *Frontiers in Geographical Teaching* (p. 114)

Author's acknowledgements

The production of this book has been dependent upon advice, stimulation and help from a number of people and institutions. Peter Haggett, still a person but in some danger of becoming an institution, gave early encouragement. To John Everson, Brian Fitzgerald, Mike Archer, Rex Walford and Tony Crisp, members of a fierce and successful 'ginger group' dedicated to the reform of geographical work in schools, the author respectfully acknowledges his debt for various helpful discussions. Howard Andrews of the University of Sussex and Bernard Thompson of the Brighton College of Education were both kind enough to read certain sections and offer comments. A number of teachers, including Margaret Caistor, Tom Aubrey and Chris Colthurst, gave invaluable help and criticism on Section 1.

Finally the author wishes to thank his wife Elizabeth for her comments as a potential user of the book, for her services as typist, proof reader and production assistant, and for much else besides.

Acknowledgements

We are grateful to the following for permission to reproduce copyright material. The Association of American Geographers for extracts from their Annals 'Man Against His Environment: A Game Theoretic Framework' by P. Gould, Vol. 53, 1963, 'Exceptionalism in Geography' by F. Schaefer, Vol. 43, 1953, author for 'The Quantitative Revolution and Theoretical Geography' by Ian Burton from *The Canadian Geographer* volume 7; author and *The Journal of the American Institute of Planners* for 'An Historical Review of the Gravity and Potential Concepts of Human Interaction' by Gerald A. P. Carrothers, Volume XXII, No. 2, Spring 1956; authors and *Tijdschrift voor Economische en Sociale Geografie* for 'Theory, Science and Geography' by W. K. D. Davies, from T.E.S.G. 1966, and 'A Quantitative Expression of the Pattern of Urban Settlements in Selected Areas of the United States' by L. J. King, from T.E.S.G. 1962; *Economic Geography* for 'The Functional bases of the Central Place Hierarchy' by B. J. L. Berry and W. L. Garrison from Vol. 34, No. 2, and 'The Determination of the Location of Retail Activities with the use of a Map Transformation' by A. Getis from Vol. 39, No. 1; author and American Marketing Association for 'Defining and Estimating a Trading Area' by David L. Huff from *Journal of Marketing*; New York University Institute of Retail Management for 'New Concept: Subjective Distance' by D. L. Thompson (1963) from *Journal of Retailing* 39, 1–6; author and The American Geographical Society of New York for 'The Negro Ghetto: Problems and Alternatives' by Richard L. Morrill from *Geographical Review*, Vol. 55, 1965; author for 'Perception of the Drought Hazard on the Great Plains' by T. F. Saarinen, Dept. of Geography, University of Chicago (1966); author for 'A Theory of Location for Cities' by Edward L. Ullman from *American Journal of Sociology*, Vol. 46, *Geography as Spatial Interaction*: *Studies in Regional Development, Cities and Transportation*, University of Washington Press, Seattle 1969; University of Pennsylvania for 'Connectivity of the Inter-State Highway System' by W. L. Garrison (1960) from *Papers and Proceedings of the Regional Science Association*, Vol. 6 (slightly adapted).

Preface

'... human geography is entering a most exciting phase ... It is of vital importance in this field as in others that the thread linking research, university teaching and school teaching, a thread already pulled taut, should not be allowed to part.'

Peter Haggett, *Frontiers in Geographical Teaching* (p. 115)

This book is about human geography and seeks to explain some of the striking changes that have occurred in the discipline in the past two decades. When academic subjects go through a period of rapid development, as they all do (or should), problems of communication and evaluation arise. Those who were trained before the trends were reflected in their university or college course and those who have not yet begun any higher education are both placed in a difficult position. The facilities for refresher courses for teachers are generally less than adequate, while work at the frontiers of research is not represented in journals taken by schools. In human geography an additional problem arises in the idiom used by much recent work. The use of mathematical symbols tends to give an impression, not borne out by the facts, that a great deal of advanced mathematics is involved. Those who teach and learn in school are therefore partly cut off from interesting developments and their horizons are limited, quite reasonably, by the available textbooks and the crushing need to cover the existing syllabus. Change in what is taught is largely dependent on change in the content of the syllabus and that in turn is dependent on the availability of textbooks which reflect new trends at an appropriate level. Having said this there is little further need to spell out the aim of this book.

The title

Some justification should be offered for the title. In Section 1 I have ventured to question the value of *regional description* as a framework for study and have suggested that a much better framework might exist in a form of study best summed up in the phrase *spatial analysis*. The words 'description' and 'analysis', as a short survey of reputable dictionaries will show, do have different meanings. To describe something is to represent it, to depict it, to conjure it up. Analysis involves the resolution of some complex phenomenon into its essential components so that one can see how it 'works'. The description of a work of art, perhaps a piece of music or a painting, can be undertaken by anyone who feels moved by it; its analysis is a more penetrating and demanding process which requires some specialist expertise on the part of the analyst. The analogy with human geography, while not exact, is near enough. Description of an area can be undertaken with some success by anyone who can write well, be he geographer, novelist or journalist. The analysis of the functioning of that area demands more specialised skills. The material contained in this book provides an introduction to some of these skills so that analytical as well as descriptive work can be carried out.

There are other adjectives apart from 'analytical' which partly sum up the type of work contained in this book. 'Locational' might have been acceptable but it has been pre-empted by Peter Haggett.[1] 'Theoretical' would have given a very reasonable idea of the new orientation. A great deal of recent work has been directed towards the building up of a body of theory relating to geographical analysis in view of the discipline's conspicuous lack of this vital commodity in the past. But such a title might also have given the misleading impression that work of the sort contained in this book is not applicable to practical problem solving. In any case the word has been used in the title of a very original and stimulating book by Bunge.[2] 'Statistical' has also been used in at least one recent title,[3] and again the emphasis seems slightly wrong. Although statistical techniques are invaluable tools, they are complementary to, not a substitute for, original thought and the development of new theory. 'Mathematical' would be completely misleading. While it is accepted that most of the papers are demanding in other ways, comprehension of them does not depend upon any great mathematical expertise. Only two papers, those by Garrison and Gould, use any mathematical techniques beyond calculating a square root or raising a value to a power. A third paper, that by Berry and Garrison, uses the statistical technique of regression analysis. In these three cases the central principles of the paper can be appreciated even if the details of the techniques are not fully understood.

Two other possible titles suggested themselves. 'Quantitative Human Geography' would have conveyed the idea that a mixture, albeit weak, of statistics and mathematics was involved but a similar title has been used in a recent collection of work by Garrison and Marble.[4] The best title to sum up the orientation of the work would perhaps have been 'Scientific Human Geography'. This would have given the correct idea that observation, measurement, theory building, experimentation and quantitative testing were all involved. It would also have led to hopeless confusion on the part of many people who firmly believe that physical geography is 'science' and human geography is 'arts', and what on earth can this title mean? In deference to them, and out of consideration for bolder authors who may wish subsequently to adopt it, this rather intriguing title has been left unused.

The selection of material

The material for inclusion has been chosen with several criteria in mind. Primarily, each extract or paper had to be a clear example of some principle, or set of principles, concerning the measurement or explanation of spatial distributions. Since the aim was to keep to reasonably simple work, several rather early papers have been included. Ullman's paper on Central Place Theory, for example, has been followed by a great deal of more advanced literature. But since it was the first important statement of the theory in English and was designed to explain the main ideas to those not familiar with them, it seemed suitable for the purposes of this book.

Another important consideration guiding the selection of material has been the need to complement material which is already relatively easily accessible. This particular group of papers was chosen because in most cases they would otherwise be very difficult for students or teachers to obtain. This consideration has led to the exclusion of several excellent but more readily accessible pieces of work. Reference to some of this related reading has been made at the end of each section.

Anyone attempting a collection of this sort, unless he is particularly widely read, is bound to reflect his research interests in his choice of papers. It will not take much detective work to identify the editor's preoccupation with research into service centre analysis and shopping activity. No apology is attempted for this bias in the subject matter. The main criterion adopted has been set out above; that each paper should contain important principles which can be used to analyse movement patterns and distributional patterns. These principles relate to many types of human activity. The fact that three or four of the papers included relate specifically to service activity is of little consequence.

Even more obvious is the North American flavour of the book. Apart from the two papers from a Dutch journal, all the material comes from North American publications (although the nationalities of the authors are rather more diverse). Partly this is due to the conscious attempt to include material not easily available in Britain. More fundamentally it reflects the extent to which human geographers in North American departments have led the way in the development and use of new analytical concepts. British, New Zealand and Swedish geographers have been closely involved in this process but the backing for research, both in terms of money and facilities, has been more easily obtained in the

United States and Canada than elsewhere. Only the most chauvinistic would take exception to this situation. Knowledge is, or should be, a commodity that knows no frontier except the partial frontier erected by language. At one time various European countries led the field in the development of new ideas and techniques in human geography. At present the big North American departments have taken over. Soon perhaps the pendulum will swing back. The academic geographer will accept this situation philosophically and will continue to examine interesting ideas no matter what their source, and try to build upon them. Fortunately ideas emanating from the other side of the Atlantic are not subject to the language barrier to any great extent, although some of the syntax used by American authors and the split infinitives scattered liberally around may cause raised eyebrows.

The plan and content of the book

The book is designed in a rather unusual fashion. The aim of the introductory essay is to set the collection of papers in context. The changes in *method and approach* which the papers embody are contrasted to the much less significant changes that have occurred in the *subject matter* of geographical study. The regional and systematic approaches are compared and emphasis is placed on the emerging idea of *human geography as the study of a dynamic spatial system*.

The introductory notes to each section form an integral part of the book and try to achieve a number of ends. They are designed partly to précis the papers that follow (so that the reader gains some idea of what to expect), partly to simplify difficult concepts or language, partly to evaluate and comment on the papers and partly to relate them to each other and to other work in the field of human geography. These aims constitute jointly an ambitious undertaking and it would not be surprising if in some cases there remained a considerable gap between the aims and the achievement. Each section includes a list of further reading much of it more advanced than the material contained in this book. Some sections also include suggestions concerning practical work or experiments that might be carried out to illustrate some of the principles embodied in the papers. The concluding section attempts to draw the various papers together by emphasising their common concern with the idea of locational analysis and tries to identify some key concepts which might assist in carrying out this type of analysis at all levels of enquiry.

The book is arranged in what is hoped is some kind of logical order in that it proceeds from general methodology to the measurement of simple elements, to more complex theories of settlement and then to problems of perception, decision and prediction. This does not mean that it must necessarily be read in this order. If for example the subject matter of Section 4 is specially relevant for some purpose, understanding of this section will not be seriously hampered if Section 3 has not been read. In this sense each section stands alone, although it is felt that comprehension of the papers as a whole will be helped by a consideration of the methodological material in Sections 1 and 2. To some extent, therefore, the book may be regarded as a work of reference, though the author believes, perhaps over-fondly, that a forward looking introductory human geography course at school or university level could be constructed on the basis of the material suggested.

One final comment to be made on the book is that it is very much a product both of the time and of the place in which it was written. The trends towards the use of quantification, the concern with theories and principles, the preoccupation with process and prediction, have all been evident long enough now in research activity for some reflection of this work to be needed at other levels of teaching and learning. The discipline of human geography is not changing in a vacuum. Most of the other social sciences that deal with the common subject matter of man and his behaviour in the world are undergoing similar changes. The trends represented in this book, which are equally evident in the physical side of the subject, should not be interpreted as peculiar to geography, nor are they a passing fancy. In the estimation of many professional geographers these studies represent a solid step forward in both the technical equipment and the intellectual integrity of the discipline and as such they now need to be made available for non-university geographers to read and evaluate.

The book is also a product of its immediate intellectual environment. The author is fortunate enough to teach in a university where it is quite impossible to take a narrow unidisciplinary view of anything. Frequently, in every sort of interdisciplinary situation, students and faculty are engaged in a process of explaining the viewpoint of their subject and considering the particular expertise they can bring to bear on common problems. This process ensures that aims and philosophies are thought out and methods are compared. While this constitutes a demanding environment in which to teach and learn, it also banishes any tendency to sit back in a self-satisfied or self-centred way or to be content with the methods of the past. The benefit to be gained from dialogue with related sciences is particularly valuable to a geographer because the phenomena he is trying to explain are the results of so complex a series of factors and events. Dialogue also ensures that the geographer becomes certain in his own mind of the aims and methods which organise his discipline and which make him a geographer rather than, say, a sociologist or a social anthropologist. It was partly to clarify these aims and methods that this book was written.

The University of Sussex   P.A.
July 1968

Notes and references

[1] HAGGETT, P. *Locational Analysis in Human Geography*, Arnold, 1965. A brilliant review of the literature of analytical human geography and an essential source for any advanced work in the subject.

[2] BUNGE, W. *Theoretical Geography*, rev. edn., C. W. K. Gleerup, Lund, Sweden, 1966.

[3] BERRY, B. J. L., and MARBLE, D. F. *Spatial Analysis: a Reader in Statistical Geography*, Prentice-Hall, 1968.

[4] GARRISON, W. L., and MARBLE, D. F. *Quantitative Geography*, Northwestern University, Illinois, 1967, 2 vols.

N.B. References 3 and 4 are collections of recent advanced research work. They are probably not suitable for work below undergraduate level.

1 The nature of recent developments in human geography

The subject matter of human geography

Geography is a very old discipline. The urge to make a systematic study of some area of the earth's surface is prompted not only by pure curiosity but also by expediency, since normally the material return one can gain from the environment depends upon one's knowledge and understanding of it. Geography is widely taught as a subject in schools, where most people either like it very much or are bored by it, and everybody understands in a general sort of way what it is about. This point is worth bearing in mind because when it happens that professional exponents of a seemingly easily understood subject begin to produce work in a new and uncomfortable idiom the shock is greater than if the subject were known to be obscure and technical. Recent developments at research level in geography, and to an increasing extent in the structure of university courses, have undoubtedly caused difficulties of comprehension both to those embarking upon further education in the subject and to teachers who were trained before recent trends became so widely accepted. Since the changes that are occurring are more than simply a matter of idiom, this essay will seek to examine the underlying dissatisfactions that have led to the development of new and more precise techniques of analysis and to the adoption of concepts and modes of enquiry new to geographers.

So far as the subject matter of geographical enquiry is concerned little has changed, although changes of emphasis have taken place and these will be discussed later. The geographer's field of interest, the raw material for his analyses, is enormous but relatively easily defined. It is the features, both natural and manmade, that cover the earth's surface. In addition to these natural phenomena and artifacts in themselves, the geographer is interested in the distribution patterns of both, and in the interaction of man with this spatial environment as he seeks to increase his return from terrestrial space and resources. This interaction tends to modify the spatial distribution of population and artifacts which is, of course, to a large extent dependent upon the spatial distribution of certain resources useful to man (for example, coal).

Geographers vary considerably in their interests. Some are more concerned with the natural phenomena and some with the human artifacts, while some tend to focus their attention on the man/land interactions and stress the idea of geography as 'human ecology'. But implicit in all these branches of the subject is a concern with location and spatial patterns, and a curiosity about the way in which the patterns came to be as they are. Recent developments have tended to focus attention squarely on the locational and spatial patterning aspects of the discipline. This emphasis seems to add to, rather than detract from, the 'geographical' nature of the work since it could be argued that there is no more essentially geographical activity than explaining a spatial distribution.

The changes in subject matter emphasis referred to previously result more from changes in the real world situation than in the analytical methods of geographers. In this sense they are natural rather than contrived changes. Increasingly, man is becoming urbanised. In the case of England and Wales, the move from country to town has been remarkably rapid. In 1801 only 16·94 per cent of the population lived in towns of over 20,000 inhabitants. By 1891 the proportion was 53·58 per cent. In that year the Census officially classified 72·05 per cent of the population as 'urban' and by 1911 this proportion was 80·10 per cent. In 1961 the urban proportion seemed to be virtually unchanged but the percentage of people working in towns had no doubt increased.[1] In such highly urbanised countries the daily social and economic activities of most people, and the movement patterns these form, are constrained and influenced more by the distribution of jobs, schools, shops and bus routes than of such phenomena as soil types, the presence of water, and natural routeways. In short, the 'environment' to which the majority of people in such countries are reacting, the 'land' of the man/land interaction, is not natural but has been built by man himself. This development is of fundamental importance, particularly to the human geographer since, by definition, his prime concern is with man. Thus the term 'environment', if it is to mean something that gives a partial explanation of man's observed spatial behaviour, needs to be redefined in much broader terms. It should be taken to mean not only the natural environment but also the whole complex of manmade features which are the result of past man/land interaction, and which is often referred to as the 'built environment'.

But the concept of 'environment' is wider even than this. For the distribution and location of such things as towns and specific points within towns, and the nature of physical aspects of the environment such as climate, exist in both an objective and a subjective sense. We can describe locations objectively with maps drawn to some mileage distance scale and we can characterise climate in terms of precise temperature and rainfall data. But most people are not familiar with the exact details of these maps or data. They have a 'feeling' for the relative nearness of two equally distant points. One may seem much nearer because it is either cheaper or more desirable to go there or because one grew up there. Similarly our idea of the climate of an infrequently visited place is more likely to be conditioned by the weather we experienced when we were there, or by some other generalised picture, than by the objective climatic data. In vain will Mancunians point to their fairly average annual rainfall figures; this will do little to affect the generally held belief that it is always raining in Manchester. It is pointless to talk of a 'right' or 'wrong' conception of the environment in these cases. The essential thing to establish is that there are very real differences between the subjective and the objective environments. It follows that if, as geographers, we are seeking for explanations of human behaviour in terms of an environment then our main interest is in the subjective rather than the objective one. This realisation will tend to reduce our dependence upon traditionally geographical, and rather dreary, tools such as tables of rainfall data and maps expressing distances in terms of miles. Both are, of course, essential for reference purposes but both can be highly misleading. For example it could be argued that an objective linear unit of distance such as the mile has little to commend it when analysing human movement patterns since, unless we are walking or cycling, we normally measure distance to an objective in terms of cost, time or ease of access. Even walking distances, for example in hilly country, are often measured in hours and minutes. Similarly, when considering whether or not to make a journey to a certain shop in a city centre it is the time, the inconvenience, or the cost of the door to door journey, that is important, not the distance in miles. In fact a large number of suburban and peripheral shopping centres have grown up in North America partly because in 'real' terms, as opposed to mileage terms, the centre is one of the least accessible areas of the city.

An acceptance of the vital significance of the subjectively conceived environment will lead us towards a closer interest in the ways in which man's spatial behaviour is influenced by his cultural background and by his social, or economic situation. It inevitably follows that at the undergraduate and research level we have much to gain by a closer liaison with certain neighbouring disciplines such as social psychology and social anthropology, since these examine questions of perception and the cultural traits of different societies and groups. Given the obvious desirability that the human geographer has a clear idea of the aims and basic concepts of both economics and sociology, and that time is a scarce resource, it is not surprising that few professional geographers are able to span both the human and physical aspects of the discipline in any depth. One may conclude that the human geographer's interest in purely physical aspects of the discipline may decrease as non-physical environmental phenomena become increasingly important in influencing man and as, in any case, the realisation grows that man is acting in a subjective not an objective environment. This is not to say that we have reached a stage where a comprehension of the physical landscape, and the processes affecting it, are unimportant to a human geographer. Even in the most heavily built-up areas the configuration of slopes, aspect, drainage and other physical factors are likely to be important in the explanation of the growth and pattern of activities.

In the light of this discussion of the subject matter studied by geographers it is a simple matter to attempt a statement of the aims of the discipline. These are to acquire a specialist understanding of the distribution of terrestrial phenomena, whether natural or manmade, and of the processes by which these distributions have occurred and are changing. Furthermore we may well wish to use this specialist knowledge either to increase our returns from the natural environment or to decide upon a good location for some addition to the built environment, such as a new town or transport link. It is worth pointing out here that while, within the discipline, intellectual satisfaction may well result from a good explanation of something, our subject will stand or fall ultimately by the extent to which geographers are instrumental in increasing returns from the environment or in planning the rational distribution of new artifacts. This point will be discussed more fully later.

Alternative methods of study

The subject matter outlined above is clearly enormous and extremely varied in nature. Practitioners in other disciplines, noting our apparent concern with everything that appears on the landscape whether moving or not, have often been led to believe that geography is a totally formless affair, lacking in penetrating analysis and with no clearly defined purpose. How, it might be asked, can one discipline really make any very satisfying analysis of such diverse phenomena as urban growth, frontier settlement, journeys to work, and crop choice? Yet all these concern man's interaction with the environment and his use of space so that, using the definitions set out above, they are all objects of geographical enquiry.

One answer to this question is that these various phenomena and processes may be treated in several very different ways. It will be profitable to spend a little time on a consideration of these alternative approaches. It is a common sense principle to pause sometimes to examine our methodological approach to problems as well as the problems themselves. More specifically, in relation to the subject matter of this book, recent trends in human geography have been accompanied by a swing of interest away from regional work. It is hoped that the reasons for this will become clearer as certain characteristics of the regional approach are considered.

1. Regional description

Regional descriptions have been produced since Caesar wrote his terse and vivid accounts of the people and lands in which he campaigned, and probably for long before that. Works coming under this heading vary from travelogues, which appeal to the general reader and do not pretend to be contributions to science, to academically respectable and exhaustive texts written by professional geographers. The latter may well give the impression that the geographer has begun with one basic aim: to set out the observable geographical characteristics of a region or country. This is normally done by means of maps, tables and written descriptions which all relate to the chosen study area. Work of this sort is what non-geographers generally understand by 'geography', no doubt partly because it formed the basis of their geographical training at school. Another contributory factor to this partial misapprehension is that under most library classification systems, travelogues, guide books and regional descriptions tend to dominate the geographical shelves which they share with a sprinkling of more recent analytical works. This can lead to the browsing layman being startled by pages of mathematical equations when all he wanted was a tourist guide to Chicago.

As a method of serious scientific analysis, and as a framework for college or university work, the value of the purely regional approach can be seriously questioned. Many studies of this type may be characterised as lengthy, undemanding intellectually, and dreary to varying degrees if read straight through. A common format is to begin with the geological structure of the area, proceed through the details of the landforms, soils and climate, examine the historical evolution of settlement, the present patterns of occupance and end, sometimes rather lamely, with chapters on transport, urban areas and industry. This format deals, inevitably, superficially, with an enormous range of phenomena having in common only the fact of location within the prescribed area. When, in studying a continent for example, this same system or format is used for half a dozen countries in turn (and regional courses are, in the author's experience, frequently organised in this fashion) the level of interest, both of teacher and taught, tends to fall off dramatically. There may be a number of reasons for this.

First, the student has no sense of progression; no feeling that he is passing from easier to more difficult and thought provoking concepts. The 'regional method' exists, simple and undemanding. All that need be done is to apply it to whatever region is specified by the syllabus. Thus it is not new concepts that are discovered; only new facts. It may be objected that historians have methods, analogous in their simplicity, by which they examine first one period then another. Why should geographers complain at applying a constant method of examination to different regions? One answer is that history, almost by definition, does give a feeling of progression. The phenomena studied, whether social, political or economic, evolve over time and seemingly become more complex in response to the experience of the past and to technological advance. In short (and I hope this gives no offence to historians) the methods may be relatively static but the material studied is essentially dynamic since it develops in the time dimension. By contrast, too much of regional geography is concerned with applying a relatively static method to differences occurring in the spatial dimension and with only limited emphasis on evolutionary aspects.

The second objection is related to this idea of evolution. Too often descriptive regional geography is concerned with the detailed characterisation of the country or region as it exists today. Thus a cross-section through time is attempted almost as if the phenomena presented were an end product. Since regional textbooks are usually expensive to buy and must be kept in use for long periods, the cross-section they represent soon becomes out of date. The other difficulty when trying to represent an end product is that, at least as far as human development or the physical landscape is concerned, such a thing simply does not exist. Everything is in a state of evolution. By using a method which inevitably emphasises a static picture, attention is drawn away from the reality of the situation. This reality is that, both in human and physical geography, the essential things to understand are the processes at work, the dynamics of the situation. Once we can explain how a crop pattern or an urban growth pattern came into existence in the recent past, we have a very clear idea not only of why it exists as it does but also of how it might change in the near future. This introduces a key idea, the idea of prediction, which will be further developed later.

Before proceeding it should be made clear that although the traditional bulky regional textbook has been criticised from a number of standpoints, its value as a work of reference is also recognised. It is often a useful compendium of information on the growth of settlement of an area and on the distribution of crops, farming types, settlement types and other geographical phenomena within it. Like a land use map, it has normally been carefully compiled from personal work in the region by an experienced geographer and it may well be excellently illustrated. Despite this it is maintained that at college and university level, and perhaps before, works of this sort should be adjuncts to the main lines of geographical enquiry and not central to them. In other words, a wide knowledge of the facts of the physical and human landscape of a region should not be an end in itself. The central aim should be to acquire a knowledge of the principles and processes governing the spatial distribution of the phenomena observed. To study these principles and processes, clearly, reference must be made to some regional examples, and here the traditional textbook (supplemented with other sources of data such as census publications and yearbooks) plays an important rôle. But this rôle should be seen as illustrative of principles; the principles should not come a poor second to a close and often boring concern with the minutiae of the landscape phenomena in a region.

It is, of course, not legitimate to criticise one method of arranging material, of teaching and learning, unless constructive suggestions are made about alternative methods. The 'regional approach' is well established both in Advanced Level syllabuses (to the extent that sometimes it seems that 'regional' is regarded as synonymous with 'human' as a course description) and in degree course structures. If the usefulness of so sacred a cow is to be questioned, to what alternative species might one turn? One alternative species has been developing and multiplying fast during the past ten or fifteen years. Its progenitors seem to be not in *regional* but in *systematic* geography, that is, in a method of study that sets out to understand and explain the workings of certain processes, which themselves give rise to regional characteristics. These processes may concern such disparate phenomena as depressions, urban growth, the development of transport networks, the spread of ideas, or slope formation. And since phenomena of this sort tend to occur all over the world, examples are taken from a wide variety of regions in order to increase understanding of the processes at work.

One can discern fairly clearly some of the main features of the new species. Berry[2] has characterised the beast as 'the quantitative bogeyman'. The increased use of quantitative methods is certainly one aspect of the new approach but there are others of at least equal importance. Perhaps a more significant feature is that an observed distribution pattern, for example a settlement map, is often the starting point for analysis rather than the end product as has frequently been the case in the past. Much of the new work has tended to choose a particular distribution, let us say the distribution of people over retirement age, and to analyse the factors that have brought it about. No attempt is made to focus attention on a widely varied range of features which have in common simply the fact that they are located within a prescribed area. Instead attention is focused on certain spatial regularities and patterns which, because they reflect fundamental aspects of human behaviour such as the desire to better oneself by migrating, to maximise returns from agriculture, or to live with people of one's own status or religion, can occur virtually anywhere in the world. And if, to further our analyses of the land use patterns created by these desires, we are led to draw on examples from all over the world there is little point in organising our courses and material regionally. Because our interest in these aspects of behaviour stems primarily from the land use patterns they produce, and because it is often the observed land use pattern that is the starting point of the geographer's enquiry, it seems reasonable to categorise this sort of work under the collective term 'spatial analysis'.[3] It is this approach which is suggested as an alternative to the regional method.

2. Spatial analysis

At least as far as the human side of the discipline is concerned, spatial analysis is now emerging as the focal point and the organising framework for much geographical research. The central concern here is to disentangle the basic regularities that occur in urban and rural land use patterns, to analyse the processes that bring these patterns about and to use the knowledge gained in this way to predict their future development. The patterns can relate to any phenomena traditionally studied by geographers: crops, routes, settlements, industry, ethnic groups, and many others. Three key ideas emerge here, *spatial pattern regularity*, *process analysis* and *prediction*, and each of these will be considered more fully.

There is nothing new in the idea of recognising *spatial pattern regularity*. For many years geographers have learned that villages grew up along spring lines, that towns grew up in gaps, that the chalk hills are covered in sheep and that cities have concentric rings of different morphological and ethnic types. Making generalisations about apparently repeating spatial patterns is, of course, a useful activity. But many of the generalisations about these regularities, including those above, are either drastic oversimplifications or just plain wrong, and should not be taught at any level. The dangers of unsubstantiated generalisation can be gauged by the present low esteem in which the idea of environmental determinism is held. The great intuitive leaps that the early determinists made as they generalised about the effects of climate and landforms on man's physique and socio-economic organisation have dealt this rather promising line of enquiry a series of blows from which it has not yet recovered. The moral is that we must look much more closely and carefully at the patterns and regularities that seem to exist. Nothing, or very little, is entirely random about such things as the choice of crops or the growth and spacing of towns. Truly random spatial patterns, those that we can think of no possible rules to explain, are extremely rare. One could instance the pattern made by a skyful of stars on a clear night as being random in this sense. This is because it is the two-dimensional representation of a three-dimensional reality. In this situation it is presumably just as likely for a group of bright stars to appear close together as for a group of dull stars. We group the bright stars together into constellations and give them fanciful names but we do not understand the ways in which change will occur in the pattern. This is because it is likely that no functional relationship exists between the stars which, to us, form a group.

By contrast the patterns made by, for example, the distribution of towns above a certain size in Britain is not random. This is because these towns are functionally related to each other, to the world outside Britain, and to the lesser towns, villages and open country that surround each of them. Certain of these functional relationships are easy to understand (for example, people go from villages to towns to buy new clothes) and some are much more complicated (for example, a range of economic considerations cause large industrial complexes to grow up at certain locations). If we understand sufficient of the principles in operation, we see that regularities exist in the location of large towns. For example they tend to be located on estuaries, in areas of dense rural population, or near mineral resources. Regularities exist not only in the spacing of settlements but also in many other spatial (and temporal) patterns. The first tasks of the geographer are to look for these patterns, to examine them closely to see whether they are well marked, and to formulate suggestions, or hypotheses, to explain them. The testing, refinement or abandonment of these hypotheses is an obvious next step but one which must often be left to the academic researcher (or to more junior researchers on school field courses).

The formulation of hypotheses to explain observed spatial patterns inevitably leads us to a consideration of the second of the key ideas outlined earlier, the idea of *process analysis*. As has been previously made clear, the geographical phenomena we observe and measure are in a constant state of change. It may be helpful to categorise these phenomena into three reasonably separate groups; places, fields and routes. Places (towns, etc.) may be envisaged as small areas (or conceptually, points) of high density human activity in such spheres as industry, commerce, political administration and so on. Fields, in this context, are the larger areas of lower density human activity in a much more limited range of spheres (farming, recreation, etc.). Clearly, essential functional inter-relationships occur between the places and the fields. These take the form of flows of goods, people, money, and less tangible things like ideas, social values and inventions. These flows take place along the routes that link not only place and field but also place and place. When spatial phenomena are looked at in this way, it is evident that the key dynamism in the system made up of places, fields and routes is the flows that occur. Because of these flows routes develop or decline, cities evolve, land uses change, and areas undergo social or economic transformation. The flows themselves actually define the specific field/place relationships because a town's hinterland is accepted as being that area having a strong functional relationship with it. And the best index of the strength of a functional relationship between two locations is the amount of flow taking place between them.

This concept of a *spatial system* is of central importance. The analogy is often made with a domestic water system consisting of a tank, pipes and water. Despite its obvious shortcomings this analogy is useful since it contains the idea that an event in any one of the elements (say, a break in a pipe) inevitably affects all the other elements. The same is true of the geographer's spatial system. For example, the addition of a factory with a hundred jobs to a town may bring in three hundred people directly, may produce a few hundred extra jobs in shops, schools and other services, may entail new road schemes and may affect the pattern of farming around the town. The vital difference between the two cases is that in the water system the water is inanimate and has no power to bring about change in the system (if long-term changes due to corrosion are ignored). By contrast, the geographical space system has been built up and defined by past and present flows of people, goods, and so on. It changes constantly in response to human decisions; individual or collective, forced or voluntary, conscious or unconscious. It follows that if we want to achieve a satisfying and penetrating understanding of the geographical phenomena that surround us we must focus our attention firmly on the processes that work to produce flows and we must consider the decision making agencies that bring them about. These agencies include departments of central government, local planning authorities, individual industrialists and developers and, on a smaller but still important scale, ordinary individuals who choose a place to live, to work, to play and to shop in accordance with their own understanding of what the environment offers them.

If the argument is accepted so far, it is a small step to accepting that some reorientation is required in the way geographers approach their task of explaining spatial distributions, whether in small-scale field surveys or in more formal research work. For example, a field survey is not an end in itself; an exercise to be carried out because geographers have always done fieldwork. A rural land use survey, a commonly carried out field exercise at all levels of study, should be based upon a previous evaluation of the main determinants of land use in the chosen area. These will include the recent trends in agricultural subsidies, the known physical characteristics of the area, its distance from large urban markets, and the local population density. Having discussed these, the group can go into the field knowing what to look for and with some theories about what to expect. The survey then becomes a type of experiment to test the validity of a set of previously thought out hypotheses. If statistical analysis of the results of the survey indicate that the hypotheses were not wholly correct, then one embarks upon the invaluable task of rethinking and refining them.

The alternative strategy is to carry out the survey with little prediscussion and then to try to account for the pattern. This lacks the stimulation of an experiment since one cannot be proved right or wrong. Perhaps partly for this reason, the explanation of the pattern is likely to be less systematically thought out than the theorising attempted in advance of the survey. In the same way, a field study of urban land use changes should be based on an examination of the workings of agencies which are actually bringing about city redevelopment. These agencies include estate agents, property developers, local planning authorities, and in important cases like central London, central government departments. Some understanding of the complex ways in which these agencies cooperate and conflict, and of the means by which land use decisions are finally made, is surely an essential prerequisite to any really penetrating study of urban areas. It is for this reason that the development of rôle-playing games as an aid to geography teaching at all levels is to be warmly welcomed.[4] Apart from the sheer enjoyment of playing the games, the student immediately becomes aware that changes in land use come about not in some mystical fashion but as the result of the interplay of conflicting interest groups.

It may well be objected that we are geographers, not politicians, agriculturalists, developers or city planners. Why should we concern ourselves with the history of planning legislation and with the finer points of decision-making processes relating to urban and rural land use? There are really two answers to this. One is that the finer points can safely be left to the professional practitioners in the process so long as we have some basic understanding of the principles and agencies involved. The other is that if we pay no attention to these important processes, which actually and literally change the face of our cities and countryside, we leave ourselves in a very unsatisfactory position. We shall be mapping and describing, in laborious detail, distributions which we conceive to be the end product of processes which we hardly conceive at all. This position is unacceptable both in its intellectual incompleteness and in the possibility that it will lead to the production of geography graduates with a limited will and ability to participate in the vitally important task of bringing about more efficient and rational land use patterns. It may also have given rise to the widespread (but even now mistaken) belief on the part of those outside the discipline that the only thing the geography graduate is fitted to do is to teach geography. Inbreeding, as in other contexts, is likely to lead to disaster. The best way for human geography as a discipline to avoid this charge is to look outwards. This means, first, becoming aware of the viewpoints, basic concepts and techniques of closely related social science disciplines and, second, recognising the central rôle played by decision making agencies in bringing about land use changes. Until our teaching structures and syllabuses, both at school and university, reflect these interdisciplinary interests we may be doing less than justice to our enormously varied subject material and failing in our supposed rôle as synthesisers.

The question of fieldwork has been considered at some length because it embodies an important methodological difference that has a wide implication in human geography. To observe before theorising leads not only to inefficient observation but also to uncertain conclusions because no specific idea has been identified and tested. To theorise before observing forces the observer to think through the processes that may be at work, focuses the attention on a manageable number of ideas and limits the observations to selected phenomena only. This seems to be not dissimilar to the difference between regional and spatial analysis approaches. In the regional method an attempt is made to observe and record everything, often with a very inadequate attempt at explanation. The spatial analysis method concentrates on the pattern made by a particular set of phenomena. The researcher will then theorise about the processes producing the pattern, make a prediction based on these theories and collect only the evidence necessary to test and refine his theories. If his predictions are not good he must think again about his appreciation of the processes so that all the time his attention will be on the functioning of the spatial system. The describer of a region can, if he likes, spend nearly all his time characterising observable phenomena and very little time analysing how they got there.

The idea of *prediction* constitutes the third key theme of the space analytical approach. Process analysis and prediction are inextricably linked in several ways and for several reasons. The study of any dynamic and continuing process cannot easily disregard the future. If we formulate a set of hypotheses to explain an observed occurrence (let us say rural to urban migration over the past ten years) we are naturally interested to know whether our ideas seem to be good ones. The best way to find this out is to look into the future and to predict, on the basis of the hypotheses, how much migration will take place over the next ten years. On a more immediately practical level a decision making agency, for example a firm of property developers considering investing some capital in building a new shopping centre, are interested to know how much business they are likely to do and so they will have to attempt some predictions. 'Interested' may be too weak a word here as the penalty for inaccurate prediction may be very costly. In fact if, in either of these two examples, the geographer by his expertise can contribute to better prediction he will be highly valued.

It is the incorporation of predictions of one sort or another in so much of modern analytical geography that marks it out as distinct from a great deal of what has gone before in the discipline. Many very challenging problems, methodological and substantive, are raised by this attempt to predict. In common with many other social scientists (but later than most) human geographers are grappling with these problems. The central problem is perhaps not 'Is man's collective action ever predictable?' since daily life would be impossible if it were not based on all sorts of instinctive predictions about how other people and institutions will behave. The operational question is 'Are we ever likely to know enough about the way people behave and interact in groups, and in the environment, to enable us to carry out valid predictive work rather than purely descriptive work?' Many social scientists, including human geographers, are showing implicitly in their research, and explicitly in their methodological statements, that they believe the answer to the second question to be 'Yes'. It should be borne in mind that prediction in this sense does not depend upon the accurate forecasting of the actions of every individual over a given future period. What is involved is the statement, within specified levels of probability, that a human group will tend to behave in a certain way given a stated choice of possible alternatives.

Prediction in human geography depends upon other preconditions apart from the assumption that some sort of predictability exists in human behaviour. There must be a willingness to turn the general knowledge already gained about some aspect of behaviour into specifically formulated and testable hypotheses. There must be a willingness to combine a number of hypotheses about this aspect into a *model* or simplification of reality (this will be discussed more fully in Section 6) and to test and refine this model. And in order to carry out work of this sort effectively there must be a willingness to use statistical techniques both to measure data and distributions and to test models against reality. These techniques will include not only the standard ones used by most other scientists[5] but also those being invented or used by geographers specifically to deal with spatial phenomena.[6] These are formidable pre-conditions but to accept them is to accept scientific methodology and it is likely that the geographical enquiries that are built on them will not be journalistic or descriptive but genuinely analytical and predictive.

We may now return to the question posed earlier. How can one discipline make legitimate claim to deal in any scientific manner with the whole range of phenomena on the earth's surface; surely the very breadth of this subject matter must lead to shallow examination and to inadequate explanations with little practical applicability? The geographer's answer to this is that all these phenomena have certain vital features in common; they all have location and they all form spatial patterns. In fact location and pattern are two of the fundamental attributes of any terrestrial phenomenon and it is the human geographer's task to study these fundamental aspects, to develop techniques to measure and analyse them and, by understanding the processes that bring them about, to make predictions about how they will change. This is a challenging task and one of great potential usefulness. The processes, as we have seen, will often be economic, social or political in nature. Thus to increase our understanding we shall have to develop our knowledge of the concepts and methods of one or more of the disciplines which examine them in a non-spatial way. This can most effectively be done by concentrating as early as possible on the systematic branches of the subject, social geography economic geography and so on, and by using regional examples in a primarily illustrative rôle. It is for these reasons that a systematic orientation, with the emphasis on process that this inevitably entails, seems much more likely than a regional approach to lead both to a more satisfying analysis of space and land use and to the production, in co-operation with other disciplines, of genuinely useful results.

The timing and rationale of recent trends

The modern development of interest in a more scientific methodology, with all that this implies in the way of theory building and careful measurement, may be dated roughly from the middle and late 1950s. Researchers in certain American universities (notably the University of Washington) and in Sweden (notably at Lund University) began to build upon a body of theoretical and empirical thinking which stemmed partly from the work of Christaller and other location analysts of the 1930s and 1940s. It is a relatively simple matter to outline the timing of the changes, but a much more complex one to account for them. Why has attention swung so obviously towards new methodologies and why are researchers writing and speaking in terms that are not only untraditional but also inconveniently difficult? The answer can perhaps be summed up in one word—dissatisfaction. Academic disciplines evolve constantly, partly because the natural world and society are themselves evolving. Indeed it could easily be argued that those which are not developing in some way are dead. A period of rapid evolution in a discipline occurs when a sizeable minority of people within it become dissatisfied either with its intellectual content, or with the value of its contribution to society, or with both. The intellectual restlessness that results is augmented when external advances in technology make available, comparatively suddenly, new aids to analysis. This may then lead to the splitting of disciplines (for example, barbers no longer undertake surgery) or, more rarely, to their merging (as for example in the growing discipline of urban planning).

It seems that the dissatisfaction in geography, both physical and human, has taken several forms. Too often the intellectual content has been undemanding. It has been argued earlier that the regional method contains little that is really challenging and the result is often boredom, the most stultifying and depressing type of dissatisfaction. Another source of disquiet has been the apparent lack of impact that the discipline has had in recent years on the world outside. This shows itself in many ways and it would be dishonest not to draw attention to some of them. For example, how often do geographers pronounce on the mass media about current land use planning issues or about developments in their subject? How frequently are planning teams led by geographers? And even in the traditionally geographical field of exploration how many parties are dominated and led by geographers? These questions are of fundamental importance to the discipline and the answers do not give rise to complacency. Geography graduates are valued objectively by the outside world and the positions they achieve reflect the value of their training. If it is observed that the outside world does not value geographers particularly highly that is a reflection not of the blindness of the outside world to our talents but of the shortcomings of our training. It may well be that many of the researchers whose methodological and empirical contributions have done so much to foster recent trends have intuitively or subconsciously, if not explicitly, recognised these shortcomings. Certainly any attempt to comprehend their more difficult papers demands a level of penetrative thinking and quantitative understanding that, if it were present in every geographer, would soon attract the interest of employers in many professional fields.

Dissatisfaction within the discipline has occurred at a time when external developments in technology, principally the invention of the computer, have suddenly opened up new possibilities for the large scale manipulation of data. Whether there is a causal relationship between these events is too intricate a matter to discuss here. It is evident, however, that the fact of the computer, with its ability to do a very large number of sums extremely quickly, has had a considerable impact on geographical enquiry in several ways. The sheer amount of data that can be handled, and the complex ways in which it can be manipulated to test hypotheses and build models, is itself an invitation to feed more and more variables into our analyses. As soon as one begins to use a computer in research it becomes apparent that this is a mixed blessing since the urge to feed in a mass of data in an indiscriminate manner can lead not only to sloppy thinking but also to 'data indigestion', nonsense correlations, and expensive computer bills. At a later stage it becames evident that, wisely used, the computer can help research in ways other than its ability to make rapid calculations. Often it forces the researcher to visualise and design the final tables in advance. This leads to much of the hard thinking about the project being done at the proper time—before the survey. Similarly, because of the expense, it forces him to consider much more carefully exactly what he is trying to show and thus exactly what things he should measure to show it. This is a precisely similar approach to that suggested previously for the rural land use survey. If it is adopted, one of the old accusations against geographers, that they go into the field and try to record everything, falls to the ground. Thus because of the discipline imposed by the computer, analysis in the social sciences generally is likely to become methodologically sounder. In the special case of human geography, the computer has been a powerful impetus in the swing from a descriptive regional approach to a space analytical approach.

One other important point should be made at this stage. It would be of relatively little help to us to adopt a theory-building approach, and to have the use of sophisticated computers, if the raw material we handle is of the sort that is not readily measurable. Disciplines in which qualitative judgment inevitably plays a large rôle, for example history and politics, and those where social attitudes are central to the enquiry, for example social psychology, may have great difficulty in adapting their raw material to quantitative analysis. By contrast much of the raw material of geographical enquiry is fairly easily quantifiable. Distances and areas (however measured), populations, crop yields, movements, transport costs, settlement patterns, ethnic distributions and many other variables of fundamental interest to us are normally expressed in some numerical form. There are, of course, other important factors such as social status, distance perception, and neighbourhood coherence that present difficulties. Indeed one of the skills of the researcher is to make a wise choice between variables which can safely be quantified and those which, perhaps for the moment, should not. Looked at on balance, however, it seems clear that the human geographer is well placed to measure his material and to carry out quantitative analysis. The extent to which geography has lagged behind other sciences in this respect does not, therefore, seem to reflect the nature of the data. It could be argued that it stems more from the myopic and compartmentalised way in which geography has been studied and taught, both in schools and universities.

Introduction to the collected material

The papers and extracts set out in this book are presented as examples of the sort of work that has gone to make up the 'quantitative revolution'. It is evident that the themes of careful measurement, theory building, prediction and decision making are all present. It should be equally clear on reflection that much of the work done, and certainly the theoretical and predictive work, carries with it the implicit assumption that regularities exist in human behaviour with respect to space use and land use. The very act of suggesting a predictive model would be meaningless without this assumption.

The first group of papers deals with general problems of geographical methodology. Methodological writing has been characterised, perhaps unfairly, as being about anything under the sun except methods. Whether or not this is true, it is essential in any intellectual pursuit to spend some time considering what one is doing, why one is doing it, and how it fits in with what other people are doing. It is by these means that important questions of aims and techniques are raised for discussion. Section 3 provides an introduction to techniques that have recently been developed to make more accurate measurements of two elements of the spatial system—places and routes. One paper suggests methods of giving quantitative expression to settlement distributions so that one pattern can be compared to another in some more objective and precise way than saying one is more 'dispersed' than the other. The second paper deals with measurements that can be made of a transport network to express, for example, the extent to which it is well or poorly connected. Section 4 provides a short and simple introduction to the core ideas of Central Place Theory and also includes a paper dealing with the problem of

ANALYTICAL HUMAN GEOGRAPHY

defining an urban hinterland. Central place theory, which has been described as the main body of theory in human geography, sets out to explain the size and spacing of urban settlements, or 'central places'. Inevitably, since the problem is so enormously complex, it is only partially successful in explaining the observed distribution. Nevertheless, certain of the statements or assumptions upon which the theory was built have themselves provoked a considerable amount of hypothesising and field research and the theory has perhaps been as useful for the subsequent work it has prompted as for the completeness of its explanation of reality. One of its central ideas, that service hinterlands for towns of equal size do not overlap, is implicitly repudiated by the paper by Huff on problems of hinterland delimitation.

Section 5 deals with the idea that the subjective environment which we perceive around us differs quite considerably from the objectively measured environment. The extract from a recent study by Saarinen deals with the ways in which farmers on the American Great Plains misjudge the frequency and severity of drought, while another paper considers the way in which people subjectively shorten or lengthen actual distances in accordance with how much they wish to make a specified journey. The third contribution illustrates that by distorting geographical space into something more meaningful, in this case consumer expenditure space, the observed distribution of a certain landscape feature can be more adequately explained. The sixth section contains papers dealing with a range of geographical models which are all concerned, to a greater or less extent, with making predictions. The paper dealing with crop choice sets out a procedure by which, given stated inputs of possible crops, climatic data and market prices, a rational choice of crop combinations can be made so as to maximise returns. The review of the gravity model traces the history of this particular set of ideas in considerable detail and considers a number of refinements developed to make the model more realistic and meaningful. The final paper presents a predictive model simulating the spatial diffusion of Negroes in a North American city. In the concluding section a new definition of the subject is offered in the light of the material contained in the book. In addition, certain key geographical concepts are identified and the way in which each of these concepts bears on a wide range of geographical problems is discussed.

Notes and references

[1] These figures are taken from ASHWORTH, W. *The Genesis of Modern British Town Planning*, Routledge & Kegan Paul, 1954, and Table 1 of the 1961 Census, *Migration* volume, H.M.S.O., 1965.
[2] BERRY, B. J. L. 'The quantitative bogey-man', *Econ. Geogr.*, 1960, facing p. 283.

[3] The emphasis on space and location has found expression in the titles of a number of recent works in geography—see, for example, the books by Haggett and by Berry and Marble referred to on page xvii.

[4] An interesting series of rôle-playing games, dealing with geographical situations and suitable for a wide range of ability levels, has recently been developed by Rex Walford of the Maria Grey College, Twickenham.

[5] There are a number of excellent introductory textbooks on statistics. They include MORONEY, M. J. *Facts from Figures*, Penguin, 1956.

An equally useful book dealing specifically with geographical examples is GREGORY, S. *Statistical Methods and the Geographer*, Longmans, 1963.

[6] For example, the 'nearest neighbour' technique used in the paper by L. J. King in Section 3.

Suggested practical exercise

Factors affecting farming strategies

Make a list of up to ten factors, physical, economic, locational or cultural, that might be operating in the minds of local farmers as they make decisions about what crops to plant, what livestock to rear or what combination of crops and livestock to adopt. Arrange these factors into what is thought to be their order of importance (making separate lists if appropriate for crops and livestock or even for subdivisions within these categories).

Carry out a small survey of representative local farmers and ask them to range the factors in their actual order of importance (using the same crop and livestock subdivisions). How closely does the expected and the actual ordering coincide? Does it coincide more closely for some crops or livestock than for others? In the farmers' estimation, has there been any recent change in the order of importance of the factors? Is any change in the order foreseen and if so what would be the implication for the pattern of land use in the area?

2 The methodological foundations of change

Methodological debate has been variously characterised as a sign of health, a defence mechanism, or a waste of time. This latter reaction tends to be expressed in some such terms as 'Why doesn't he stop writing about the way he is doing geography and get on and do it?' This is unfair because nobody ventures into methodological writing without first having done a fair amount of substantive work. It is in the process of carrying out actual research studies that questions of aims and methods are raised.

The defence mechanism interpretation may arise from the particular position in which the social sciences find themselves at the present time. Although this group of disciplines is growing fast in terms of university applicants and places, there is still a widespread lack of understanding about the aims and nature of social science. The old misapprehension that it has something to do with the training of social workers is by no means dead. To clarify their distinctive central concepts, to demonstrate their internal coherence, in fact to justify their comparatively youthful existence, various of the social sciences are engaged in methodological discussion.[1] Apart from this consideration there is the hoary debate, as active now as it was in the mid-nineteenth century, about the extent to which those sciences devoted to the study of man can adopt, or adapt, the proven methods of the physical sciences.[2] This debate has been brought well to the forefront of current methodological writing in geography because it is precisely with the natural scientific themes of careful measurement, theory-building, prediction and experimentation that the 'quantitative revolution' is most concerned.

Perhaps it would not be too complacent to see this sort of debate as a sign of health. Certainly the attempt on the part of any discipline to clarify aims, to consider methods, to relate to other disciplines and to trade in techniques must be of some benefit in our over compartmentalised and overspecialised educational system. Those of us who try to make a scientific study of man and his behaviour, from our various disciplinary viewpoints, may find ourselves in the same position as the group of people in a darkened room with an elephant; it is not always evident that all the bits we are in contact with belong to the same animal. At school, where interdisciplinary work is very difficult to arrange and where, say, geography, history and economics are studied at different times and places and with different textbooks and teachers, it is easy to lose sight of the essential unity of the study of man's behaviour. For this reason it seems that methodological discussion could well begin before entry into a university or other course of higher education.

Although this sort of debate is generally accepted to be a beneficial exercise it is possible to have too much of a good thing and the dose should be judiciously controlled. For that reason it might be as well if the three papers that follow are not read consecutively. They vary a great deal in their emphasis, but running through all three is the feeling that geography should be moving towards more scientific and precise methods of analysis and towards the development of a more satisfying body of theory relating to spatial distributions. The paper by *Burton* is perhaps a good starting point since it is clear, readable, and gets as close to humour as one can expect in work of this sort. Certainly his comments on the way in which the 'conventional wisdom' can be recognised and his characterisation of quantifiers are agreeably lighthearted. The easy tone should not be allowed to mislead. Burton is making, very clearly, the essential point that good measurement and good theory are intimately related in human geography. Sophisticated quantitative work without any explicit statement of theory is no more to be accepted than is generalised theorising without any attempt at substantiation by measurement. His repeated assertion (in 1963) that the quantitative revolution is over and that we all accept the need for more precise techniques of measurement may well have been optimistic since a certain lack of receptivity to new methods is still distinctly discernible in the schools, and even the universities. Burton gives an example of what he means by 'theoretical geography' right at the end of his paper, where he draws attention to the interest of geographers in networks of all sorts; drainage, transport, social, and so on. These all have points, links and flows in common and they could all conceivably be studied in terms of a branch of mathematics called graph theory. This idea is referred to here because in the final section of this book an attempt is made to identify a number of geographical concepts, including the idea of a network, and to suggest that they might form the basis of a more conceptual and theoretical mode of geographical study.

The contribution by *Davies* is well documented, brief and to the point. He contrasts the rather high-sounding pronouncements made by various revered figures about the scientific nature of geography with the work, much of it descriptive and subjective, that has actually been produced. With reference to a number of nineteenth-century thinkers, including Ritter, he questions whether the inductive methods they adopted could possibly foster the type of theoretical insight and intuition shown by, for example, Galileo, Newton and Darwin. Davies sees the late nine-teenth-century growth of physical determinism, following the emphasis given by Darwinian thought to the idea of adaptation to an environment, as an acceptably scientific methodology since it was based on the search for laws and principles. The move to a possibilist approach and a regard for the intuitive grasp of the unique 'personality' of regions is seen as a retreat from scientific methodology. He sees the recent renewed search for lawful regularities in human behaviour as a return to a scientific ap-proach but is careful to differentiate social laws, which are generalisa-tions about observed phenomena, from other types of laws such as chains of command (and, one might add, inflexible causal relation-ships).

Davies rejects Hartshorne's view that the essential characteristics of geography have been determined for us by its past development since he feels that such a view is pre-scientific and, like the guild system of medie-val towns, constraining. Some consideration is given to whether geo-graphy is primarily concerned with the general or with the unique and it is concluded that perhaps the two are not mutually exclusive since descriptions of unique regions can be organised into generalised theo-retical structures and tested. The danger is that an overemphasis on regional description, which is essentially subjective, classificatory and 'artistic', can reduce the amount of time and energy spent on theory building and that this will lead to work that is not scientifically creative. He illustrates this point in an interesting way by suggesting that artistic creativity does not build directly upon previous workers in the field whereas scientific creativity does, since it is dependent upon a body of previously tested theory. He concedes that prediction in human geo-graphy may always have to be based on the 'uncertainty' principle, since the behaviour of individuals is not completely predictable. This is no disgrace since, increasingly, theoretical physicists are becoming aware that events at the atomic level cannot be observed with certainty and that prediction in what was thought to be one of the most exact sciences is now based on laws of probability. (An example of a 'stochastic' geo-graphical model, which incorporates the effects of sheer chance, is des-cribed in the paper by Morrill contained in Section 6.) The paper ends by characterising much of our present methodology as 'pre-quantum' and calls for more hypothesis and theory building as an alternative to 'a morass of regional description'.

The paper by *Schaefer*, whose death in 1953 deprived geography of a very original thinker, is a substantial re-examination of the historical basis of what he terms 'exceptionalism'. This term he uses to sum up the viewpoint that, for a number of reasons which are set out, geography is methodologically distinct from all other sciences. These reasons include the idea that geography is the only 'integrating' science and that the dualism represented by the regional versus systematic approaches is also distinctive to geography. Schaefer entirely rejects these exceptionalist ideas since he clearly feels they do not help us to adopt the scientific procedures used by related disciplines. He is especially critical of the descriptive regional approach: 'Description, even if followed by classification, does not explain the manner in which phenomena are distributed over the world. To explain the phenomena one has described means always to recognize them as instances of laws.' By reference to physics and economics he shows the essential weakness of Hartshorne's view that the heart of geography is regional work and that systematic work can be left to those who like it or are temperamentally fitted to pursue it. (Incidentally, neither Hartshorne nor Schaefer elaborate on the temperament required.)

Schaefer traces exceptionalism back to some early and immature passages by the philosopher Kant. These included the statement: 'Geography is a description'. These views propagated in 1756 by a non-geographer have, in Schaefer's estimation, been instrumental in shaping the form our discipline has taken. They were adopted and developed by Hettner who considered that since no two phenomena or regions were alike, geography was essentially concerned with describing unique occurrences. Since there are no laws for the unique there was little point in searching for laws in geographical analysis. Hettner is also seen as responsible for the penetration into geographical thought of the 'anti-scientific spirit of historicism'.[3] This is interpreted as a belief that if one arranges past events accurately in order their meaning will become clear. Translated into geographical terms, if one makes an accurate spatial ordering of regions their 'meaning' will be understood. If one adopts this philosophy the obvious course is to make full and accurate descriptions of regions, dealing both with where they are and what they look like, and await events. Schaefer obviously considers this whole approach to be unsound and unhelpful. These general trends of thought have been powerfully injected into the English language tradition of geography by Hartshorne who seems to have adopted the Hettner position fairly whole-heartedly and whose two books[4] were for thirty years or more the obvious sources for the keen student of methodology to consult. Schaefer quotes Hartshorne's view that 'generalizations in the form of laws are useless, if not impossible, and any prediction in geography is of insignificant value'.

Schaefer criticises the Hettner/Hartshorne position from several points of view. He maintains that while it is obvious that all objects (and all regions) are unique it is equally obvious that certain laws (for example, gravity) are operating on them and that events are brought about by these laws acting in combination or opposition. Natural science would be unthinkable without studying and applying laws, and there is no reason to think that social science cannot also recognise and apply laws. With regard to regional thinking, Schaefer points out that a region can be recognised only in terms of a limited and specified number of phenomena (say relief, climate and soils) or perhaps of only one (say an ice-cap). Change the phenomena studied and you change the boundaries of the region. From this it follows that 'the notion of a region in itself explains therefore nothing'.

To base geographical methodology on a notion that means nothing in isolation, or on the rather mystic idea that the region is in some way more than the sum of its parts is, Schaefer implies, unsatisfactory. In regard to the rejection of the work of certain over-enthusiastic searchers for deterministic laws relating human development to the physical environment he writes:

> The contemporary reaction against these exaggerations is understandably strong. But to fight them from the standpoint of science is one thing; to fight geographical determinism in order to fight science and its underlying idea of universal lawfulness is another thing.

Schaefer concludes by urging that geography must search for laws. These laws take different forms; they can be physical laws affecting the processes of physical geography, laws of location and spatial arrangement (partly derived from economics) or 'process laws' which we must search for in combination with other social scientists. We can contribute to this search for laws by using our professional skill to analyse the spatial factors involved in their operation.

This paper has been included despite its length and difficulty because although it was published in 1953, before the great upsurge of interest in more scientific approaches in geography, it forms a firm philosophical foundation for these approaches. It has been unduly neglected, perhaps because it is a little obscure in places, but a number of subsequent original thinkers, for example Bunge,[5] have drawn heavily upon it. It should be pointed out that Hartshorne has replied to some of the criticisms advanced in the paper both in a direct rejoinder[6] and in the more recent of his two books. It is not proposed to examine this disagreement in any further detail. All that need be said is that the body of work contained in the present book, and the underlying philosophy it represents, stems from Schaefer rather than from Hartshorne.

Notes and references

[1] A useful book outlining the aims and methods of a number of the social sciences is MACKENZIE, N. *A Guide to the Social Sciences*, Weidenfeld & Nicolson, 1966.

[2] See, for example, several of the essays in BRAYBROOKE, D. *Philosophical Problems of the Social Sciences*, Macmillan, 1965.

[3] The most influential recent treatment of historicism, in a context much wider than geographical study, is POPPER, K. R. *The Poverty of Historicism*, Routledge & Kegan Paul, 1957.

[4] HARTSHORNE, R. 'The nature of geography', *Ann. Ass. Am. Geogr.*, 29 (1939), and *Perspective on the Nature of Geography*, Rand McNally, 1959.

[5] See note 2, p. xvii.

[6] HARTSHORNE, R. 'Exceptionalism in geography re-examined', *Ann. Ass. Am. Geogr.*, 45 (1955) 205–44.

The quantitative revolution and theoretical geography*
Ian Burton

In the past decade geography has undergone a radical transformation of spirit and purpose, best described as the 'quantitative revolution'. The consequences of the revolution have yet to be worked out and are likely to involve the 'mathematisation' of much of our discipline, with an attendant emphasis on the contruction and testing of theoretical models. Although the future changes will far outrun the initial expectations of the revolutionaries, the revolution itself is now over. It has come largely as the result of the impact of work by non-geographers upon geography, a process shared by many other disciplines where an established order has been overthrown by a rapid conversion to a mathematical approach.

Geographers may look with the wisdom of hindsight on a recent statement by Douglas C. North who points out that in the field of economic history 'a revolution is taking place. . . . It is being initiated by a new generation of economic historians who are both sceptical of traditional interpretations of U.S. economic history, and convinced that a new economic history must be firmly grounded in sound statistical data.'[2] North's paper has a familiar ring in geographical ears, but is not primarily concerned with where the revolution is likely to lead. If the example of other social sciences is any criterion, it will lead to a more mathematical, not solely statistical, economic history.

The movement which led to the revolution in geography was begun by physicists and mathematicians, and has expanded to transform first the physical and then the biological sciences. It is now strongly represented in most of the social sciences including economics, psychology, and sociology. The movement is not yet strongly represented in anthropology or political science, and has scarcely been felt in history, although early rumblings may perhaps be heard from a new journal devoted to history and theory.[3]

This paper presents a discussion of the general characteristics of the quantitative movement; describes in somewhat greater detail the coming of the quantitative revolution to geography; and attempts an assessment of the value of quantitative techniques in the development of theory. Some scholars have chosen to regard the revolution in terms of a qualitative-quantitative dichotomy. It does not help to cast the debate in this form. For 'what is philosophically distinctive about contemporary science is its disinterest in dubious dichotomies or disabling dilemmas',[4]

* Reprinted from *The Canadian Geographer* 7 (1963), 151–62, by permission of the publishers.

which fascinate and ensnare the mind because they give the illusion of coming close to the essential nature of things. O. H. K. Spate, in his paper on 'Quantity and quality in geography', goes so far as to cry 'down with dichotomies',[5] but fails to heed his own advice and apply it to the title of his paper. Furthermore, to specify the presence or absence of an attribute or quality is merely to begin the process of measurement at its lowest level on a nominal scale. Viewed in this manner, observations of qualitative differences are but the prelude to measurements of a higher order on ordinal, interval, or ratio scales.

The quantity-quality dichotomy has also been allowed to embrace and perhaps conceal a number of related but distinct questions. These include measurement by instruments versus direct sense-data; rational analysis versus intuitive perception; cold and barren scientific constructs versus the rich variety of daily sense-experience; continuously varying phenomena versus discrete cases, nomothetic versus ideographic, and the like.

The desire to avoid this confusion reinforces my inclination to side-step the quality-quantity issue, and to view the movement toward quantification as a part of the general spread and growth of scientific analysis into a world formerly dominated by a concern with the exceptional and unique.

Quantification as Indeterminism

Geography has long been a 'following' rather than a 'leading' discipline. The main currents of thought have had their origins in other fields. The mechanistic approach of much nineteenth-century science was represented to some extent among the environmental determinists from Ratzel (if he *was* a determinist) to Semple, Huntington, and Griffith Taylor. They were preoccupied by the notion of cause and effect, and were constantly seeking 'laws'. A similar mechanistic flavour is present in much of the recent work by the 'quantifiers'. It is as if geography is re-emerging after the lapse into ideography which followed the retreat from environmental determinism. The quantitative revolution is taking us back much closer to environmental determinism. It is surely not coincidental that the quantitative revolution is contemporaneous with the appearance of neodeterminism in geography.[6]

It seems clear that a strong reaction to environmental determinism has served to delay the coming of the quantitative movement to geography, and has postponed the establishment of a scientific basis for our discipline that the quantifiers hope to provide (and which the determinists were seeking, although for the most part did not find).

It is not so surprising, therefore, that the quantitative revolution was resisted most strongly by American geographers, for it was in the United States that the reaction to environmental determinism was strongest. Characteristically, the source of strongest opposition is now the source of greatest support, and the United States has achieved a very favourable balance of trade in the commodity of quantitative techniques.

Although quantification in geography has been mechanistic, new techniques being used and others being developed are in line with the contemporary trend in science in that they are probabilistic. The probabilistic approach as exemplified in Curry's work on climatic change,[7] and Hägerstrand's simulation of diffusion[8] offers a most promising vista for future research. As Bronowski notes, statistics 'is the method to which modern science is moving. . . . This is the revolutionary thought in modern science. It replaces the concept of inevitable effect by that of probable trend.'[9] It is more accurate, therefore, to refer to some of the later examples of quantification in geography as indeterministic. With Jerzy Neyman, 'One may hazard the assertion that every serious contemporary study is a study of the chance mechanism behind some phenomena. The statistical and probabilistic tool in such studies is the theory of stochastic processes, now involving many unsolved problems.'[10]

Of great significance in the development of laws in the social sciences is the scale of analysis. As Emrys Jones explains:

'The lack of stringency lies in the finite numbers dealt with in the social sciences as opposed to the infinite numbers dealt with in the physical sciences. At this latter extreme, statistical regularity is such that it suggests extreme stringency or absolute validity; while at the other end statistical variations and exceptions are much higher, and deviations themselves warrant study.'[11]

The end of a revolution

Although its antecedents can be traced far back, the quantitative revolution in geography began in the late 1940s or early 1950s; it reached its culmination in the period from 1957 to 1960, and is now over. Ackerman remarks that:

'Although the simpler forms of statistical aids have characterized geographic distribution analysis in the past, the discipline is commencing to turn to more complex statistical methods—an entirely logical development. The use of explanatory models and regression, correlation, variance and covariance analysis may be expected to be increasingly more frequent in the field. In the need for and value of these methods geography does not differ from other social sciences.'[12]

Similarly, Hartshorne says that:

'to raise ... thinking to the level of scientific knowing, it is necessary to establish generic concepts that can be applied with the maximum degree of objectivity and accuracy and to determine correlations of phenomena with the maximum degree of certainty. Both purposes can best be accomplished if the phenomena can be fully and correctly described by quantitative measurements and these can be subjected to statistical comparisons through the logic of mathematics.'[13]

Spate, although somewhat sceptical about quantitative methods, concedes that 'increasingly young geographers will feel that they are not properly equipped without some statistical nous',[14] and adds parenthetically that he is relieved not to be a young geographer.

An intellectual revolution is over when accepted ideas have been overthrown or have been modified to include new ideas. *An intellectual revolution is over* when the revolutionary ideas themselves become a part of the conventional wisdom. When Ackerman, Hartshorne, and Spate are in substantial agreement about something, then we are talking about the conventional wisdom. Hence, my belief that the quantitative revolution is over and has been for some time. Further evidence may be found in the rate at which schools of geography in North America are adding courses in quantitative methods to their requirements for graduate degrees.

Many would concur with Mackay's comment that 'the marginal return on arguing for the need of quantitative methods is now virtually nil'.[15] This does not deny that many ramifications of the revolution remain to be worked out. Nor does it mean that the ramifications will be painless. It is not easy to agree with Spate's argument that the need for statistical nous applies only to young geographers. Is the field to progress only as rapidly as the turnover in generations? The impact of cybernation is already creating unemployment at the white collar level. Its impact on the managerial and professional strata is likely to mean more work, not less. It is no flight of fancy to foresee the day when geographers, if they are to remain abreast of developments, must re-learn their craft anew every decade. Nor is it difficult to see that the present generation of quantifiers may rapidly be replaced by younger men more thoroughly versed in mathematics.

Although the quantitative revolution is over, it is instructive to examine its course because to do so tells us something about the sociology of our profession, and because it provides a background for the question, 'quantification for what?' considered below.

The course of the quantitative revolution in geography

Although the origins of the revolution lie in the fields of mathematics and physics, the direct invasion came from closer to home. A list of the more important antecedents, having a direct or indirect impact on geography, would include Von Neuman (a mathematician) and Morgenstern (an economist) for their *Theory of Games and Economic Behavior*,[16] first published in 1944; Norbert Wiener, whose 1948 volume on cybernetics[17] emphasised the necessity of crossing academic boundaries; and Zipf, who published *Human Behavior and the Principle of Least Effort*[18] in 1949.

Geographers began to look for quantitative techniques that could be applied to their problems, and some non-geographers began to bring new methods to bear on old geographic questions. One example is physicist J. Q. Stewart's paper, 'Empirical Mathematical Rules Concerning the Distribution and Equilibrium of Population', published in the *Geographical Review*[19] as early as 1947.

Stewart has been a leader in the development of social physics, and the declaration of interdependence signed by a group of physical and social scientists at the Princeton conference in 1949 is a landmark in the growth of the application of mathematics to the social sciences.[20] That economists were engaging in methodological debate at this time, in a way that geographers were to do five years later, is evidenced by the Vining and Koopmans controversy in the *Review of Economics and Statistics* for 1949.[21]

The impact of quantification began to be felt in geography almost immediately. It was initiated by a number of statements calling for quantification. Such calls had been issued earlier. For example, in 1936 John Kerr Rose, in his paper on corn yields and climate argued that 'the methods of correlation analysis would seem especially promising tools for geographical investigation'.[22] This call went largely unheeded. Similar statements in 1950, however, were followed up. An outstanding early plea was made by Strahler in his attack on the Davisian explanatory-descriptive system of geomorphology,[23] and his endorsement of G. K. Gilbert's dynamic-quantitative system.[24]

Quantitative geomorphology and climatology

If Gilbert's 1914 paper was as sound as Strahler seems to think, why was it not adopted as a signpost to future work in geomorphology, instead of being largely forgotten and ignored for thirty years? The answer may be, as Strahler himself seems to imply, that geomorphology was a part of geography. Hydrologists and geologists did not direct their major interest towards such matters, or when they did they followed Davis. The followers included Douglas Johnson, C. A. Cotton, N. M. Fenneman, and A. K. Lobeck. Strahler held that they made 'splendid contributions to descriptive and regional geomorphology', and 'have provided a sound base for studies in human geography',[25] but they did not greatly advance the scientific study of geomorphological process. This is not to say that there was no quantitative work in geomorphology prior to Strahler.[26]

One immediate response to Strahler's attack on Davis came from Quam, who wondered whether mathematical formulae and statistical analysis might not give a false impression of objectivity and accuracy.[27] A more violent response, however, came from S. W. Wooldridge, who notes that:

'There has been a recent attempt in certain quarters to devise a 'new' quasi-mathematical geomorphology. At its worst this is hardly more than a ponderous sort of cant. The processes and results of rock sculpture are not usefully amenable to treatment by mathematics at higher certificate level. If any 'best' is to result from the movement, we have yet to see it; it will be time enough to incorporate it in the subject when it has discovered or expressed something which cannot be expressed in plain English. For ourselves we continue to regard W. M. Davis as the founder of our craft and regret the murmurings of dispraise heard occasionally from his native land.'[28]

Lester King is inclined to support Strahler.

'Statistical analysis is essentially the method of the bulk sample, and is admirable for the study of complex phenomena and processes into which enter a large number of variables. As yet few geomorphic topics provide data suited directly to statistical treatment, and methods may have to be adapted to the new field of enquiry, so that too facile results should not be expected. The net result must be, however, a greater precision in geomorphic thinking.'[29]

Several geomorphologists, including Chorley,[30] Dury,[31] Mackay,[32] Wolman,[33] and others, in addition to Strahler, are using quantitative methods, and the practice seems likely to spread.

There has been little argument about the application of quantitative techniques to climatology. This branch of our subject embraces the most apparently manageable and quantifiable continuum that geographers have been concerned to study. Thornthwaite and Mather,[34] Hare,[35] Bryson,[36] and others have been applying quantitative techniques to climatic problems for some time, and with great effect. The quality of their work has virtually silenced the potential critics.

Quantification in human and economic geography

By far the greatest struggle for the acceptance of quantitative methods has been in human and economic geography. This is not surprising in view of the possibilist tradition.[37] It is here that the revolution runs up against notions of freewill and the unpredictability of human behaviour. Here the comparison with physical science is helpful. Physicists working on a microcosmic level encounter the same kinds of problems with quanta and energy that social scientists do with people. The recognition of such parallels is cause for rejoicing, not for despair. To be accepted and accorded an honoured place in our society, social science needs to acquire demonstrable value as a predictive science without a corresponding need to control, restrict, or regiment the individual. A social science which recognises random behaviour at the microcosmic level and predictable order at the macrocosmic level is a logical outgrowth of the quantitative revolution.

The catalogue of claim and counterclaim, charge and countercharge that appeared in the literature in the 1950s is a long one. It includes Garrison's[38] comment on Nelson's[39] service classification of American cities; the Reynolds[40]-Garrison[41] exchange of 1956 on the (then) little use of statistical methods in geography; the Spate-Berry editorial exchange in *Economic Geography* in which the former reminds us that 'Statistics are at best but half of life. The other half is understanding and imaginative interpretation',[42] and the latter defends the quantifiers for their clear distinction between facts, theories, and methods, and in turn accuses his critics of creating a quantitative bogey-man and tilting at windmills;[43] Dacey's[44] criticism of Burghardt's[45] conclusions on the spacing of river towns, and Porter's defence with the fable of 'Earnest and the Orephagians';[46] the Zobler[47]-Mackay[48] exchange on the use of chi-square in regional geography; Arthur Robinson's classification of geographers into 'Perks and Pokes';[49] the debate between Lukermann[50] and Berry[51] on a 'geographic' economic geography, and so on.

By 1956, the quantifiers were arguing with each other through the medium of the professional journals as well as with their opponents. In so doing, they occupied an increasing amount of attention and space. In 1956 also the Regional Science Association was established and gave further impetus to quantification in geography.

The erstwhile revolutionaries are now part of the geographic 'establishment', and their work is an accepted and highly valued part of the field.

The opposition to quantification

The opposition to the quantitative revolution can be grouped into five broad classes. There were those who thought that the whole idea was a bad one and that quantification would mislead geography in a wrong and fruitless direction. If such critics are still among us they have not made themselves heard for some time. There were those like Stamp who argued that geographers had spent too long perfecting their tools (maps, cartograms, and other diagrammatic representations) and should get on with some real building. Stamp was 'a little alarmed by the view that the geographer must add to his training a considerable knowledge of statistics and statistical method, of theoretical economics and of modern sociology. Sufficient perhaps to appreciate what his colleagues are doing so that team work may be based on mutual appreciation seems to me the right attitude.'[52] This seems to be another dubious dichotomy. The notion that geographers either improve their tools or engage in research with available tools seems false. Surely advances in technology are most likely to occur at the moment when we are grappling with our toughest problems. Furthermore, to argue that geographers should not use statistical methods comes close to defining geography in terms of one research tool—namely the map. One weakness of this position has been well demonstrated by McCarty and Salisbury who have shown that visual comparison of isopleth maps is not an adequate means of determining correlations between spatially distributed phenomena.[53]

A third kind of opposition holds that statistical techniques are suitable for some kinds of geography, but not all geography, because there are certain things that cannot be measured. This may be true for some variables. However, even with qualitative characteristics, nominal observations can be made and there is an expanding body of literature on the analysis of qualitative data.[54] A variant of this argument is that the variables with which geography is concerned are too numerous and complex for statistical analysis. Quantifiers claim that it is precisely because of the number and complexity of the variables that statistical techniques are being employed.

Another class of objections is that although quantitative techniques are suitable and their application to geographic problems is desirable, they are nevertheless being incorrectly applied; ends are confused with means; quantitative analysis has failed on occasion to distinguish the significant from the trivial; the alleged discoveries of the quantifiers are not very novel; and so on. That these criticisms have a grain of truth cannot be denied, but to the valid, correct use of quantitative methods (and this is surely what we are concerned with) they are merely irrelevant. Incorrect applications have been and no doubt will continue to be made, and in some cases for the wrong reason such as fashion, fad, or snobbery. More often, however, they are genuine and honest attempts to gain new knowledge and new understandings.

A final kind of criticism to note is in the *ad hominem* that quantification is alright but quantifiers are not. They are perky, suffer from over-enthusiasm, vaulting ambition, or just plain arrogance. To this charge also perhaps a plea of guilty with extenuating circumstances (and a request for leniency) is the most appropriate response. When you are involved in a revolution, it is difficult not to be a little cocky.

The consequences of the revolution

The revolution is over, in that once-revolutionary ideas are now conventional. Clearly this is only the beginning. There is a purpose other than the establishment of a new order. If the revolution had been inspired by belief in quantification for its own sake, or by fad and fashion, then it would have rapidly run its course and quickly died. But the revolution had a different purpose. It was inspired by a genuine need to make geography more scientific, and by a concern to develop a body of theory. Dissatisfaction with ideographic geography lies at the root of the quantitative revolution. The development of theoretical, model-building geography is likely to be the major consequence of the quantitative revolution.

Description, or as some have said, 'mere description',[55] may be an art or at least call for the exercise of certain talents best described as artistic. Nevertheless, description is an essential part of the scientific method. In examining the real world, our first task is to describe what we see, and to classify our observations into meaningful groups for the sake of convenience in handling. The moment that a geographer begins to describe an area, however, he becomes selective (for it is not possible to describe everything), and in the very act of selection demonstrates a conscious or unconscious theory or hypothesis concerning what is significant.

In his examination of significance in geography, Hartshorne rejects the notion that significance should be judged in terms of appearance, that is, as in objects in a landscape, and establishes as an alternative the criterion that observations should express 'the variable character from place to place of the earth as the world of man'.[56] In many geographic pursuits, man is the measure of significance, and spatial variations the focus. But how else can significance to man be measured except in terms of some theory of interrelationships?

In this connection there is reason to question Strahler's assertion, quoted above, that the Davisian geomorphologists 'provided a sound basis for studies in human geography'. The genetic and morphological landform classifications they produced may have provided a sound basis for most studies in human geography prior to 1950, but they are not truly anthropocentric. No attempts to assess significance to man were made until the work was substantially completed. This can be contrasted with Sheaffer's recent stream classification,[57] based on flood-to-peak interval, a variable known to be of significance for human adjustment.

The observation and description of regularities, such as these in the spatial arrangement of cultural features, human activities, or physical variables, are first steps in the development of theory. Theory provides the sieve through which myriads of facts are sorted, and without it the facts remain a meaningless jumble. Theory provides the measure against which exceptional and unusual events can be recognised. In a world without theory there are no exceptions; everything is unique. This is why theory is so important. As Braithwaite puts it, 'The function of a science is to establish general laws covering the behaviour of empirical events as objects with which the science in question is concerned . . . to enable us to collect together our knowledge of the separately known events, and to make reliable predictions of events yet unknown.'[58]

The need to develop theory precedes the quantitative revolution, but quantification adds point to the need, and offers a technique whereby theory may be developed and improved. It is not certain that the early quantifiers were consciously motivated to develop theory, but it is now clear to geographers that quantification is inextricably intertwined with theory. The core of scientific method is the organisation of facts into theories, and the testing and refinement of theory by its application to the prediction of unknown facts. Prediction is not only a valuable by-product of theory building, it is also a test by which the validity of theory can be demonstrated. Scientific inquiry may or may not be motivated by the desire to make more accurate predictions. Whatever the motivation, the ability to predict correctly is a sound test of the depth of our understanding.

Given the need to comply with the rigorous dictates of the scientific method, the need to develop theory, and to test theory with prediction, then mathematics is the best tool available to us for the purpose. Other tools—language, maps, symbolic logic—are also useful and in some instances quite adequate. But none so well fulfils our requirements as mathematics.

The quantification of theory, the use of mathematics to express relationships, can be supported on two main grounds. First, it is more

35

rigorous. Second and more important, it is a considerable aid in the avoidance of self-deception.

These points may be illustrated by reference to a paper by Robinson, Lindberg, and Brinkman on rural farm population densities in the Great Plains.[59] The authors point out that the statistical-cartographic techniques which they use may be properly employed after the establishment of 'tentative descriptive hypotheses regarding the mutuality that may exist among the distributions of an area, inferred through the study of individual maps and other sorts of data. Coefficients of correlation and related indices provide general quantitative statements of the degree to which each hypothesis is valid.'[60]

My submission is that the testing of hypotheses does not make much sense unless these hypotheses are related to a developing body of theory. High correlation does not necessarily confirm a hypothesis, and it is well known that nonsense correlations are possible. The authors propose rural farm population density as a dependent variable and proceed to examine spatial variations using average annual precipitation, distance from urban centres, and percentage of cropland in the total land area as explanatory variables. Having calculated correlation coefficients, the authors conclude that the general hypothesis concerning the association of spatial variations of these variables is confirmed.[61] This use of quantitative techniques demonstrates rigour to the extent that precise measurements of association are made. It also demonstrates the need and possibility of avoiding self-deception.

Nowhere in the paper is it possible to find an explicit statement of theory. Nowhere are we told why rural farm population density is highly correlated with average annual precipitation. Perhaps the explanation lies in the fact that as precipitation decreases, larger farm units are required to support a farm family, owing to lower yields of the same crops, or the cultivation of less remunerative crops. This is a theory, and a test of it would be to examine rural farm population density and farm size. It is conceivable that these two variables are not closely correlated. If this is the case, the theory will need revision. It is surely not much of an explanation, however, to correlate rural farm population density with precipitation. If there is a causal relationship here, it is an indirect one and several links have been omitted.

A more logical treatment would relate farm population to farm size, farm size to yields and land use, yields and land use to precipitation; but it is by no means certain that the causal chain of relationships could be carried so far. The correlations which John K. Rose[62] obtained between corn yields and July precipitation are not as high as Robinson, Lindberg, and Brinkman obtained for average annual precipitation and rural farm

THE QUANTITATIVE REVOLUTION

population. Admittedly, the two studies were concerned with different measurements, in different areas, at a different point in time. Nevertheless, it is significant that the Robinson group was able to show higher correlation between remotely connected variables than Rose could show between much more closely connected variables.

Robinson's study is deficient because it is not related to an explicit statement of theory. Quantitative analysis of variables cannot be justified for its own sake. The mere restatement of accepted ideas in numerical form instead of in 'plain English' is not what the quantitative revolution is about. Examination of spatial variables of rural farm population of the Great Plains in terms of an explicit theory would have led Robinson *et al.* to select other, or at least, additional, variables than those considered. Some might argue that the hypothesis relating rural farm population and average annual precipitation is a theory. If so, it sounds dangerously like the old deterministic hypotheses and has the same quality of inferring a causal relationship without any explanation or testing of a connecting process leading from cause to effect.

Conclusion

Quantitative techniques are a most appropriate method for the development of theory in geography. The quantitative era will last as long as its methods can be shown to be aiding in the development of theory, and there can be no end to the need for more and better theory. It follows that any branch of geography claiming to be scientific has need for the development of theory, and any branch of geography that has need for theory has need for quantitative techniques.

Not all statements of theory need to be expressed quantitatively in their initial form. Firey, for example, has developed a general theory of resource use[63] without resort to hypothesis testing in a formal sense. Such statements of theory are extremely valuable, and many more of them are needed in geography. Once formulated they should not long remain untested, but the testing need not be undertaken by the same person, or even by persons in the same discipline.

The development and testing of theory is the only way to obtain new and verifiable knowledge and new and verifiable understandings. As Curry points out:

'Methods of representing various phenomena of nature and speculation about their interrelationships are closely tied together. It is too often forgotten that geographical studies are not descriptions of the real world, but rather perceptions passed through the double filter of the author's mind and his available tools of argument and representation. We cannot know reality, we can have only an abstract picture of aspects of it. All our descriptions of relations or processes are theories or, when formalised, better called models.'[64]

Curry relates model building to another element in recent geographical work—the problem of perception which may soon come to merit a place alongside the quantitative revolution in terms of significant new viewpoints.[65]

Our literature is replete with ideographic studies. There is a strong urge to get something into the literature because it has not been described before. If these ideographic studies and new discriptions are to have lasting value, their theoretical implications must be shown. In an increasing number of cases, the relationship to theory can best be shown in quantitative terms. In some instances a simple description of an exceptional case may serve to highlight defects in theory. The theory can then be revised or modified to take account of another kind of variation not previously noted, or the theory may have to be abandoned. Theories are not usually abandoned, however, because a few uncomfortable facts do not happen to fit. Theories are abandoned when newer and better theories are produced to take their place. Although observation and description of exceptional cases may be achieved without quantification,[66] the eventual incorporation of modifications into a theory will normally require the rigour of statistical techniques to demonstrate their validity.

There is not a very large literature in theoretical geography. Our discipline has remained predominantly ideographic.[67] A small proportion of the large volume of central place literature can be described as theoretical.[68] It is appropriate to speak of central place theory as one relatively well-developed branch of theoretical economic geography. A recent volume by Scheidegger has emphasised the theoretical aspects of geomorphology.[69] Wolman comments that 'the emphasis on principles that Scheidegger stresses directs attention to interrelationships and hopefully lessens the tendency to observe, measure, and record everything because it's there'.[70] This remark can be applied with equal value to the development of theory in other branches of geography.

Geographers are now making a conscious effort to develop more theory. A recent volume on theoretical geography[71] attempts to develop theory basic to some areas of the subject. In particular, the author presents a measurement of shape and discusses a general theory of movement and central place theory. This volume will help to focus the attention of geographers on the need for theory. Perhaps a rash of attempts to develop geographic theory will begin. Such a development seems unlikely, however. For while the use of quantitative methods is a technique that can be learned by most, few seem to have that gift of insight which leads to new theory. North comments that a difficult problem is 'the development of the theoretical hypotheses necessary for shaping the direction of quantitative research'.[72]

Attempts to develop theory in geography need not mean a wholesale shift in emphasis. Many an ideographic study could be of greater value if it contained but two paragraphs showing the theoretical implications of the work. This is often easier or at least possible for the author, while it is more difficult or even impossible for others who try to use the work at a subsequent time to develop or test theory. Of course, if case studies are designed with a theory in mind, it is likely that they will differ considerably from studies unrelated to a conscious statement of theory.

Theoretical geography does not mean the development of an entirely new body of theory exclusive to geography. Scheidegger has not attempted to develop new laws of physics, but has merely refined and adapted these laws to the study of geomorphological phenomena and processes. Central place theory is in keeping with some schools of economic theory. One rôle of an economic geographer is to refine and adapt available economic theory. In doing so he will improve the theory he borrows. If the Anglo-Saxon bias in economics has been to ignore the spatial aspects of economic activity, the geographer is one of those to whom we should look for the remedy. It need not be thought that the growth of regional science completely fills the gap. Those geographers who study drainage networks, highway networks, power distribution systems, flood problems, airline routes, social organisation, and the venation of leaves all have in common a concern for a 'flow' between 'points' over a network of links arranged in a particular pattern. Graph theory is a branch of mathematics concerned with networks and may be adapted to fit all manner of collection, distribution, and communications systems. It is conceivable that a body of useful theory could be built up around the application of graph theory to geographical problems.[73] This is an example of what is meant by theoretical geography. It is a direction that an increasing number of geographers are likely to follow. Let us hope that the effort will meet success.

Acknowledgements

During the preparation and revision of this paper, I have benefited from discussions with Brian J. L. Berry, J. W. Birch, W. C. Calef, Michael Church, John Fraser Hart, Robert W. Kates, Leslie King, and Jacob Spelt.

Notes and references

[1] A shorter version of this paper was presented at the 13th annual meeting of the Canadian Association of Geographers, Quebec City, June 1963.

[2] NORTH, D. C. 'Quantitative research in American economic history', *Am. Econ. Rev.* 53 (1961). 128–30.

[3] See, for example, BERLIN I. 'History and theory, the concept of scientific history', *History and Theory* 1 (1960) 1–3.

[4] LERNER, DANIEL, ed. *Quality and Quantity*, New York, The Free Press, 1961, from the editor's introduction, p. 22.

[5] SPATE, O. H. K. 'Quantity and quality in geography', *Ann. Ass. Am. Geogr.* 50 (1960) 377–94.

[6] See, for example: SPATE, O. H. K. 'Toynbee and Huntington: a study in determinism', *Geog. J.* 118 (1952); also SPATE, O. H. K. *The Compass of Geography*. Canberra, 1953, pp. 14–15. 'There are signs of at least a neodeterminism, more subtle than the old, less inclined to think of environment as exercising an almost dictatorial power over human societies, but convinced that it is far more influential than the current view admits; and with this trend I would identify myself.' (Quoted in JONES, EMRYS, 'Cause and effect in human geography', *Ann. Ass. Am. Geogr.* 46 (1956) 369–77 (see p. 370)). See also: MARTIN, A. F. 'The necessity for determinism', *Trans. and Papers, Inst. Brit. Geogr.* 17 (1951) 1–11.

[7] CURRY, LESLIE. 'Climatic change as a random series', *Ann. Ass. Am. Geogr.* 52 (1962) 21–31.

[8] HÄGERSTRAND, TORSTEN. 'On Monte Carlo simulation of diffusion', unpub. paper; and *The Propagation of Innovation Waves*, Lund Stud. in Geog., B, 4, 1952, Dept. of Geog., Royal Univ. of Lund.

[9] BRONOWSKI, J. *The Common Sense of Science*, New York, Random House, 1959.

[10] NEYMAN, J. 'Indeterminism in science and new demands on statisticians', *J. Am. Stat. Ass.* 55 (1960) 625–39.

[11] JONES, 'Cause and effect in human geography', p. 373.

[12] ACKERMAN, EDWARD A. *Geography as a Fundamental Research Discipline*, Univ. of Chicago, Dept. of Geog., Research paper no. 53 (1958) p. 11.

[13] HARTSHORNE, RICHARD. *Perspective on the Nature of Geography*, pub. for Ass. Am. Geogr., Chicago, Rand McNally, 1959, p. 161. (Monograph Ser. of Ass. Am. Geogr. no. 1.)

[14] SPATE, 'Quantity and quality', p. 386. Spate makes a similar statement in 'Lord Kelvin rides again', guest editorial, *Econ. Geogr.* 36 (1960) preceding page 95.

[15] Personal communication, 30 March 1963.

[16] VON NEUMAN, JOHN, and MORGENSTERN, OSKAR. *Theory of Games and Economic Behavior*, Princeton, Princeton Univ. Press, 1944.

[17] WIENER, NORBERT. *Cybernetics*, New York, Wiley, 1948.

[18] ZIPF, G. K. *Human Behavior and the Principle of Least Effort*, Cambridge, Mass., Addison-Wesley Press, 1949.

[19] STEWART, J. Q. 'Empirical mathematical rules concerning the distribution and equilibrium of population', *Geogr. Rev.* 37 (1947) 461–85.

[20] —— 'The development of social physics', *Am. J. Physics* 18 (1950) 239–53.

[21] VINING, RUTLEDGE. 'Methodological issues in quantitative economics', *Rev.*

Econ. and Stat. 31 (1949) 77–86. See also T. C. Koopman's reply and Vining's rejoinder, pp. 86–94.

[22] ROSE, J. K. 'Corn yield and climate in the corn belt', *Geogr. Rev.* 26 (1936) 88–102. For a much earlier paper on a similar topic, see: HOOKER, R. H. 'Correlation of the weather and crops', *J. Roy. stat. Soc.* 70 (1907) 1–51.

[23] STRAHLER, A. N. 'Davis' concepts of slope development viewed in the light of recent quantitative investigations', *Ann. Ass. Am. Geogr.* 40 (1950) 209–13.

[24] GILBERT, G. K. *The Transportation of Debris by Running Water*, U.S. Geol. Surv., Prof. Paper no. 86, Washington, G.P.O., 1914.

[25] STRAHLER, 'Davis' Concepts', p. 210.

[26] Strahler notes that important work was initiated in the Soil Conservation Service in the middle and late 1930s. In addition, in 1945 there is R. E. HORTON's classical paper on quantitative morphology, 'Erosional development of streams and their drainage basins: hydrophysical approach to quantitative morphology', *Bull. Geol. Soc. Am.* 56 (1945) 275–370.

[27] See QUAM, LOUIS O. 'Remarks on Strahler's paper', *Ann. Ass. Am. Geogr.* 40 (1950) 213.

[28] WOOLDRIDGE, S. W., and MORGAN, R. S. *An Outline of Geomorphology*, London, Longmans, 1959. The quotation is from the preface to the 2nd edn., p. v.

[29] KING, LESTER. *Morphology of the Earth*, Edinburgh and London, Oliver & Boyd, 1962, p. 231.

[30] See, for example, CHORLEY, R. J. 'Climate and morphometry', *J. Geol.* 65 (1957) 628–38.

[31] See, for example, DURY, G. H. 'Contribution to a general theory of meandering valleys', *Am. J. Sci.* 252 (1954) 193–224; also 'Tests of a general theory of misfit streams', *Trans. and Papers, Inst. Brit. Geogr.* 25 (1958) 105–18; and 'Misfit streams: problems in interpretation, discharge and distribution', *Geogr. Rev.* 50 (1960) 219–42.

[32] MACKAY. 'Pingos of the Pleistocene Mackenzie Delta area', *Geogr. Bull.* 18 (1962) 21–63; and *The Mackenzie Delta Area, N.W.T.*, Dept. of Mines & Tech. Surveys, Geog. Branch, Mem. no. 8, Ottawa, 1963.

[33] See, for example, WOLMAN, M. G. *The Natural Channel of Brandywine Creek, Pa.*, U.S. Geol. Surv., Prof. Paper no. 271, Washington, G.P.O., 1955.

[34] Much of the work of C. W. THORNTHWAITE and J. R. MATHER has appeared in the Thornthwaite Assoc. Laboratory of Climatology, *Publications in Climatology*, Centerton, N.J.

[35] See, for example, HARE, F. K. 'Dynamic and synoptic climatology', *Ann. Ass. Am. Geogr.* 45 (1955) 152–62; also 'The Westerlies', *Geogr. Rev.* 50 (1960) 345–67.

[36] See, for example, HORN, L. H., and BRYSON, R. A. 'Harmonic analysis of the annual March precipitation over the United States', *Ann. Ass. Am. Geogr.* 50 (1960) 157–71; also SABBAGH, M. E., and BRYSON, R. A. 'Aspects of the precipitation climatology of Canada investigated by the method of harmonic analysis', *Ann. Ass. Am. Geogr.* 52 (1962) 426–40.

[37] A useful summary is provided by TATHAM, G. 'Environmentalism and Possibilism', in Taylor, G., ed. *Geography in the Twentieth Century*, New York, 1953, 128–62.

[38] GARRISON, WILLIAM L. 'Some confusing aspects of common measurements', *Prof. Geogr.* 8 (1956) 4–5.

[39] NELSON, H. J. 'A service classification of American cities', *Econ. Geogr.* 31 (1955) 189–210.

[40] REYNOLDS, R. B. 'Statistical methods in geographical research', *Geogr. Rev.* 46 (1956) 129–32.

[41] GARRISON, W. L. 'Applicability of statistical inference to geographical research', *Geogr. Rev.* 46 (1956) 427–29.

[42] SPATE, 'Lord Kelvin rides again'.

[43] BERRY, B. J. L. 'The quantitative bogey-man', guest editorial, *Econ. Geogr.* 36 (1960) preceding p. 283.

[44] DACEY, M. F. 'The spacing of river towns', *Ann. Ass. Am. Geogr.* 50 (1960) 59–61.

[45] BURGHARDT, A. F. 'The location of river towns in the central lowland of the United States', *Ann. Ass. Am. Geogr.* 49 (1959) 305–23.

[46] PORTER, P. W. 'Earnest and the Orephagians: a fable for the instruction of young geographers', *Ann. Ass. Am. Geogr.* 50 (1960) 297–99.

[47] ZOBLER, L. 'Decision making in regional construction', *Ann. Ass. Am. Geogr.* 48 (1958) 140–48.

[48] MACKAY, J. ROSS. 'Chi-square as a tool for regional studies', *Ann. Ass. Am. Geogr.* 48 (1958) 164. See also ZOBLER, 'The distinction between relative and absolute frequencies in using chi-square for regional analysis', *ibid.*, 456–57; and MACKAY and BERRY 'Comments on the use of chi-square', *ibid.* 49 (1959) 89.

[49] ROBINSON, ARTHUR H. 'On Perks and Pokes', guest editorial, *Econ. Geogr.* 37 (1961) 181–83.

[50] LUCKERMANN, F. 'Toward a more geographic economic geography', *Prof. Geogr.* 10 (1958) 2–10.

[51] BERRY, 'Further comments concerning "geographic" and "economic" economic geography', *Prof. Geogr.* 11 (1959) 11–12, Part I.

[52] STAMP, L. DUDLEY. 'Geographical agenda: a review of some tasks awaiting geographical attention', Pres. address, *Trans. and Papers, Inst. Brit. Geogr.* 23 (1957) 1–17 (see p. 2).

[53] MCCARTY, HAROLD H., and SALISBURY, NEIL E. *Visual Comparison of Isopleth Maps as a Means of Determining Correlations between Spatially Distributed Phenomena*, Univ. of Iowa, Dept. of Geog., Pub. No. 3, 1961.

[54] MAXWELL, A. E. *Analysing Qualitative Data*, London, Methuen, 1961.

[55] SHAEFER, FRED K. 'Exceptionalism in geography: a methodological examination', *Ann. Ass. Am. Geogr.* 43 (1953) 226–49.

[56] HARTSHORNE, *Perspective on the Nature of Geography*, chap. 5, pp. 36–47.

[57] SHEAFFER, J. R. 'Flood-to-peak interval', in White, G. F., ed. *Papers on Flood Problems*, Univ. of Chicago, Dept. of Geog., Research Paper no. 70, 1961, pp. 95–113. Also BURTON, I. *Types of Agricultural Occupance of Flood Plains in the United States*, Univ. of Chicago, Dept. of Geog., Research Paper no. 75, 1962, represents a similar attempt to classify flood plains on the basis of characteristics significant for agricultural occupance.

[58] BRAITHWAITE, R. B. *Scientific Explanation*, Cambridge University Press, 1955.

[59] ROBINSON, ARTHUR H., LINDBERG, JAMES B., and BRINKMAN, LEONARD W. 'A

correlation and regression analysis applied to rural farm population densities in the Great Plains', *Ann. Ass. Am. Geogr.* 51 (1961) 211–21.

[60] *Ibid.*, p. 211.

[61] *Ibid.*, p. 215.

[62] ROSE, 'Corn yield and climate', pp. 95–7, figs. 7 and 8.

[63] FIREY, WALTER. *Man, Mind and Land: a theory of resource use*, New York, The Free Press, 1960.

[64] CURRY, 'Climatic change', p. 21.

[65] One recent publication in this newly developing field of geography is KATES, ROBERT W. *Hazard and Choice Perception in Flood Plain Management*, Univ. of Chicago, Dept. of Geog., Research Paper no. 78, 1962. See also papers by Ian Burton and Robert Kates, and by Robert Lucas and Dean Quinney, *Natural Resources Journal*, vol. 3 (1963/64).

[66] See, for example, my description of a dispersed city as an exception to the classical central place theory in 'A restatement of the dispersed city hypothesis', *Ann. Ass. Am. Geogr.* 53 (1963).

[67] SIDDALL, WILLIAM R. 'Two kinds of geography', guest editorial, *Econ. Geogr.* 37 (1961) preceding p. 189.

[68] BERRY, B. J. L., and PRED, ALLAN. *Central Place Studies: A Bibliography of Theory and Applications*, Bibliog. Ser. no. 1, Philadelphia, Regional Science Research Inst., 1961.

[69] SCHEIDEGGER, ADRIAN E. *Theoretical Geomorphology*, Berlin, Springer-Verlag, 1961.

[70] WOLMAN, Review of *ibid. Geogr. Rev.* 53 (1963) 331–33.

[71] BUNGE, WILLIAM. *Theoretical Geography*, Lund Stud. in Geog., C, 1, 1962, Dept. of Geog., Royal Univ. of Lund.

[72] NORTH, 'Quantitative research', p. 129.

[73] Some recent work has been done in this direction. See GARRISON, 'Connectivity of the interstate highway system', *Papers and Proc., Regional Sci. Ass.* 6 (1960) 121–37; NYSTUEN, JOHN D., and DACEY, MICHAEL F. 'A graph theory interpretation of nodal regions', *ibid.* 7 (1961) 29–42; KANSKY, KARL. *Structure of Transportation Networks: Relationships between Network Geometry and Regional Characteristics*, Univ. of Chicago, Dept. of Geog., Research Paper no. 84, 1963; BURTON, IAN. 'Accessibility in northern Ontario; an application of graph theory to a regional highway network', unpub. rept. to Ont. Dept. of Highways, Toronto, 1962.

Theory, science and geography*
Wayne K. D. Davies

Throughout its history geography has been characterised by an unceasing methodological debate upon its scope and content, a debate that has occasionally scorched the pages of its varied journals.[1] Today an apparently new perspective has been opened up under the impact of the so-called quantitative revolution.[2] Statistical methods have been introduced to attain a desired level of objectivity, and a search for laws and theories has proceeded apace. All are devoted to the fundamental conception of geography as a science. Indeed, many of the exponents of this new perspective adopt an almost Lutheran stand. 'The basic approach to geography is to assume that geography is a strict science, and then proceed to examine the substantive results of such a conclusion.'[3] Such attitudes of conviction tend to give a false impression of the fact that geography has always been considered as a science—Humboldt,[4] Ritter,[5] Davis,[6] and even Vidal de la Blache[7] have all evoked the necessity of considering its scientific nature and searching for laws, whilst Hartshorne has enshrined this general conception. 'Geography accepts the universal scientific standards of precise, logical reasoning based on specifically defined, if not standardised concepts. It seeks to organise its field so that scholarly procedures of investigation and presentation may make possible, not an accumulation of unrelated fragments of individual evidence, but rather the organic growth of repeatedly checked and constantly reproductive research.'[8] Such a statement of faith contrasts strikingly with the descriptive and subjective approaches that generally characterise the present. As Ackerman observes 'the end product of geographic research still has been the contemplation of the unique. Small wonder that the subject was open to characterisation as an art. The only ready way of integrating unlike entities has appeared to be through an intuitive process, and geography appears to be concerned with unlikes at a critical step.'[9] He proceeds to point out that the intuitive 'leaps' of areal differentiation that were made especially by the teachers of the early years of this century were certainly admirable, but 'at the same time they confuse our view of the frontier of fundamental research in the discipline'.[10]

Reconciliation or explanation of this apparent contradiction between the state of the discipline, and its scientific nature, can only be made by

* Reprinted from 'Tijdschrift voor Economische en Sociale Geografie' 57 (July/August 1966), 125–30, by permission of the publishers.

the use of the unfashionable historical method. An appreciation must be made of the changing nature of 'science' and especially scientific method. Hanson[11] has recently demonstrated how facts are very much affected by the sort of attitude that the observer possesses, so that the views of past geographers need to be interpreted in the light of current knowledge about their attitudes, convictions and prejudices.

It is significant that Humboldt and Ritter both died in the year that Darwin published his *Origin of Species*. Their organisation of material was certainly based upon the prevalent philosophical views of their age, for they sought to interpret the underlying unity of nature. This unity was conceived in a teleological sense by Ritter, but was more aesthetic in the case of Humboldt.[12] Similarly their method of analysis was in line with current thinking, for Ritter rejected the *a priori* theories of the rationalists, believing that 'one must not proceed from opinion or hypothesis to observation, but from observation to observation'.[13] This essentially inductive approach had long been characteristic of scientific thinking, certainly going back to Bacon[14] and it achieved a new vigour in the educational principles of Pestalozzi.[15] He indicated the necessity of fact acquisition, their integration and finally the discernment of the general system. In geography the integration was spatial, but the laws were certainly not forthcoming from this sort of approach. Indeed it is significant that it was not until 1865 that Bacon's inductive process was attacked with any success by Liebig, the first to do so from the standpoint of modern science.[16] Yet whilst this inductive approach was considered the ideal it is without doubt that the major scientific advances were not conceived in such a manner. Galileo, Newton and Darwin all possessed in considerable degree a theoretical insight by which their observations were correlated, their 'flash of intuition' was certainly not inductively derived. But whilst Ritter and Humboldt observed, their work was devoted to describing a 'natural unity' of the world, a romantic conception that has often survived into the present day.

The impact of Darwin's evolutionary thesis was not confined to biology, for its implications and methodological conceptions permeated science. The mechanism he postulated as an explanation of the variation of organisms was that of the survival of the fittest, a survival that depended upon adaptation to the environment. This cause/effect doctrine led, in the determinist school of geography, to the human phenomena in space being considered as determined by their physical background. Causal connections were substituted in cases where the interrelation was only casual. Yet despite its over elaboration, and the often untenable positions into which it floundered, it is significant that the determinists used the logical methodology that lies at the heart of science today. Its conclusions were expressed as laws, that were deductively connected into theories, whilst the importance of the generalisation was stressed. Thus although W. M. Davis can be criticised for maintaining that the relationships he described were seen from 'the modern principle of evolution —the adaptation of all the earth's inhabitants to earth',[17] he went on to express views upon the relation of the general and the particular that would not be contradicted today. 'I believe it is possible to discover and establish general principles in geography (as in physics and geometry) and to teach individual items chiefly as illustrations of the principles under which they fall . . . they may, perhaps, be . . . aided in perceiving the proper relation of the specific to the general in their own subject.'[18]

Rejection of the determinist thesis by the possibilist school unfortunately led to the abandonment of much of this scientific methodology— the structure or logic was discarded because of the inadequacy of the premises. The historical perspective certainly corrected the corruption of relations that the determinist school had exemplified in their more rigid works. However many of the ills that have been diagnosed by certain young geographical doctors of philosophy, Bunge[19] and Berry,[20] certainly stem from this rejection. Lip service was paid to law development and scientific description, and the stress upon man's free will inevitably led to the contemplation of the unique case,[21] and to the enshrinement of regional description as the true goal of geography.[22] To apply orderly logical analysis and experimentation to the sort of description that stressed the 'personality' of areas was impossible. The intuitive process that integrated the unique crystallised as an art.

A rapprochement with modern science has taken place at an accelerating pace within the last ten years. It has been realised that social phenomena can be regarded as law giving, if the laws are regarded as generalisations, not chains of command.[23] But it must be stressed that the critics of the established field have not attempted to reject all that has gone before. The attempt has been made to reformulate the material upon a more systematic basis and in a scientific fashion.

Although it has been shown that the conception of geography as a science has meant different things at different times, it seems necessary at this stage to answer the question of 'what is a science'. The *Oxford Dictionary* defines science as 'systematic and formulated knowledge; pursuit of this or principles regulating such pursuit',[24] an interpretation that is wide enough to include the classificatory lawfulness of Aristotle[25] and the scientific method of Bacon.[26] This does, however, lend support to the view that the aim of science has probably been the same at all times. 'For science in its totality the ultimate goal is the creation of a monistic system in which . . . the world's enormous multiplicity is reduced to something like unity'[27] or as Whitehead has put it 'to see what is general in what is particular'.[28] However the method by which this aim is arrived at has changed over the centuries. Bacon's inductive approach was designed to prepare the mind for the ultimate truth by cleansing it of anticipation and prejudices.[29] Modern scientific methodology, however, differs. 'Science never pursues the illusory aims of making its answers final . . .',[30] indeed it is essentially a way of thinking that creates a body of empirically supported propositions that are related within a particular theoretical structure. This creation has occurred as a result of experimentation and observation that are fruitful for further experimentation and observation.[31]

Davis has observed that 'geography will become more and more a scientific study in proportion to the use that is made of the fully developed scientific method'.[32] Looking at the results of the fifty years since this statement was made, and within the context of the modern, not a Baconian, conception of a science, then it must be accepted that geography is still ill qualified to consider itself a science. The mere accumulation of facts, even if obtained objectively,[33] does not make a science in the modern sense. It is the way of approaching these facts that distinguishes a science. 'Out of the uninterrupted sense experiences, science cannot be distilled, no matter how industriously we gather and sort them.'[34] This is the essential difference between alchemy purged of its magic and chemistry.

Essentially, therefore, it is by the standard of current organisational techniques used by fellow workers that the science of geography must be judged. We cannot afford to agree with Hartshorne that 'the essential characteristics of geography have been determined for us by its past development . . . [and] . . . can only [sic] be considered as binding or restrictive on our freedom of research only if one fails to observe the full expanse and depth of the field which that tradition provides'.[35] Such a view is prescientific in that it projects attitudes to the golden past, not to the future. To adhere to such a historically determined methodology is to erect a guild system upon our thought. Indeed one of the essential characteristics of modern science is that it is cumulative and progressive, ever re-examining its concepts in the light of evidence that has been discovered. An analogy is useful to demonstrate this point. What would be the current position of physics if its concern had been limited to gross matter. The heart of physics is now seen to be the science of events, not particles, and the general principle of indeterminacy has had a profound influence on all scientific thinking.

Inevitably some of the findings of the other sciences are influencing geographical thought so that it is not surprising that the Hettner-Hartshorne conception of methodology[36] is being challenged. Bunge, following on from Schaefer,[37] has observed that a single methodology cannot incorporate the general and the unique, at least not in the sense that Hartshorne seems to contemplate, and still remain a science.[38] This dichotomy is not the only one that has arisen in geographical thinking and Hartshorne has clearly demonstrated how ill founded many of them are.[39] Yet this general/unique difference remains, and it is pertinent, in view of its basic significance, to examine its origin and nature.

Geography studies the spatial variations of phenomena,[40] and with a romantic conception of the unity of nature these variations were perceived on the basis of their integration in regions. A region is, however, essentially an intellectual concept,[41] though the possibilist monographs seemed to give them an identity of their own, so that they seemed far more than an illuminatory device. Yet once one accepts the region, as being the prime unit of study, i.e. the place where the integration of spatial variation occurs, then one is accepting the unique. It is bound to be unique because of the multitude of possible combinations that could occur amongst all the available phenomena. To consider the region as the culminating core of geography is to elaborate the doctrine of the unique. Sets of discoveries formulated upon such a basis cannot therefore be connected together. The only possible way of connecting these together is to hold some romantic view of the underlying unity of nature as in the mid nineteenth century, or to put forward some deterministic philosophy. In the terms of the latter then, it is the physical basis in any area that has determined the human manifestation. From this base the spatial variation is explained. Yet it is the spatial variation in phenomena and their connections that is ultimately the prime cause of these regional differences, not vice versa. It is not place that gives these differences, but the space that holds them. An analogy with the concepts of atomic structure will demonstrate this point.

By the early nineteenth century, chemists realised that the different elements that they could recognise were constructed of atoms with certain properties—hence the atomic weights table. Subsequent research has shown that each atom is merely a special case of a number of basic particles, the distinctive atom being the result of a special connection of these particles. So it is the organisation of the structure, not the early conception of the building block, that is important and basic to understanding and further work. Different planes of understanding have therefore been elaborated, material, element, atom, particle etc., but it is the organisation of the structure at any level that gives it distinctiveness. The properties of any structure can be described at each level, but one is only accounting for the differences, not illustrating how they are derived. So by conceiving of the phenomenon in terms of its structure and connections, one can proceed to a different level of understanding. Although the analogy can be pushed too far, regions in geography could be conceived as attempts at different planes of understanding, that is if we ignore any direct connection with atomic structure. Hence the connections and structure of the regions are all important. To formulate a region, or look at a material, and then simply to describe it will not get us far, for this is an elaboration of the unique. Science can only deal with populations, only then does its laws hold good and can the scientific method of orderly analysis be applied. Inevitably the process of analysis breaks down when the object of study is changed from a population of electrons to a single one. Yet this is what geography is attempting in its enshrinement of the region—it is building up the unique and then looking for laws. Little wonder they have not been forthcoming.

In essence it must be accepted, as Bunge puts it, that 'a single methodology cannot embrace both the unique and the general'.[42] This has involved some re-thinking about the concept of a region, but once it is conceived as a generic, not a unique, fact then the difficulty is resolved. So Schaefer is able to observe that 'regional geography is like the laboratory in which the theoretical physicists' generalisations must stand the test of use and truth'.[43]

The paradoxical situation that began this discussion has now been resolved. Acceptance of geography as a science can only be made if it places itself within the current methodological conception of a science, and uses its techniques, instead of harking back to the science of other eras. But the two schools of thought are not as opposed as one might expect at first glance, and the new generation of geographers does not reject all that has gone before, quite the reverse.[44] It is possible to achieve useful work and results even under a different philosophy. What is radical about the new approach is the desire to make the discipline more productive, and it is necessary to demonstrate how this is being achieved.

Objections are sometimes made that descriptions are unscientific. However all science began as description. Facts relevant to each particular perspective were chosen and they were then organised. The advances came when the discoveries were fitted together into theoretical structures and tested. The early geographers also began by describing the facts relevant to their discipline, and their organisation showed well conceived spatial notions and stimulating conceptions as to the interrelations between objects. In essence this organisation is a theory, or at least a hypothesis and the connection of facts is carried out by means of an intuitive theory.[45] However these intuitive connections were rarely formulated in a way that made the testing of the propositions possible. For any discipline to advance scientifically the theories, once suggested, should be removed from the intuitive level and be made specific.[46] The theory should then be formulated as precisely as possible and tested, this is what students of geography have rarely attempted except in limited fields. Concern with the region *per se* as the organisational framework has led to the compilation of inventories, a series of facts about a particular zone. This traditional approach, formalised in the geology, soils, climate, settlement etc. progression has had a stultifying effect upon geography, because, as we have seen, it leads to the contemplation of the unique. Inventories have been the organisational medium, not theories. Yet there is a way out of this impasse once the geographic variations are conceived in space rather than in place. Then description is not made equivalent to inventory, but is directed towards theory formulation and the translation of the intuitive into the specific. Goal directed or problem orientated programmes can then be conceived,[47] and with successive building upon different works the end process must be creative since it is not only conceived for itself. Thus the work of an individual can be built upon in a way that is impossible in art, since it is not scientifically creative. T. S. Eliot need not necessarily have had a Shakespeare before him in order to produce his work, but Newton certainly needed Galileo.

Whilst the work of a scientist should be conceived as putting forward and testing theories, the initial stage does not necessarily call for logical analysis. Einstein has observed that 'the search for those highly universal . . . laws from which a picture of the world can be obtained cannot come by pure logic. There is no logical path leading to those . . . laws. They can only be reached by intuition. . . .'[48] Koestler has recently revealed the nature of this intuitive act, calling it the bisociative act,[49] and although he attempts to apply it to both science and arts there is an essential difference; in science the act leads to testable predictions. Admittedly mechanical methods and set formulas can eliminate mistakes, but eventual advance is by an intuitive flash. The importance of this for geography should be apparent, these intuitive flashes are only of use if the material has been organised in a testable way, at least if a claim to be a science is made. Problem orientation at and between places, not inventory, is the way out of the geographical dilemma, otherwise inventory leads to the enshrinement of place, the unique.

This sort of argument leads into a necessary discussion of the need for quantitative methods. They are not only significant in making geography more objective, but are important in that the theories formulated in any description can be made explicit.

The use of mathematical techniques is not necessarily a revolutionary approach,[50] it is merely a development of one that has a long history in geography. It is by the logical connection of maps and words that geographers have, in the past, linked the facts with their broad generalisations. Yet statistics act in a similar way, they represent another logical connection, but now the validity of the argument can be tested.[51] So the use of statistical techniques can fulfil three functions, the summary of data (descriptive statistics), the testing of statements that are made, and also in the formulation of models where their use as a logical process is more apparent.[52] Enough has been written upon the usefulness of these techniques to make any greater elaboration at this stage out of place, but it is certainly necessary to consider their spread as only one more example of the diffusion of scientific techniques into the modern world.

It seems to be one of the fundamental results of science that this diffusion of new techniques brings about a changing attitude about objects, for they can be manipulated in different ways. This is certainly true today, for the work of the theoretical physicists has revealed that events at the atomic level cannot be observed with certainty. A new principle, that of uncertainty, has been introduced.[53] The laws of probability, of chance, have replaced the strict determinism of Newton's laws, and quantum mechanics have given the most complete picture to date of the understanding of the world. The relation of this principle to geography has already been sketched by Emrys Jones[54] who, following Kaufmann,[55] pointed out that there are, perhaps, two kinds of laws, the cause/effect laws of classical physics, adequate at a macroscopic level, and microscopic laws or quantum laws.

> If the actions of a large number of human beings follow a pattern, however variable the human motivation, then generalisations or broad principles can be drawn up. But however broad the generalisation, it might fail in strict application to any single phenomenon. Any pattern which emerges does so as the statistical mean of the behaviour of a mass of human individuals, and any generalisation which the human geographer might find useful must be based on this behaviour.[56]

This idea will incorporate the concept of human free will since 'the course of human activity cannot . . . be adequately predicted'.[57] The analogy with the physicist is apt, for electrons are so small that individual behaviour cannot be observed without upsetting them. Thus, the uncertainty principle, if applied to the world of human action, enables us to appreciate that there is a difference between action in mass, and action at an individual plane. The latter is not determined and the former represents the answer to 'how' and not 'why'. In other words the generalisation is 'a provisional hypothesis to account for observed phenomena'.[58]

The result of this is that probability can be applied to human geography. The approach 'replaces the concept of an inevitable effect by that of a probable trend'.[59] Several workers have, by their simulation techniques, already adopted this sort of approach in their geographical writings,[60] and it is apparent that many of the models that are being used for testing data are incorporated in a stochastic framework.

Geography is, therefore, certainly being pushed down the path of modern science, at least in some quarters. The physicist or chemist who is engaged in research can go to the crux of the matter, to the heart of an organised structure for a set of scientific doctrines. In consequence a collection of generally accepted problem situations is already in existence. The hope is that geography can develop in such a way. In case the necessity of a theoretical framework is overlooked, it must be emphasised that it is only when experimentation is organised on such a basis that advances can be made. As Popper observes 'experiment is planned action in which every step is governed by theory'.[61] Organisation is therefore the key to progress, and this involves methodological questions that have been obscured in the glorification of 'the region'. Yet the type of organisation chosen does affect the results. There are many kinds of theory, so that the results must be considered upon the basis of the structure used. A recent study has outlined some of the difficulties with respect to geomorphology.[62] But these are not the only problems, science as a whole is suffering from the specialisation of its branches. Fortunately the so-called 'General Systems Theory'[63] has been formulated in order to reintegrate, the diverse aspects. Mutual relations can then be perceived, with the consequent possibility of cross fertilisation. Berry[64] has recently applied the technique to show the variety of possible approaches to regional analysis, and as a by product has shown the inadequacy of present approaches.

What is significant about these new frontiers is not so much the results that have been achieved to date, but the attitude of mind that is engendered. The search for organisational concepts and theories[65] is developing apace, fresh perspectives are being opened up upon old attitudes, problems and dilemmas. All this need not be restrictive for its ultimate aim is clarification. It is not before time that geography developed a productive methodology with an organised point of view, theoretical structure and a problem orientation. At present its methodology is largely pre-quantum. Yet the subject is not alone in its struggles. For instance, sociology is experiencing all the same internal conflicts in its advance towards the status of a science. In geography, as in sociology,[66] and like all young sciences, a great deal of energy will be devoted towards descriptive study but the value of this is only fragmentary until they can be unified with other descriptive findings. What is needed at all levels of generality is the formulation and testing of significant hypotheses. The alternative is to sink back into a morass of regional description at a subjective level. So if geography is to be a discipline in the true sense of the word, then no longer can we share the view of Wooldridge and East that 'the scope of geography is distressingly wide and its aim is far from clear'.[67] That the scope is wide should be cause of jubilation not distress, whilst its aim should be, and is being, clarified.

Notes and references

[1] For instance the reply by Hartshorne to Schaefer's article: HARTSHORNE, R. 'Exceptionalism in geography re-examined', *Ann. Ass. Am. Geogr.* 45 (1955) 205–44.

SCHAEFER, F. 'Exceptionalism in geography: a methodological examination', *Ann. Ass. Am. Geogr.* 43 (1953) 226–49.

[2] BURTON, I. 'The quantitative revolution and theoretical geography', *Can. Geogr.* 7 (1963) 151–162.

[3] BUNGE, W. *Theoretical Geography*, Lund Stud. in Geog., C, 1, Lund (Sweden), Gleerup, 1962, p. x, Introduction.

[4] HARTSHORNE, R. *The Nature of Geography*, A.A.G. Reprint, 1958, pp. 69 and 77, for Humboldt's views on geography and the sciences.

[5] HARTSHORNE, *ibid.*, p. 54, for Ritter's views.

[6] DAVIS, W. M. 'Possibly . . . geography is the most complex of all sciences', p. 38, and note discussion on pp. 41–2 in: *Geographical Essays*, ed. D. W. Johnson. Dover Publications, 1954.

[7] VIDAL DE LA BLACHE, P. He possessed 'a conception of the earth as a whole, whose parts are unco-ordinated, where phenomena follow a definite sequence and obey general laws to which particular cases are related', in *Principles of Human Geography*, trans. M. T. Bingham, London, 1926, p. 7.

[8] HARTSHORNE, *The Nature of Geography*, p. 464.

[9] ACKERMAN, E. A. *Geography as a Fundamental Research Discipline*, University of Chicago, Department of Geography Research Paper no. 53, 1958, p. 16.

[10] *Ibid*, p. 16.

[11] HANSON, N. R. *Patterns of Discovery*, Cambridge University Press, 1958.

[12] (a) HARTSHORNE, *op. cit.*, p. 65.

(b) SINNHUBER, K. 'Carl Ritter', *Scottish geogr. Mag.* 75 (1959) 153–63.

[13] Quoted in HARTSHORNE, *op. cit.*, p. 54.

[14] Francis Bacon (1561–1626), see chap. 7, pp. 526–30 in: RUSSELL, BERTRAND, *History of Western Philosophy*, London, Allen & Unwin, new ed., 1961.

[15] SINNHUBER, *op. cit.*, p. 156.

[16] LIEBIG, 'Induktion und Deduktion', quoted in POPPER, K. *The Logic of Scientific Discovery*, London, Hutchinson, 1959, pp. 25–32.

[17] DAVIS, *op. cit.*, p. 32.

[18] *Ibid.*, pp. 30–1.

[19] BUNGE, *op. cit.*

[20] BERRY, B. J. L. 'Approaches to regional analysis: a synthesis', *Ann. Ass. Am. Geogr.* 54 (1964) 2–11.

[21] The importance of the often quoted formulas of the possibilists in this respect cannot be overstressed. Thus, 'there are no necessities, but everywhere possibilities; and man as the master of these possibilities is the judge of their use', in: FEBVRE, L. *A Geographical Introduction to History* (1925), p. 236.

[22] (a) DICKINSON, R. E., and HOWARTH, O. J. R. 'The culminating point and as many would claim, the essential aim of modern geography is thus the latest phase in the development of the subject', in *The Making of Geography*, Oxford 1933, p. 233.

(b) Note also the view of E. W. GILBERT, 'It is through the region that new life has been given to the dead bones of geography. In the view of the writer geography is the art of describing the personalities of regions', in 'Geography and regionalism', chap. 15 of *Geography in the Twentieth Century*, ed. G. Taylor, Methuen, 1957, p. 346.

[23] JONES, E. 'Cause and effect in human geography', *Ann. Ass. Am. Geogr.* 46, no. 4 (1956) 369–77.

[24] *The Concise Oxford Dictionary*, 4th edn. (revised by E. McIntosh), Oxford University Press, 1950.

[25] See chapters on Aristotle, Book 1, chap. 19–23, in RUSSELL, B., *op. cit.*, pp. 173–217.

[26] See chapter on Bacon, Book 3, chap. 7, in RUSSELL, B., *op. cit.*, pp. 526–30.

[27] HUXLEY, A. *Literature and Science*, Chatto & Windus, 1963.

[28] A. N. Whitehead, 1911, quoted in RUSSELL, *op. cit.*

[29] Bacon, see Book 3, chap. 7, in RUSSELL, *op. cit.*, pp. 526–30.

[30] POPPER, *op. cit.*, p. 281.

[31] Note NAGEL, F. *The Structure of Science*, London, Routledge, 1961, pp. 1–14.

[32] DAVIS, *op. cit.*, p. 59.

[33] The distinction between objective and subjective follows the definition used by Kant. 'A justification is objective, if in principle it can be tested and understood by anybody'. 'Subjective is applied to feelings of conviction', quoted in POPPER, *op. cit.*, p. 44.

In view of the discussion which follows it must be emphasised that a 'conviction' can be converted into an 'objective justification' only by the use of adequate testing procedures. The intuitive thought can then become a specific and accepted fact.

[34] POPPER, *op. cit.*, p. 280.

[35] HARTSHORNE, R. *Perspective on the Nature of Geography*, A.A.G., London, Murray, 1960, p. 183.

[36] For instance, SCHAEFER, *op. cit.*, p. 226, and BERRY, *op. cit.*, p. 2.

[37] SCHAEFER, *op. cit.*

[38] BUNGE, *op. cit.*, p. 9.

[39] HARTSHORNE, *op. cit.*, p. 79.

[40] 'Geography is concerned with the arrangement of things and with the associations of things that distinguish one area from another. It is concerned with the connections and movements between areas'. JAMES, P. E. *American Geography at Mid Century* (29th Yearbook of the National Council for the Social Studies), Washington, 1959, p. 10.

A more explicit conception of this view is given by BERRY, *op. cit.*, pp. 2–5. He observes that 'the integrating concepts and processes of the geographer relate to spatial arrangements and distribution, to spatial integration, to spatial interaction and organisation and to spatial process'. This spatial view is, however, limited 'to the world wide ecosystem of which man is the dominant part'. Whilst this perspective of viewing a particular system is sufficient to differentiate geography from the physical and biological sciences, Berry observes that the social sciences also study the man made environment. However other distributional and organisational theories are more central to the social scientist than this spatial one so it is this spatial perspective that is important. Berry concludes by observing that 'these environments are not studied in their totality by geographers, only in their spatial aspects'. Unless geography intends to claim the whole of science this ought to be accepted. SCHAEFER (*op. cit.*, p. 227) has also drawn attention to this by emphasising that geography and history have claimed too much, they are not *the* integrating sciences.

[41] 'A region is not an objective fact; rather it is an intellectual concept', JAMES, *op. cit.*, p. 17.

[42] BUNGE, *op. cit.*, p. 12.

[43] SCHAEFER, *op. cit.*, p. 230.

[44] BUNGE, *op. cit.*, p. 6.

[45] STEBBING, S. L. *A Modern Elementary Logic*, London, Methuen University Paperbacks, 1961, p. 170.

[46] Most anthropologists also emphasise this attitude by showing the need for a clear conceptual framework and adequate theoretical basis, e.g. FORSTER, G. M. *Traditional Cultures*, New York, Harper and Row, 1962, pp. 195–217.

[47] (*a*) FORSTER, *ibid.*, p. 201.

   (*b*) BERRY, B. J. L. 'Further comments concerning "geographic" and "economic" economic geography', *Professional Geographer* 11 (1959), no. 1, part 1, p. 12.

[48] EINSTEIN, A. quoted in POPPER, *op. cit.*, p. 32.

[49] KOESTLER, A. *The Act of Creation*, Hutchinson, 1964.

[50] BURTON, *op. cit.*

[51] BUNGE, *op. cit.*, p. 37.

[52] BURTON, *op. cit.*, p. 1.

[53] HEISENBERG, W. *Nuclear Physics*, Philosophical Library, 1953.

[54] JONES, *op. cit.*, p. 370.

[55] KAUFMANN, F. A. *Methodology of the Social Sciences*, Oxford, 1944.

[56] JONES, *op. cit.*, p. 373.

[57] *Ibid.*, p. 373.

[58] *Ibid.*, p. 374.

[59] BRONOWSKI, J. *The Common Sense of Science*, New York, Random House, 1959.

[60] One of the early works in this field was HÄGERSTRAND, T. *The Propagation of Innovation Waves*, Lund Studies in Geography, B, 4, 1952, University of Lund, Sweden.

[61] POPPER, *op. cit.*, p. 280.

[62] CHORLEY, R. J. *Geomorphology and General System Theory*, Geological Survey Professional Paper 500-B, U.S. Gov. Printing Office, Washington, 1962.

[63] BERTALANFFY, L. VON. 'General systems theory: a new approach to the unity of science', *Human Biology*, 23 (1951) 303–61.
[64] BERRY, B. J. L. 'Approaches to regional analysis: a synthesis', *Ann. Ass. Am. Geogr.* 54 (1964) 2–11.
[65] For example: CHORLEY, R. J. 'Geography and analogue theory', *Ann. Ass. Am. Geogr.* 54 (1964) 127–137.
[66] MADGE, J. *The Origins of Scientific Sociology*, London, Tavistock Publication, 1963.
[67] WOOLDRIDGE, S. W., and EAST, W. G. *The Spirit and Purpose of Geography*, London, Hutchinson's University Press, 1952, p. 13.

Exceptionalism in geography: a methodological examination*

Fred K. Schaefer†

The methodology of a field is not a grab bag of special techniques. In geography such techniques as map making, 'methods' of teaching, or historical accounts of the development of the field are still often mistaken for methodology. It is one of the purposes of the present paper to help dispel this confusion. Methodology proper deals with the position and scope of the field within the total system of the sciences and with the character and nature of its concepts.

Methodology thrives on change and evolution. In an active field concepts are continuously either refined or entirely discarded; laws and hypotheses are, as the case may be, confirmed or disconfirmed or, perhaps, reduced to the status of no longer satisfactory approximations. Methodology is the logic of this process. That is why, particularly in young disciplines, methodological debate is a sign of health. Seen in this light, the methodology of geography is too complacent. Some fundamental ideas have remained unchallenged for decades though there is ample reason to doubt their power. Some others, half forgotten, lie scattered around, exposed to slow erosion like the tells in the plain of Iraq. Spethmann[1] made this point when he complained in 1928 that the methodology Hettner[2] had just published was in the main a collection of articles twenty or thirty years old, at a time when virtually all the other sciences experienced almost hectic change and progress. Turning to America, one may add that Hartshorne[3] in 1939 restated many of Hettner's views with little change or criticism. Worse than that, Hartshorne's own work, undoubtedly an important milestone in the history of American geographical thought, went itself unchallenged through the thirteen years that have passed since its publication.

The methodological literature is small. Alexander von Humboldt, rightly called the father of scientific geography, was also the first relatively modern author to pay attention to the logic of its concepts. Two generations passed before the next major contribution was made by Hettner. But only two years after Hettner's book had appeared an Austrian philosopher of science, Viktor Kraft,[4] published an essay in the

* Reprinted from *Annals of the Association of American Geographers* 43 (1953) 226–49, by permission of the publishers.

† I am much indebted to Professor Gustav Bergmann of the Philosophy Department of The State University of Iowa who has kindly read the manuscript and made many valuable suggestions.

field which is as yet unexcelled in clarity and succinctness. Hartshorne's work in this country was the only other, and is so far the last major attempt. It will appear from the following discussion that while Hartshorne follows Hettner rather closely in some respects, Kraft may be said to continue more nearly the tradition of Humboldt.

I

Geographers writing on the scope and nature of geography often begin quite apologetically as if they had to justify its very existence. And strangely, or perhaps, psychologically speaking, not so strangely, they go on claiming too much. In such writings geography, together with history, emerges as *the* 'integrating science', completely different from other disciplines, whose unique importance finds its expression in the special methods which it must use to reach its profound results. Unhappily, the actual results of geographical research, while not to be minimised, are somewhat lacking in those startling new and deeper insights which one is led to expect from such exuberant characterisations of the field. In fact, the progress of geography was slower than that of some other social sciences such as, for instance, economics. Some of this lag is perhaps due to the unrealistic ambitions fostered by the unclear idea of a unique integrating science with a unique methodology all its own. On the other hand, there is no need for the apologies which so often precede the exaggerated claims. The existence of a field is after all mainly the product of the division of labour; it needs no 'methodological' justification. In this obvious sense geography is no doubt an important field.

With the development of the natural sciences in the eighteenth and nineteenth centuries it became apparent that mere description would not do. Description, even if followed by classification, does not explain the manner in which phenomena are distributed over the world. To explain the phenomena one has described means always to recognise them as instances of laws. Another way of saying the same thing is to insist that science is not so much interested in individual facts as in the patterns they exhibit. In geography the major pattern-producing variables are, of course, spatial. Humboldt, who had come from the natural sciences, and also Ritter, accepted the proposition that all natural relations and, therefore, all spatial relations, were governed by laws. For this new type of work tools had to be provided in the form of concepts and laws. Hence geography had to be conceived as the science concerned with the formulation of the laws governing the spatial distribution of certain features on the surface of the earth. The latter limitation is essential. For, with the successful rise of geophysics, astronomy, and geology, geography can no longer deal with the whole earth, but only the earth's surface and 'with the earthly (irdischen) things that fill its spaces'.[5]

Humboldt and Ritter thus recognised as the major concern of geography the manner in which the natural phenomena, including man, were distributed in space. This implies that geographers must describe and explain the manner in which things combine 'to fill an area'. These combinations change, of course, from area to area. Different areas contain different factors or the same factors in different combinations. These differences either in the combination of factors or in their arrangement from place to place underlie the common sense notion that areas differ. Following the Greek geographers, this viewpoint is called the chorographic or chorological one, depending on the level of abstraction. Geography, thus, must pay attention to the spatial arrangement of the phenomena in an area and not so much to the phenomena themselves. Spatial relations are the ones that matter in geography, and no others. Nonspatial relations found among the phenomena in an area are the subject matter of other specialists such as the geologist, anthropologist, or economist. Of all the limitations on geography this one seems to be the most difficult for geographers to observe. To judge even from recent research they do not always clearly distinguish between, say, social relations on the one hand and spatial relations among social factors on the other. Actually, one may safely say that most of what we find in any given area is of primary interest to the other social scientists. For instance, the connections between ideology and political behaviour, or the lawful connections between the psychological traits of a population and its economic institutions do not concern the geographer. If he attempts to explain such matters the geographer turns into a jack of all trades. Like all others the geographer had better cultivate his speciality, the laws concerning spatial arrangements. But to say this is not to say that some of these 'geographical' laws are not of interest to other disciplines.

Kraft, in discussing Humboldt and Ritter, agrees with them that geography is, at least potentially, a science trying to discover laws; that it is limited to the earth's surface and that it is essentially chorological. Incidentally, he also feels that this suffices to set geography logically apart as a discipline of its own.

The chorological viewpoint presented geography with a problem that has caused more methodological controversy and misunderstanding than any other. The geographer's investigations, be he a physical, economic, or political geographer, are of two different types: either *systematic* or *regional*. A region contains, to be sure, a special, unique, yet in some ways uniform combination of kinds or categories of phenomena. The detail with which the regional geographer describes, lists, or catalogues these features at the outset of his investigation depends, of course, on the size of the region considered. Next he will want to gather information as to the spatial distribution of the individuals in each class. But this information, too, belongs to his data rather than his results. For it does not go beyond mere description. His proper task as a social scientist begins only at this stage. First, he must try to find those relations obtaining among the individuals and the classes by virtue of which the area considered has that unitary character that makes it a region. Second, he must identify the relations which obtain in this particular area as instances of the causal interrelations that hold, by virtue of general laws among such features, individuals, classes, or what have you, in all known circumstances. This second step amounts, therefore, to an application of systematic geography to the area in question. Only after both these steps have been taken can one say that a scientific understanding of the region has been achieved.

This brings us to systematic geography. Its procedure is in principle not different from that of any other social or natural science which searches for laws or, what amounts to the same thing, has reached the systematic stage. Spatial relations among two or more selected classes of phenomena must be studied all over the earth's surface in order to obtain a generalisation or law. Assume, for instance, that two phenomena are found to occur frequently at the same place. A hypothesis may then be formed to the effect that whenever members of the one class are found in a place, members of the other class will be found there also, under conditions specified by the hypothesis. To test any such hypothesis the geographer will need a larger number of cases and of variables than he could find in any one region. But if it is confirmed in a sufficient number of cases then the hypothesis becomes a law that may be utilised to 'explain' situations not yet considered. The present conditions of the field indicate a stage of development, well known from other social sciences, which finds most geographers still busy with classifications rather than looking for laws. We know that classification is the first step in any kind of systematic work. But when the other steps, which naturally follow, are not taken, and classifications become the end of scientific investigation, then the field becomes sterile.

The present lack of clarity about the relative rôle and importance of regional and systematic geography can probably be traced to the preference given to either one or the other at various periods in the history of the field. For example: the physical geographer, being closer to the impact of the development of the natural sciences, felt at times the need for adequate tools specifically his own in the form of functions, rules, or laws. Physical geography had, therefore, a phase in the late nineteenth century when it concentrated on systematic work at the expense of regional studies. Some of these authors apparently felt that regional work, since it did not lead directly to the formulation of laws, was not worth doing and had better be abandoned. Thereafter, at the beginning of the century, largely as a reaction to this exclusive concentration on systematic studies on the part of the physical geographers, when the interest began to shift towards social or human geography, the social geographer scorned the fumbling systematic efforts which, in the absence of any adequate social sciences to draw upon, attempted to find the laws regulating the spatial aspects of social variables. Any generalisation, clearly recognised as such, was considered empty and unpractical by these writers; regional descriptive geography appeared to them to be the only honourable occupation. To these men we owe the bulk of descriptive literature which, of course, contains much valuable material. Where they were actually better than their methodological creed they operated with insight or perhaps some sort of artistic feeling. In whatever methodological writing they did they aligned themselves with the opponents of scientific method.

All these confused controversies are still lingering on, so that even today hardly an article or book is free from them. Yet there is a small measure of progress. Hardly anybody maintains today that either the systematic or the regional emphasis is entirely useless and should, therefore, be abandoned. In its contemporary version the argument takes the form of the old hen and egg story, still debating the relative importance of systematic and regional work. Hettner thought that the core of geography was regional. Hartshorne believes that systematic geography is really indispensable to regional work; whoever likes it, or is by temperament fitted to pursue it, need not desert it; but the heart of geography is nevertheless regional. Just imagine a contemporary physicist maintaining that theoretical physics has its place and that its devotees should be left in peace, but that the real core of physics is experimental; or an economist who believes that only the study of a 'regional' economy that actually exists now or existed in the past is economics proper, while the systematic part of economics, which formulates its laws, is merely esoteric byplay.

Neither Humboldt nor Ritter were plagued by these pseudo-issues. ✓ As they clearly saw, systematic geography attempts to formulate the rules and laws which are applied in regional geography. Humboldt felt that the formulation and testing of laws is the highest target a scientist could aim at. The systematic geographer, studying the spatial relations among a limited number of classes of phenomena, arrives by a process of abstraction at laws representing ideal or model situations; that is, situations which are artificial in that only a relatively small number of factors are causally operative in each of them. Practically, no single such law or even body of laws will fit any concrete situation completely. In this non-controversial sense every region is, indeed, unique. Only, this is nothing peculiar to geography. As in all other fields the joint application of the laws available is the only way to exhibit and to explain what is the case. How much the known laws will explain and how complex a situation the scientist can tackle is a matter of degree, depending on the stage of development of the field. Ritter, one of the first modern geographers, had no systematic knowledge at his disposal. Conscious of this limitation, he kept regional geography, which was his primary interest, on a purely descriptive level. But he certainly made no virtue out of his choice and no methodological principle out of a practical limitation. Conversely, there is no need for regional geography to feel inferior to the systematic branch. For, systematic geography will always have to obtain its data from regional geography, just as the theoretical physicist has to rely on the laboratory for his. Furthermore, systematic geography receives a good deal of guidance as to what kind of laws it should look for from regional geography. For, again, regional geography is like the laboratory in which the theoretical physicist's generalisations must stand the test of use and truth. It seems fair to say, then, in conclusion, that regional and systematic geography are codign, inseparable, and equally indispensable aspects of the field.

One of the causes of the unnecessary argument between systematists and regionalists is, perhaps, purely psychological. Not every good theoretical physicist would make a good experimentalist, and conversely. Generally, the ability to organise a field theoretically is not always associated with the proper interest and skill in collecting its data. Also, the application of laws to concrete situations demands a special aptitude. But there is no reason why such temperamental differences should be hypostatised into pseudomethodological positions.

Hettner, and even Kraft, speak of the two complementary emphases as founding a 'dualism' which sets geography apart from all other disciplines. It should be already clear that there is, in fact, nothing unique or peculiar to geography in all this. If the term is meant to indicate opposition or conflict, then it is outright misleading. Yet, this so-called 'dualism' has been cited in support of the claim that geography is a methodologically unique discipline. Nor is the complexity of the situation that faces the regional geographer in any sense out of the ordinary so that he would have a peculiarly difficult task of 'integration', in another meaning of the glittering term. Quite to the contrary; he is at all fours with the other social scientists. When the economist applies his generalisations or laws to a given economic order, he deals not only with the complexity of the purely economic situation but takes account of the political, psychological, and social factors that influence it. This after all, is the gist of so-called institutional economics. Similarly, a sociologist or anthropologist who analyses a given primitive society, or a communist or agricultural one, deals with very complex situations. In the pretentious language of some geographers, such a sociologist 'integrates' not only heterogeneous phenomena but, clearly, also heterogeneous laws. To say that the task of those social scientists is less complex, or less integrative than that of the geographer makes no sense. If anything, it is even more complex. For, the geographer's specific task in the analysis of a region is limited to spatial relations only. Accordingly, even the most complete geographical analysis of any region gives only partial insight into it. After the geographer is done there is still much work left before one understands fully the social structure of that region. Obviously; for, how could such an understanding be attained without even considering such factors as the ecology, economics, institutions, and mores of the region. In a manner of speaking, the geographer provides only the setting for the further studies of the other social scientists. It is, therefore, absurd to maintain that the geographers are distinguished among the scientists through the integration of heterogeneous phenomena which they achieve. There is nothing extraordinary about geography in that respect. One may conjecture that this notion is a hangover from the time when there were no social sciences and not much natural science, and when such quaint and encyclopædic endeavours as natural history and cosmology still occupied their place.

We have seen that there is a whole group of ideas which are variations of a common theme: geography is quite different from all other sciences, methodologically unique, as it were. Influential and persistent as this position is in its several variations, it deserves a name of its own. I shall call it *exceptionalism*, and, for the moment, inquire into some of its historical roots.

II

The father of exceptionalism is Immanuel Kant. Though undoubtedly one of the great philosophers of the eighteenth century, Kant was a poor geographer when compared with his contemporaries or even Bernhard Varenius who died more than one hundred and fifty years before him. Kant made the exceptionalist claim not only for geography but also for history. According to him history and geography find themselves in an exceptional position different from that of the so-called systematic sciences. This grouping of geography with history has tempted many subsequent writers to elaborate the alleged similarity in order to obtain some insight into the nature of geography. This is undoubtedly one of the roots of the historicist variant of the claim to uniqueness with which we shall have to deal presently. But let us first inquire into what Kant himself said.

Kant taught a course in physical geography all through his teaching career, almost fifty times. The text of these lectures or, rather, class notes, was published in 1802, two years before his death.[6] It is in this work that one finds the statement on geography and history that has been quoted so reverently again and again by those who make it the cornerstone of geographical method. Ritter[7] used it; so did Hettner and, eventually Hartshorne. Humboldt, interestingly, neither quotes Kant nor shares his views. Neither does Kraft. But now for the words of the master:

We can refer to our empirical perceptions either according to *conceptions* or according to *time and space* where they are actually found. The classification of perceptions according to concepts is the logical one, however, that according to time and space is the physical one. By the former we obtain a *system of nature*, such as that of Linnaeus, and by the latter a geographical description of nature.

For example, if I say that cattle is included under the class of quadrupeds, or under the group of this class having cloven hooves, that is a classification that I make in my head, hence a logical classification. The system of nature is like a register of the whole; here I place each thing in its competent class even if they are found in different, widely separated places of the world.

According to the physical classification, however, things are considered in their location on earth. The system of nature refers to their place in their class, but geographical description of nature shows where they are to be found on earth. Thus the lizard and the crocodile are basically the same animal. The crocodile is merely a tremendously large lizard. But they exist in different places. The crocodile lives in the Nile and the lizard on land, also in this country. In general, here we consider the scene of nature, the earth itself and the places in which things are actually found, in contrast with the systems of nature where we inquire not about the place of birth but about the similarity of forms. . . .

History and geography both could be called, so to speak, a description, with the difference that the former is a description according to time while the latter a description according to space. Hence, history and geography increase our knowledge in respect to time and space.

... Hence history differs from geography only in respect to time and space. The former is, as stated, a report of events which follow one another in time. The other is a report of events which take place side by side in space. History is a narrative, geography is a description. ...

Geography is a name for a description of nature and the whole world. Geography and history together fill up the entire area of our perception: geography that of space and history that of time.[8]

Kant's gigantic achievements in his own field as well as the influence which this unfortunate statement has had in ours require careful criticism, systematic as well as historical. Systematic criticism proceeds along two main lines. *First*, the distinction as intended is untenable in itself. It is simply not true that such systematic disciplines as, say, physics abstract from or otherwise neglect the spatio-temporal coordinates of the objects they study. One only needs to think of Newtonian astronomy to see immediately how wrongheaded this idea is. For what are the 'systematic' laws of astronomy, such as Kepler's laws, if not a set of rules to compute from the positions of the heavenly bodies at any given moment their positions at any other moment? The error is really so obvious that one must immediately ask for a plausible cause. The answer, I suggest, is historical. When Kant wrote the passage in his youth he had probably not yet undergone the full impact of Newtonian science. Accordingly, he thinks of systematic lawfulness as essentially classificatory in the style of Aristotle and Linnaeus rather than of the process law variety of Newton. For the 'precritical' Kant of 1756 this makes sense, at least biographically. But one may well doubt whether he would still have written this passage during his critical period, in his maturity during the seventies and eighties of the eighteenth century, after he had undergone the full impact of Newton and Hume. Into this period, however, fall the achievements on which his authority rests. How unfortunate, then, that so many geographers kowtow to a patently immature idea of his youth.

Second, we noticed that the resulting notion of geography is descriptive in the narrowest sense of the term. Obviously, it does not follow that there are no laws either of geography or of the socio-historical process simply because Kant thought that there were none. The facts have long proved him wrong. Historically, one can again understand how he came to hold such views around the middle of the eighteenth century. The social sciences were virtually non-existent at that time. Their place was taken either by narrative history or by moral reflections or by a mixture of these two. The pioneer work of Bodin was forgotten; Macchiavelli was hated or refuted as a diabolic tempter; Montesquieu was more often praised than understood; the great contributions of Voltaire, Hume and Adam Smith were either still in the future or had not yet penetrated into the academic precincts of provincial Koenigsberg. (One look into Kant's *Moral Geography* or, as we would now say, comparative anthropology, suffices to convince one that it is as crudely and clumsily classificatory and enumerative as his *Physical Geography*.) The biological disciplines were at that time still largely classificatory or, as one says in this case, taxonomic. So it was not unnatural after all, that Kant in 1756 conceived of geography exclusively as a catalogue of the spatial arrangement and distribution of taxonomic features. What he formulated was therefore not so much the methodological schema of what we now call geography but, rather, in unusually abstract terms, the pattern of the then fashionable cosmologies whose literary history goes back to the Middle Ages. Humboldt's *Kosmos* is the last and, because of its stylistic merits, the most famous specimen of this literary genre. So it is forgotten that Humboldt himself in his other writings distinguished very well between cosmological description on the one hand and geography on the other. The literary charm of *Kosmos* has, unfortunately, overshadowed this fact. Yet, to judge Humboldt as a geographer by what he says in *Kosmos* is like judging Darwin's contribution to biology from the diary that he kept on the Beagle. For that matter, even in the introductory chapter of *Kosmos* Humboldt[9] patiently explained to the general public the difference between science and cosmology. All sciences, according to him, search for laws, or, as the later term goes, are nomothetic. Cosmology is *not* a rational science but at best thoughtful contemplation of the universe. Such contemplation has its place. Whatever else assumes the 'pretentious name of a system of nature' is nothing but taxonomy, a mere catalogue of phenomena. Having delivered himself briefly of these fundamental observations, Humboldt, naturally enough in the introduction to his own cosmology, goes on to discuss the field of cosmology, only occasionally touching on geography. Cosmology is descriptive, something like an art. He advises it should not be studied without a good previous training in such systematic sciences as physics, astronomy, chemistry, anthropology, biology, geology, and *geography*. It is unfortunate that Hettner and, following him, Hartshorne, mistake this discussion for one of the methodology of geography. Humboldt is really not an authority properly cited in support of exceptionalism. One must not be misled by the circumstance that the great Kant in his day called geography what in Humboldt's terminology is *cosmology*.

One who is critical of the presentation just given may well ask why Humboldt, if he held such views, spent so much time, effort, and enthusiasm on cosmology. The question deserves an answer, which, in the nature of things, must again be historical. Humboldt lived at a time when a man of genius could still grasp and make significant contributions to virtually all the sciences. His own technical research was done in close personal co-operation with such founders of modern science as Gay-Lussac, Lalande, Arago, Thénard, Fourcroy, Biot, Laplace, Couvier, Gauss, and many others. Soon after Humboldt's time such versatility transcended human strength for good. Humboldt's grasp, however, was still universal as well as technical, in the sense that he could keep up with the most specialised developments in many fields. A man of this calibre may well conceive of the idea of a great synopsis that could contribute to the intellectual enjoyment and enlightenment of a larger number of readers. A presentation or, as one would say today, a popularisation of this kind would have to be descriptive rather than analytic. This may be submitted as the rationale behind Humboldt's enthusiasm for cosmology. In other words, he thought of his *Kosmos* as a piece of literature rather than a contribution to science. One more circumstance can be adduced in support of this view. Humboldt was, after all, a leader of the romantic movement, a contemporary of Herder and Schelling, and had in his youth embraced the pantheism of Goethe. Nothing is more characteristic of romanticism than the yearning for a synoptic view of the universe. Humboldt's *Kosmos* and his love for cosmology in general are therefore easily understood as his tribute to the romantic 'Zeitgeist'. *Kosmos* was indeed a great success throughout the world, also in this country. But from our point it is most important to see clearly that Humboldt, though he thought that cosmology had a legitimate place of its own, did not confuse it with what he clearly recognised as the science of geography. On the nature of the latter he did, therefore, not agree with Kant. The superficial appearance to the contrary is due to the fact that Humboldt treated history and cosmology as special disciplines outside of the sciences. Kant did make the same claim for history and geography. The point is that what Kant called geography Humboldt called more judiciously cosmology, at the same time emphasising the scientific nature of geography proper.

III

Hettner's great prestige helped to perpetuate the confusion that has just been unravelled. Invoking the formidable authority of Kant, Hettner successfully impressed upon geography the exceptionalist claim in analogy to history. On this basic fallacy he built an elaborate argument. The principles of natural history or cosmology were forced upon geography. Spurious similarities between history and geography were constructed. Thus geography was laid open to the invasion of a whole host of nonscientific, not to say antiscientific, ideas: the typically romantic argument from uniqueness; the hypostatisation of the quite uncontroversial fact that variables must be expected to interact into an antianalytical holism; in connection with this the spurious claim for a specific integrating function of geography; and, finally, the appeal to the intuition and artistic touch of the investigator in preference to the sober objectivity of standard scientific method. Some at least of these points must now be taken up in detail.

Let us begin with a brief statement of Hettner's position in one of its two major aspects. Both history and geography are essentially chorological. History arranges phenomena in time, geography in space. Both, in contrast to the other disciplines, integrate phenomena heterogeneous among themselves. Also, these phenomena are unique. No historical event and historical period is like any other. In geography no two phenomena and no two regions are alike. Thus both fields face the task of explaining the unique. Such explanation is, therefore, unlike all scientific explanation which 'explains' by subsumption under laws. But there are no laws for the unique; little use, then, in looking for historical or geographical laws or prediction. The best one can hope for is, in Dilthey's fashion, some sort of 'understanding' or, more frankly, empathetic understanding. An idiomatic difference between German and English has been instrumental in obscuring the basically antiscientific bias of this doctrine. Hettner calls history 'time-Wissenschaft' and geography 'space-Wissenschaft'. Hartshorne, as far as the dictionary goes quite correctly, translates this into 'time science' and 'space science'. The point is that the German term Wissenschaft is much wider than the English 'science' or, for that matter, the French 'science'. Wissenschaft for a German is *any* organised body of knowledge, not only what we call a science. Law is called Rechtswissenschaft; literary criticism or even numismatics, if cultivated with the proper Teutonic thoroughness and erudition, may acquire the status of Wissenschaften in their own right. That much for Hettner's position and terminology. Now for criticism.

The use of the term history in methodological discussion is tantalisingly ambiguous. For the sake of precision it will here for the moment be given a very narrow meaning. History or historical research is the ascertainment of events that occurred in the past. Of course, not all past events are of equal interest to the historian. What he cares for are such phenomena as, say, the movement of the American frontier during the nineteenth century, or the reception of Roman law at the end of the Middle Ages. However, there is no need to begin with a methodological distinction between these and other past events. Historically significant facts are simply those which interest the historian in view of the patterns into which he hopes to arrange them. It should be granted without argument that the ascertaining of past events, even if they are not as elusive as the thought and motives of dead people, is by no means a simple matter. Quite to the contrary. Many sciences and also the most elaborate 'scientific method' of inference from traces and relics to what they are the traces and relics of, must be put into the service of this most difficult undertaking of ascertaining the historical course of events. In this non-controversial, auxiliary sense history certainly makes use of science and its methods. But what it thus achieves is nevertheless mere description and, in the nature of things, a very selective description at that. Science or, perhaps, Wissenschaft begins only when the historian is no longer an historian in the narrow sense and tries to fit his facts into a pattern. This, whether they know it or not, is what all historians try to do. What then, logically speaking, are they doing? At this point the argument begins. A baffling variety of analyses has been proposed. Basically there are two views, the scientific approach and historicism.

The scientific view, which is here taken, claims that all the data, which the historian in the narrow sense of the term collects, are nothing but raw material for the social scientist. The historian, in constructing his pattern is, therefore, whether he knows it or not, a social scientist. In other words, apart from all the technical difficulties which were just mentioned, there is no difference in principle between a social scientist's use of the last census report on the one hand and his use of what historians have found out about the census variables in ancient Rome on the other. At this point, the terminological awkwardness of defining history as narrowly as it has been done for the sake of precision becomes obvious. For no worthwhile 'historian' will stop there. Assume, for instance, that he is interested in the market prices that prevailed in ancient Rome during a certain period. Naturally, he will first have to find out what they were. But then he will wish to go beyond that limited goal and try to find out how demand and supply interacted with each other and the other relevant social factors to produce those prices. The causal relations on which he draws for such 'explanation' are *not* special historical laws but obviously, such as they are, the laws of economic theory. Similarly in all other instances. This is the point. With reference to geography, it follows that the historian who goes, as all historians do, beyond mere fact finding, is comparable to the regional geographer. In getting the facts the historian does what the regional geographer does in getting his. In trying to understand or, better, to explain them he does exactly what the regional geographer does in applying systematic geography to his region. In this broader sense of history, history is a science or, less ambiguously, history is social science applied to the conditions of a special 'historical situation'. Turned this way Hettner's analogy is acceptable. But then we have merely followed his words, not his meaning. What is this meaning? This brings us to the other view, historicism.

Historicism maintains that there is an alternative, radically different way of understanding the past or, for that matter, the present as a product of its past. The gist of it is the belief that by merely arranging the past events in their temporal order some sort of 'meaningful' pattern, cyclic, progressive, or otherwise, will appear. To understand anything it is necessary and sufficient to know its history. Again, there is no argument if one takes that to mean that knowledge of the past state of a system *and of the laws of its development* leads to the knowledge of its present state. But what understanding can be gained merely from contemplating the successive stages of an unfolding process is hard to see. In other words, in the historicist interpretation the 'genetic method' yields nothing.

For better or worse the antiscientific spirit of historicism was one of the major intellectual forces of the nineteenth century. Through Hettner it has penetrated geographical thought and, as we see it, powerfully affected its course. Characteristically, the very first sentence of Hettner's methodological work reads: 'The present can always be understood only from the past.' Also, his work on social and cultural geography exemplifies the genetic method applied to geography. And, as one would expect from a man of his breadth and vision, much of the material is not at all geographical but anthropological, cultural, or political.[10] To be sure, that makes for good reading. But Humboldt's *Kosmos*, too, makes good reading; yet it is not geography. Among American geographers, Carl Sauer is perhaps the outstanding representative of historicism, building his geography consistently on Hettner's premise stated above.

The argument for the uniqueness of the geographical material stems both logically and historically from historicism. The main protagonist of this line of thought in America is Hartshorne. So it is easily understood why he makes so much of the old Kantian parallelism between history and geography. If history, according to the historicist, deals with unique events and if geography is like history, then geography, too, deals with the unique and must try to 'understand' rather than search for laws. The formal syllogism is beyond reproach. To refute it one must, as we have tried to do, attack its premise. So let us first turn to the uniqueness argument as such and only then to the use Hartshorne makes of it.

The main difficulty of the uniqueness argument is that, as Max Weber has pointed out, it proves too much. Are there really two stones completely alike in all minute details of shape, colour, and chemical composition? Yet, Galileo's law of falling bodies holds equally for both.

Similarly, limited as our present psychological knowledge is, it seems safe to say that no two people would register identical scores on all tests as yet devised. Does it follow that our psychologists have so far discovered not a single law? What it all comes down to is a matter of degree. In the physical sciences we have succeeded in discovering a set of variables such that if two objects or situations, no matter how different they are in other respects, agree in these variables or indices, then their future with respect to these indices will be the same and predictable. To what extent and how soon any other field will reach a state as satisfactory as this is a matter of fact, to be decided by trial and error, not to be prejudged by pseudomethodological argument. Of course, the social sciences are not as well developed as physics. This is, indeed, what we mean when we call them less developed. On the other hand, it is also true that sciences which are less developed in this sense often resort with remarkable success to the search for statistical laws. Whether this kind of lawfulness is a measure of our temporary ignorance or must be taken as ultimate is a purely speculative point. Surely, the recent development in physics should give pause to anybody who attempts to deny on these grounds the logical unity of the sciences. To apply all this to geography, the claim is, then, that the difference between the differences between two 'unique' regions on the one hand and the equally numerous differences between our two stones, on the other, is again a matter of degree.

There is still another misunderstanding that prevents some from fully ✓ appreciating this point. Stones do not really, as Galileo's formula tacitly assumes, fall in a vacuum. And they fall differently according to the characteristics of the medium through which they travel. Airplanes, by the way, do not fall at all in the ordinary course of events. Does that mean that Galileo's law is false; or that there are as many laws as there are atmospheric conditions; and still another set of laws for airplanes? Obviously, this is not the way science operates. What scientists do is, rather, this. *They apply to each concrete situation jointly all the laws that involve the variables they have reason to believe are relevant.* The rules by which these laws are combined, thus reflecting what is loosely called the interaction of the variables, are themselves among the regularities science tries to discover. In fact, these are among the most powerful laws of nature and their very existence refutes the exaggerated claims of various brands of holism or gestaltism. There is thus no point in challenging, as Hartshorne does, the social scientist to produce a single law that would explain as complex a situation as the geography of New York Harbour. Descriptively the situation is indeed unique in the obvious sense that there has and will never be a region or location exactly like New York Harbour with all the services it supplies for its hinterland.

Nor will there ever be any law to account for it. For, what point would there be in a law that takes care of one and one case only? But, on the other hand, urban geographers do by now know a few systematic principles which, jointly applied to New York Harbour, do explain quite a bit though not all of its structure and functions. This is the point. Or shall we give up the attempt to explain because we cannot as yet explain everything? In this respect geography finds itself once more in the same boat with all other social sciences. Or should we really reject sociology because the prediction of election results is not yet as reliable as some wish; or because we cannot tell for sure whether the Argentine will be a dictatorship or democracy five years hence? Such councils of despair are now heard again. Surely, they are merely a sign of the intellectual crisis of the age.

Hartshorne, like all rigorous thinkers, is quite consistent. He does, in fact, reject all social science and is particularly sceptical of the future of sociology. With respect to uniqueness he says that, 'While this margin is present in every field of science, to greater or less extent, the degree to which phenomena are unique is not only greater in geography than in many other sciences, but the unique is of the very first practical importance.'[11] Hence generalisations in the form of laws are useless, if not impossible, and any prediction in geography is of insignificant value.[12] Thus he comes after lengthy discussions to the same conclusion as Kant. 'Both history and geography might be described as naïve sciences, examining reality from a naïve point of view, looking at things as they are actually arranged and related, in contrast to the more sophisticated but artificial procedure of the systematic sciences which take phenomena of particular kinds out of their real setting.'[13] One may say that Hartshorne goes Kant even one better. For Kant geography is description; for Hartshorne it is 'naïve science' or, if we accept his meaning of science, naïve description. As one would expect from all this, and as has been mentioned before, regional studies are for Hartshorne the heart of geography. The terminology he uses stems in part from the German historicist philosopher Rickert who distinguishes between idiographic and nomothetic disciplines. The former describe the unique; the latter search for laws. Geography according to Hartshorne is essentially idiographic. Whenever laws are discovered or applied one is no longer in the area of geography. All it contributes is facts. 'In its [geography's] naïve examination of the interrelation of phenomena in the real world it discovers phenomena which the sophisticated academic view of the systematic sciences may not have observed, shows them to be worthy of study in themselves and thus adds to the field of the systematic studies.'[14] In other words, Hartshorne takes permanently and systematically as narrow a view of geography as we have, temporarily and for the sake of the argument, taken of history.

Mainly through Hartshorne's efforts, American geographers have come to look at Hettner as the major recent authority in support of the idiographic conception of their field. Under these circumstances, it is important to point out that the picture Hartshorne paints of the German author is as one-sided as his quotations are selective. As has been hinted before, there is another side of Hettner's work. He could just as effectively be cited in support of the nomothetic position. Consider, for instance, the following excerpts from one of his earlier papers:

> Therefore, if we assume in geography the necessity of relations and, as in the natural sciences, exceptions in these only as apparent ones, as gaps in our knowledge, then with the frequent appearance of similar conditions we obtain the possibility of establishing anthropogeo-graphical laws.
>
> We cannot say that similar conditions produce everywhere and always the same effects. Such a statement would ignore the fact that people differ and therefore can act differently under similar natural conditions. Also wrong, of course, would it be to say that similar people act alike under different natural conditions. Anthropogeo-graphical laws have to take into account the difference in conditions of existence as well as the difference among people. Of course, in reality there will never be a repetition of exactly the same condition. Each situation is individual, unique, as a result of which no law will be able to explain the totality of a given phenomenon as in the natural sciences. There will always be a rest which must be explained under a different law or will remain unexplainable. . . .
>
> There are no absolute relations between man and environment which are valid for all time. With the development of mankind changes the nature of relationships between man and environment. *The development of these relationships rests on the constancy of effects although the causes which produced these effects may have disappeared some time go.* (italics added.)[15]

Nor was this an incidental remark that did not fit into Hettner's final thought. In his main work of 1927 one can still find passages like the following:

> As much as the individualising method is appreciated and needed, one must say that geography received only through the generalising method its stricter scientific character. Only the generic treatment which concentrated many properties and features into one word, made

a concise and relatively short and easily conceived description possible. *Thereby it created the basis for a more concise form of explanation resting on comparative investigation and leading to laws.* In doing this, modern geography is far advanced over history. (italics added.)[16]

One may agree or disagree with such passages which, as far as we know, have never before been translated into English. But one can hardly deny that, even taken by themselves, they amount to a programmatic declaration in favour of the conception of geography which is here advocated and which has been so vigorously opposed. Nor has this side of Hettner's thought been overlooked by all American geographers. Isaiah Bowman, for example, one of the pioneers of American geography, has declared that the search for laws and prediction based on laws is 'the measure of a science'.[17]

To emphasise this systematic side of Hettner is not to accuse Hartshorne of reading into him what is not there. Hettner undoubtedly advocated at different times and at different places the idiographic as well as the nomothetic conceptions of geography and, for all the complexity and subtlety of his thought, did not succeed in integrating them. This requires some comments, logical as well as historical. Logically, it must be noted again that there is in fact no conflict or opposition between the descriptive and systematic aspects of geography or, for that matter, of any other science, either physical or social. Difficulties arise only when the descriptive component is, in the German manner, rationalised into the idiographic method which is then conceived as coordinate with that of explanatory science. Historically, it seems plausible to say that the reason Hettner did not see this clearly is to be found in the preponderant historicism of his environment. The strength of historicism in German thought, academic or otherwise, ever since Hegel and up to the present is a matter of record. However, the German universities became during the same period one of the centres, perhaps the main centre, of the rising natural sciences and, in connection with this, of what is sometimes called the positivistic philosophy of science, which stresses the search for laws and the methodological unity of all inquiry. These two philosophies have never been reconciled in the German mind. Nor is Hettner, and with him geography, the only victim of this sterile struggle. Perhaps the most tragic case, certainly the one with the most tragic and far-reaching consequences, is Karl Marx. There is no doubt that Marx made some historically important contributions to economics. In this respect he continued, characteristically, the work of the British classical economists, who thought of their field as a systematic discipline and were quite free from the Hegelian influence. Nor can it be denied that Marx's attempt to analyse the historical process, no matter how one-sided and biased his view of it may have been, represents a daring attempt to apply scientific thought to concrete situations. The historicist bias appears in Marx's conception of history as an 'understandable' progression. From there it is but a small step to conceiving of history as a progress toward a desirable goal. In other words, history itself takes care of our aspirations. This is the basic teleology of historicism. Logically, this error is much more vitiating and, if you please, vicious than Marx's preoccupation with the economic variables.

IV

The impact of exceptionalism on geography has been profound. That is why it has been necessary to devote so much space to its refutation. Methodological discussion is indeed essentially dialectical in that much clarification is to be derived from the mutual criticism of contending viewpoints. Nor is such treatment as sterile and merely polemical as it might appear at first sight. Even so, with exceptionalism disposed of, we had now better turn to a group of more specific comments. There is, first, the general issue of pure versus applied science. Next, attention must be given to some of the difficulties geography shares with the other social sciences. Third, a few comments on geography's specific tools will be in order. Fourth, our dominant interest in structure, rather unlike that of the other social sciences, has certain logical aspects. They lead, fifth, to a re-examination of the idea of the region and, in connection with that, to the claims of holism. Sixth, comparative geography and typology must be recognised for what they are. Seventh, some recent claims of a more metaphysical nature in connection with the freedom of the will require that we understand clearly the much worried idea of geographical determinism. In conclusion, some remarks about the relations of geography to its sister disciplines now and in the foreseeable future will, perhaps, not be out of place.

Like others, we have occasionally spoken of applying the laws and concepts of systematic geography to the regional material. As a manner of speaking this is harmless enough. Yet it is false or, at least, misleading to oppose systematic and regional geography to each other as an instance of pure and applied science. The point is, very radically, that there is no such thing as a methodological distinction between pure and applied science. There is only science and science applied. Whatever distinction there is, is practical, a matter of either interest or emphasis. The laws for which the 'pure' scientist looks are in no way different from those which he himself or his 'applied' colleagues use. Conversely, some of the most important theoretical ideas have been suggested by engineering problems. To draw once more upon a field in which all these things have long been straightened out, engineering physics is not a branch of physics comparable with or coordinate to, say, thermodynamics or mechanics. Nor is, for that matter, the notion of application itself as unambiguous as one may think. It has at least two meanings. The regional geographer who explains some features of a region by the use of laws applies the latter in one sense of the term. The regional planner or soil conservationist applies the same laws in a different sense of application. He is a social engineer. The high prestige of, and the justified concern with, application in the sense of social engineering is, for better or worse, one of the outstanding features of our civilisation. The following syllogism needs, therefore, to be guarded against: applied science is the core of science; regional geography is applied science; hence, regional geography is the core of geography.

In order to clarify some logical points, repeated use has been made of physics, which is unquestionably the most highly developed of all sciences. To do this is not to deny that there are important differences among the various disciplines. But here, too, geography does not stand by itself in splendid isolation. It shares most of its methodological peculiarities with all other social sciences. Though this is not the place for an exhaustive treatment, some of these characteristics should be mentioned. The most serious difficulty, which all social sciences share, is the very limited scope or complete lack of experimentation. It is true enough, and has been frequently pointed out, that one cannot experiment in astronomy either; yet astronomy is the oldest, most precise and most successful natural science. But this is rather by way of the exception that confirms the rule. It just so happens that the celestial processes are periodical or very nearly so and depend on a very limited number of variables. For another difficulty, quantification, which permits us to draw upon the rich resources of mathematical inference, is not easily achieved in the social disciplines. In this respect geography and economics are, it would seem, somewhat better off than, say, political science and sociology. In the absence of easy experimentation and quantification the body of reasonably reliable laws in the social disciplines is not as impressive as in physics or, even, biology. It is only too true that social scientists, and geographers among them, are often still in the dark as to which variables are the relevant ones in any given situation. Naturally, for if we knew the variables, it would not be hard to guess at the law. And if we could experiment we would not need to guess. As has been pointed out once before, statistical techniques prove to be a powerful tool in making the best of the situation. Like all other social scientists, geographers have come to appreciate this tool. There are thus many important differences between the natural sciences and the social sciences. Logically, it is submitted, these are differences of degree, not kind. Whether, finally, the social sciences will ever be as perfect as the natural ones is a matter of fact. To assert that it must be possible for us to reach that stage would be dogmatic. But any assertion to the contrary is equally *a priori*. Upon examination it usually reveals itself as a romantic plea for such metaphysical ideas as the freedom of the will.

There is one major aspect in which geography does differ from the other social sciences. The latter, as they mature, concentrate more and more on the discovery of process laws, that is, to repeat, laws that are in one important aspect like the laws of Newtonian astronomy. Given the state of a system at a certain point in time, process laws allow for the prediction of the changes that will take place. Geography is essentially morphological. Purely geographical laws contain no reference to time and change. This is not to deny that the spatial structures we explore, are, like all structures anywhere, the result of processes. But the geographer, for the most part, deals with them as he finds them, ready made. (As far as physical geography is concerned, the long-term processes that produce them are part of the subject matter of geology.) Let us in this connection consider Koeppen's Hypothetical Continent. The word hypothetical merely indicates that he neglected, for the purpose of his climatological generalisation, all but a few variables. For the remaining ones he states a spatial correlation that is a morphological law. To call such comparatively crude correlations patterns rather than laws is perhaps laudable modesty. But to think that patterns, in this sense of pattern, are different from laws, would be a mistake. This absence of the time factor within physical geography is the source of a peculiar phenomenon within all branches of human geography. The 'social process' is, as the very term indicates, a process in the logical sense; and this process interacts with geographical factors. Assume for the sake of the argument two regions to be alike in all relevant physical aspects. They may, and as a rule will, differ with respect to some or all of the variables that interest the economic or social geographer. The reason for this is that the populations of the two regions went through different processes. Settlement patterns, for instance, may vary according to the state of technology at the time of occupation. What we are faced with in this case is not a failure of geography as a social science nor, as some would have it, with a breakdown of 'causality'. What we have uncovered is, rather, the exact point where the geographer must cooperate with all the other social scientists if they are jointly to produce more and more comprehensive explanations. Whether the geographer should stick to strictly morphological work which he can do by himself or, on the proper occasion, cooperate with the other social scientists is not a theoretical but a practical question to which we shall return at the end of the paper.

Technically, the morphological character of geography finds its expression in its own specific tool, maps and cartographic correlation. Mapping has been called the shorthand of geography. True as far as it goes, this clever simile fails to do justice to our technique in at least four respects. First, a map is not just a shorthand description but, in a quite literal sense, a picture exactly as a blueprint is a picture of a machine. For example, a map which preserves distance is in this respect a literal picture of the region mapped. It is, as logicians and mathematicians say, an isomorph of it. The techniques of geographical analysis are to a considerable extent based on such isomorphisms. Second, the pictures which we make by means of the various cartographic symbols are deliberately selective in two respects. We map only those features in which we are at the moment interested, and we neglect all the differences among the entities which we represent by the same symbols. One hardly needs to elaborate how useful it is to have such a convenient and selfregulating vehicle for the process of abstraction. Third, since maps are spatial isomorphs, they depict directly not only the various features which we try to correlate spatially, but also these correlations themselves. In other words, they serve the same function, or very nearly the same function, as charts, diagrams and other representations of functional connections. Much of what other social scientists achieve in this manner the geographer achieves by the technique of cartographical correlation. By the single device of superimposing maps with isopleths such correspondences as, say, that between precipitation and crops can be discovered, at least in a preliminary and qualitative fashion, at a glance. This is more than just a different technique in the narrow sense of the word. It is a special tool of generalization and analysis used by no other science as much as by geography.

Cartographic correlation leads to two related topics, so-called comparative geography and typology. The term, comparative geography, is of old standing. Humboldt used it occasionally; Ritter and Hettner were quite fond of it. Both liked to 'compare' very large and complex geographical phenomena, whole continents, or vast regions which, for all their complexities, exhibited some similarities. Now, the main point to be made here is that there is not, either in geography or elsewhere, any such thing as a comparative method as such. To put the same thing differently, the comparative approach is not a third possibility in addition to the descriptive and systematic one. Much of what goes on under the name of comparative geography is really systematic geography though, more often than not, of a rather rudimentary kind. Much other work that is called comparative is more or less naïve regional description. Nor is it accidental that the most interesting attempts of this kind deal with large areas. If several such areas, differing in many respects as large areas naturally would, also show some marked similarities, it is, indeed, reasonable to consider these similarities as indicative of certain basic patterns. But then, we have seen before that to speak of such basic underlying patterns is but a covert way of referring to systematic lawfulness. Furthermore, while large-scale comparisons may well yield valuable hints as to the underlying lawfulness, such intuitions must still pass the test of independent verification in further areas of all kinds and sizes. Logically speaking, comparative geography is, therefore, a half-way house between systematic work and regional description.

The same goes for typology. English and German geographers have not unsuccessfully tried to establish types of landschaft belts. Climatic regions, natural regions, wheat belts, coal mining regions are examples. Again it is not implausible that comparisons among the various specimens of such types will yield hunches. Exceptionalists will speak of the intuitive grasp of types, just as antiscientific psychologists speak of empathetic understanding of personality patterns. Advocates of the scientific method will recognise those hunches for what they are, educated guesses at systematic lawfulness. This is not to disparage this anticipatory stage. After all, science is educated guessing. But there is also no particular mystique about the notion of type. A type is just a class. An intelligent classification either anticipates or is based on some sort of lawfulness. If, therefore, the material itself suggests some sort of classification by mere inspection, one may hope to be on the track of some lawfulness.

If the notion of type is once clarified by being recognised as no more and no less than a fruitful classification, then the key to one of the most fundamental concepts of geography, the idea of the region, is also at hand. For, a region is defined conventionally as an area homogeneous with respect to one or two *classes of* phenomena. As has been pointed out by Palander,[18] one of the keenest critics of economic geography, the notion of a region in itself explains therefore nothing. In particular, it is no substitute for the notion of a morphological or any other law. Rather, it enters into that notion. A morphological law is, in many cases, nothing but a statement of the lawful spatial relations within a region or between regions defined by different criteria. From a purely methodological standpoint this is really all that needs to be said about the notion of a region. This does not mean that we underestimate the rôle it plays in geography. The importance of a scientific concept is measured by its fruitfulness in application, not by how much can be said about it logically.

Regions and other geographical entities have been considered by many geographers as wholes in the sense of the doctrine of holism or gestaltism. A whole, in this peculiar doctrine, is more than the sum of its parts; also, it is unique in the sense that its various properties cannot be accounted for by applying standard scientific methods to its compound parts and the relations that obtain among them. Hartshorne, in arguing against such holists, is rightly opposed to the use of that doctrine in the definition of the geographical area and the region.[19] But after this rejection he finds it necessary to reintroduce the doctrine into geography when, later on, he defines cultural regions and, by the way of example, farm units as 'primary wholes' the parts of which can be understood only in terms of the whole.[20] This is, indeed, different from 'the merely analytic method of Hettner' says Passarge as quoted by Hartshorne. Now, the complete logical analysis of holism is an elaborate matter and cannot be taken up here in detail.[21] What it all comes down to is this. Whenever the one side insists that it has a whole, the other side claims that we simply do not as yet know enough to explain its behaviour by standard scientific methods. In many crucial cases such explanation has actually come forth later on. One may, therefore, doubt whether there is such a thing as a whole in the holist's sense anywhere in nature. Within our field, the earlier discussion of the geography of New York Harbour is a case in point. Hartshorne who calls it unique, would consistently also have to call it a whole whose parts, like those of a farm unit, can only be understood from the whole. We, in turn, from our viewpoint, doubt whether any geographical entity, region or not, is a whole in this methodological sense.

Whoever rejects the scientific method in any area of nature, rejects in principle the possibility of prediction. In other words, he rejects what is also known as scientific determinism. The intellectual motif behind this attitude is in most cases some version of the metaphysical doctrine of free will. This may seem a farfetched allegation in a field like geography. A look at some recent publications[22] should suffice to allay any such doubt. Generally, the many interrelations between the various holisms, uniqueness doctrines, and free will philosophies are a matter of record.

If determinism is taken to mean that nature is lawful throughout, permitting of no 'exceptions', then it is the common ground of all modern science. And if freedom of the will means that human decisions are not determined by their (physiological and/or sociopsychological) antecedents, then the will is indeed not free. At any rate, most scientists proceed on this assumption and are more than willing to leave the debate to the metaphysicians. However, the word determinism has still another meaning. Those, for instance, who blame Marx for his 'economic determinism' do not need to reject the idea of universal lawfulness. What they reject is, rather, the doctrine that one who knows everything about the economic and technological conditions of a society, could in these terms alone predict its 'super-structure' and its future development. Scientific determinism as such must therefore be carefully distinguished from the various determinisms with an adjective, such as economic determinism. These latter determinisms are specific scientific theories, to be accepted or rejected on the basis of the empirical evidence. Geography has been bedevilled by its own kind of determinism. Geographical determinism or environmentalism attributes to the geographical variables the same rôle in the social process as Marxism does to the economic ones. There is no good reason to believe that either of these two special determinisms is anything but a gross exaggeration of some admittedly valuable insights. There is nothing wrong with investigating the influence which the physical environment exercises, positively or as a limiting condition, on the social process. Most geographers would expect to find lawful connections in this area; that does not make them geographical determinists. Ratzel was the first to think originally and imaginatively along these lines. Like Marx, he was not quite as bad as some of his latter day disciples. In this country Semple was a student of Ratzel. In Ellsworth Huntington's writings geographical determinism reaches some of its dizziest heights. In France, Demolins insisted that if French history had to happen all over again it would essentially run the same course on account of the natural environment. The contemporary reaction against these exaggerations is understandably strong. But to fight them from the standpoint of science is one thing; to fight geographical determinism in order to fight science and its underlying idea of universal lawfulness is another thing.

We cannot and need not, as geographers, settle the future of science. But we may wonder what can reasonably be said about the future of geography as a discipline, an organised unit within the intricate division of intellectual labour. This is not strictly a methodological question and depends on many extraneous factors. Yet, it has a theoretical core that is not unrelated to methodology. So we shall venture a few remarks in conclusion. Science, to repeat once more, searches for laws. What then, one may ask, are the peculiarities of the laws we look for and which would make it advisable that they be kept together in one discipline? From this viewpoint, we believe, the laws of geography fall into three categories. Typical of the first are most of the laws of physical geography. These are not strictly geographical. Many of them are specialisations of laws independently established in the physical sciences. These we take as we find them, apply them systematically to the various conditions that prevail on the surface of the earth and analyse them with particular attention to the spatial variables they contain. To be specific, the climatologist uses much physics (meteorology), the agricultural geographer, applied biology (agronomy).

Typical of the second category are many laws of economic geography, for instance, the now flourishing theory—for it has, indeed, reached the stage where one can speak of a theory in the strict sense of a whole group of deductively connected generalisations—of general location. As everybody knows, this theory investigates the spatial relations obtaining between the places at which the various economic factors, raw materials, producing units, means of communication, consumers, and so on, are to be found in any region. As far as they are morphological, these laws are genuinely geographic. The pioneer work in this area has, in fact, been done by economists, if we except Christaller who is a geographer.[23] But, as the theory is being refined, the geographer's skill will increasingly come into its own. For, he is more expert than others in the treatment of spatial factors and he knows from his rich store of experience with which others they typically interact. As far as these laws are not morphological, they belong to the third category.

This is a crucial point. We touched on it before when we used as an illustration two similar regions showing different settlement patterns because of the different processes their population had undergone. Let us try to state the case more generally. Mature social science looks for process laws. Knowing such laws one can ideally predict the whole course of history in a region, provided one also knows the influences that flow into it from without, if one knows its physical factors and the characteristics of the population that occupied it at a given time. Such laws are, of course, not geographical laws, nor do they belong entirely within any of the other now current divisions, such as anthropology or economics. The variables one must expect to occur in them extend over the whole range of systematic social science. Spatial variables are essentially and inevitably among them, but they are no more self-sufficient than those of economics or traditional sociology. It is our task to make explicit the rôle these geographical variables play in the social process. In other words, we must try to explore what else would be different in the future if, all other things being equal, the spatial arrangements in the present were different from what they actually are. To insist on this is, as we saw, not geographical determinism. The real danger here is geographical isolationism. For, we have also seen that the search for these laws can only proceed in cooperation with the other social sciences.

What may one infer from all this for the future of geography? It seems to me that as long as geographers cultivate its systematic aspects, geography's prospects as a discipline of its own are good indeed. The laws of all the three categories which we have distinguished are no doubt both interesting and important. And they all contain spatial factors to an extent that requires special skills and makes the professional cultivation of these skills well worth while. We, the geographers, are these professionals. I am not so optimistic in case geography should reject the search for laws, exalt its regional aspects for its own sake and thus limit itself more and more to mere description. In this event the systematic geographer will have to move much closer and eventually attach himself to the systematic sciences.

Notes and references

[1] SPETHMANN, H. *Dynamische Länderkunde*, Breslau, 1928, p. 119.

[2] HETTNER, A. *Die Geographie, ihre Geschichte, ihr Wesen und ihre Methoden*, Breslau, 1927.

[3] HARTSHORNE, R. 'The nature of geography', *Ann. Ass. Am. Geogr.* 29 (1939) 171–658; reprinted in book form. Page references cited are to the 4th edn., 1951.

[4] KRAFT, V. 'Die Geographie als Wissenschaft', in *Enzyklopädie der Erdkunde*, ed. O. Kende, Leipzig, Wien, 1929.

[5] RITTER, C. *Über die historischen Elemente in der geographischen Wissenschaft*, Berlin, 1833, p. 45.

[6] KANT, IMMANUEL. *Physische Geographie*, ed. F. T. Rink, Koenigsberg, 1802. In fairness to Kant it should be said that according to Adickes, the famous Kant scholar, the text as edited by Rink and used by Ritter, Hettner and Hartshorne is of doubtful authenticity. Four-fifths of the manuscript is not in Kant's handwriting. It probably consists of notes taken by students during the very first semester in which Kant gave that course. Also, editing was done shortly before Kant's death when, as Adickes points out, he was too ill to make any alterations in what he had written or dictated in class before 1756. Quite apart from this, Erich Adickes in his book *Untersuchungen zu Kant's physischer Geographie*, Tübingen, 1911, is rather distressed about the geographical ignorance displayed by his philosophical idol.

[7] HARTSHORNE, *op. cit.*, p. 136, maintains that Ritter 'does not appear to have stated the comparison as clearly as either Kant or Humboldt'.

[8] KANT, *Physische Geographie*, ed. F. T. Rink, vol. 1, pp. 6–8.

[9] HUMBOLDT, ALEXANDER VON, *Kosmos. Entwurf einer physischen Weltbeschreibung*, Stuttgart, Tübingen, 1845, vol. 1, p. 66.

[10] HETTNER, A. *Vergleichende Länderkunde*, vol. 4, Leipzig, Berlin, 1935; *Das Europäische Russland*, Leipzig, Berlin, 1905.

[11] HARTSHORNE, *op. cit.*, p. 432.

[12] *Ibid.*, p. 433.

[13] *Ibid.*, p. 373.

[14] *Ibid.*, p. 461.

[15] HETTNER, A. 'Die Geographie des Menschen', *Geogr. Z.*, Leipzig, 1907.

[16] HETTNER, *Die Geographie, ihre geschuchte, ihr Wesen und ihre Methoder*, pp. 222–3.

[17] BOWMAN, ISAIAH, 'Commercial geography as a science. Reflections on some recent books', *Geogr. Rev.* 15 (1925) 285–94; see also his *Geography in Relation to the Social Sciences*, Report of the Commission on the Social Studies, part V, American Historical Association, New York, 1934.

[18] PALANDER, T. *Beiträge zur Standortstheorie*, Dissertation, Uppsala, 1935, pp. 17–20.

[19] HARTSHORNE, *op. cit.*, pp. 263–6.

[20] *Ibid.*, p. 351.

[21] For a discussion of holism see BERGMANN, G. 'Holism, historicism and emergence', *Philosophy of Science* 11 (1944) 209–21. Also, by the same author, 'Theoretical psychology', in *An. Rev. Psychol.* 4 (1953), Stanford.

[22] PLATT, ROBERT S. 'Determinism in geography', *Ann. Ass. Am. Geogr.* 38 (1948) 126–32; and, by the same author, 'Environmentalism versus geography', *Am. J. Sociol.* 53 (1948) 351–8.

[23] THÜNEN, J. H. VON. *Der isolierte Staat*, Rostock, 1842. LÖSCH, A. *Die räumliche Ordnung der Wirtschaft*, Jena, 1940. HOOVER, EDGAR M. *The Location of Economic Activity*, New York, 1948. CHRISTALLER, W. *Die zentralen Orte in Süddeutschland*, Jena, 1933.

3 Some techniques of measurement

The papers included in this section represent attempts to bring greater precision of measurement to the distribution and characteristics of two fundamental spatial elements; point locations and networks. The various indices included in the papers are expressed in the form of simple formulae but this should present little difficulty to anyone who has taken any secondary school mathematics at all. The confusion at seeing a statement in symbolic terms in work relating to geographical distributions will soon be overcome if a few examples are invented and worked out.

These papers do not attempt measurement simply for the sake of measurement. Such an attempt would, nevertheless, be defensible. Previously the most accurate way in which we could categorise, for example, a settlement pattern was by using such terms as 'nucleated' or 'scattered' and these terms are obviously an imprecise foundation for the comparison of patterns. But the intention goes beyond this. In the last paragraph of *King's* paper, hypotheses are suggested about the way in which the value of R (the statistic used) might be related to other characteristics of the areas analysed. For example, uniform spacing of settlement might correlate with a high percentage of land in crops. It is obviously much easier to test such hypotheses, and thus to add to the quality of the geographer's explanation of an area, when information is expressed in terms of quantitative values as well as words. And it is exactly these processes of making and testing hypotheses, thus building one analysis upon another, which contribute to the scientific creativity referred to in Davies's paper in Section 2.

The nearest neighbour analysis carried out by King on selected areas of the United States raises a number of problems of definition. Since, in reality, towns are not points but areas some central point within the town has to be chosen for the purpose of measuring intertown distances. It is relatively easy to select this central point in a roughly circular town but more difficult with elongated settlements. Also, as King points out, no account is taken in this particular study of the size of each settlement and a small town is given as much locational 'weight' as a large city. Theoretically, there is no real difficulty here since the analysis could equally well be carried out separately for towns of various size classes. For example, it may be felt that there are good grounds to expect small service-oriented towns to be more regularly (as well as more frequently) spaced than large industrial towns. Whether or not this is a reasonable expectation is for the reader to decide. Whether or not it is true would depend on a nearest neighbour analysis of the distributional patterns made by the two different types of town. The measurement of intertown distances is another problem. Should they be road distances (either in miles, time or cost) or straight line distances? For the purposes of this paper straight line mileage distances are used since they simplify considerably the rather mechanical task of measurement.

In essence, the R statistic is the ratio between, on the one hand, the average of all *actual* distances measured from each town to its nearest neighbour and, on the other, the value of this average *to be expected* if the towns were randomly distributed over the area. Clearly, if the observed average distance is considerably less than the distance to be expected in a random distribution ('random' in this context is defined early in the paper) then the towns must be closer together than expected. This leads to a value of R well below unity and this expresses a clustered or nucleated pattern. The value of $1 \cdot 00$ should not be taken too seriously as a definitive indication that the pattern is random. The usefulness of the statistic lies more in the comparison it allows than in the verbal definitions of different settlement patterns one can make with it.

As a result of analysing the urban settlement pattern of twenty selected sample areas, King was able to make a number of tentative explanations of the observed patterns. For example, it seems that towns are most uniformly spaced in the Midwestern states. Here the generally level terrain, rectangular road network, and the quarter section settlement patterns may be among the reasons for this uniformity. In the case of the Ohio survey area, the settlement pattern north of the Maumee River differs slightly from that to the south and King suggests why this might be. Elsewhere clustering is seen to be related to a linear disposition of settlement. The reader is left (until he reads the paper) to consider why this might be and to suggest the direction this linearity might take, for example, in North Dakota. This last example demonstrates a weakness of the technique in that a pattern that is indicated by the statistic to be random may obviously not be random when the actual configuration of settlement on the map is examined. Similar defects, mostly relating to the inadequate way in which the unmodified technique allows for linear clustering, have been discussed in an interesting and amusing series of papers by various authors.[1] Despite these limitations, the technique is a useful one. From the way in which King relates his results to other characteristics of the survey areas it is evident that he regards it not simply as a statistical 'toy' to be played around with, but as a genuine tool to improve the analyses that geographers make of settlement distribution patterns.

The paper by *Garrison*, which suggests a number of ways in which important characteristics of transport networks may be measured, is perhaps not the ideal paper on this topic for the purposes of this book. But since the ideal paper does not exist, and since the paper does contain a number of important ideas, it has been included. Garrison wrote the paper for a fairly specialist readership (the members of the Regional Science Association) and the style is terse and technical. For example, graph theory terminology is used but the meaning of terms such as 'vertex' and 'edge' is carefully explained. At one point knowledge of the branch of mathematics known as matrix algebra is assumed, but this passage is not central to the understanding of the other measurement devices dealt with. In other respects the paper is clear, and most of the indices suggested can be worked out by anyone who can count, multiply and divide.

The early part of the paper is full of suggestive ideas. For example it is pointed out that the development of a rapid highway system of the type which has been built up in the United States causes cities to 'move about' relative to each other.[2] This relates directly to the ideas of objective and subjective distance discussed in Sections 1 and 5. Garrison also suggests that the Interstate System is more like an airline or railway system than an ordinary road network because it tends to link city centres and to disregard the smaller settlements between cities. It may be visualised as having been superimposed suddenly on an existing transport system that had grown up over several hundred years. Thus while the essential interrelationships of town development and route development are rightly stressed in the paper, the towns concerned in this particular route system are, generally, large ones only.

As in King's paper, problems of definition arise. As far as the selection of routes is concerned, definition was easy since a road is either part of the Interstate System or it is not. The question of which 'places' to include was more complex. Some places are not towns at all but are route intersections (see A, B, C and D on Fig. 4). By all the traditional geographical rules, towns should grow up at junctions and Garrison measures the characteristics of these points as if they were towns. By means of this sort of analysis it is possible to give at least some indications of the extent to which a town located at each of these points might succeed in attracting industry and trade because of its locational nodality with respect to other urban centres on the network.

A number of specific indices are suggested, some relating to the network as a whole and some to individual places on it. Examples of the former are the *degree of connectivity* (Garrison suggests that this might increase as a country becomes more developed), the *dispersion* and the *diameter* of the network. Individual places on the network can be measured in terms of their *associated number* of their *accessibility*.[3] The latter seems to be an especially useful index and it would not be difficult to calculate this value for, say, each of the ten largest towns in any British county (the county would, of course, need to be treated as an island for this purpose since external linkages would need to be ignored). Finally, Garrison attempts a rough analysis of the degree to which certain towns are better or worse served by the Interstate System than by the railway system.

This paper will probably require careful reading, recourse to a dictionary, and experiments with simple networks of the reader's own invention. It may even prod the mathematically inclined to learn some graph theory and matrix algebra. These efforts should be well repaid since a clearer idea will be gained of the implications of specific locations on a network and of the fundamental, and two-way, relationship between accessibility and urban growth.[4]

Notes and references

[1] BURGHARDT, A. F. 'The location of river towns in the central lowland of the United States', *Ann. Ass. Am. Geogr.* 49 (1959) 305–23.

DACEY, M. F. 'The spacing of river towns', *Ann. Ass. Am. Geogr.* 50 (1960) 59–61.

PORTER, P. W. 'Earnest and the Orephagians: a fable for the instruction of young geographers', *Ann. Ass. Am. Geogr.* 50 (1960) 297–9.

[2] This idea has been used in recent advertisements by railway and airline companies who claim to reduce the 'distance' between towns by introducing faster services between them.

[3] A more recent, and more advanced, treatment of the geographical applications of network theory is KANSKY, K. J. *Structure of Transport Networks: relationships between network geometry and regional characteristics*, University of Chicago, Department of Geography Research Paper no. 84, 1963.

Chapters 1 and 2 of this book form an admirably clear introduction to a number of useful measurement indices not dealt with in Garrison's paper.

[4] A good review of recent work in network theory is contained in HAGGETT, P. *Locational Analysis in Human Geography*, Arnold, 1965, chap. 3. An even fuller review (by Peter Haggett) is contained in CHORLEY, R. J., and HAGGETT, P. *Models in Geography*, Methuen, 1967, chap. 15.

A quantitative expression of the pattern of urban settlements in selected areas of the United States*

Leslie J. King

The agglomerated settlement in which there is a concentration of non-farm activities is a ubiquitous feature of the American landscape. Throughout the country these urban settlements range in population size from that of the small lowly hamlet of one hundred or so inhabitants up to the large metropolitan area of several million people. Functionally they also vary in character, although the majority of them might be considered to have basically the same *raison d'être* in that they provide some form of service to the inhabitants of the surrounding rural areas. However, the demand for goods and services originating within the farming sector of any large area can seldom be satisfied by a single urban centre. On the contrary, the physical and economic limitations to movement over the surface of the earth generally necessitate the existence of several urban settlements within any large area. Furthermore, the fact that these limitations are not constant in their effects throughout the continent, is reflected in the character of the distribution pattern of urban settlements from one area to another. The widely spaced irregular pattern of settlements characteristic of much of the semi-arid west, for example, contrasts strongly with the more compact and rectangular arrangement of settlements to be found in the Midwest. Many comparisons and contrasts along these lines have already been pointed up within the body of geographic literature.[1] However, the greater part of this descriptive work to date, has been characterised by an almost unquestioning reliance upon such qualitative terms as 'sparse', 'dispersed', 'agglomerated', or 'dense'. While these terms have meaning with reference to the context in which they are used, they lack objectivity for more extended comparative purposes. It appears desirable, therefore, that a more precise connotation be given to these descriptive terms as a means of facilitating comparative analysis and the discovery of more universal generalisations concerning the nature of settlement patterns.

The problem of deriving a mathematical expression of the pattern of settlement distribution has already received considerable attention from European geographers. In this regard, the works of Bernard,[2] Colas,[3] Debouverie,[4] Demangeon,[5] Meynier,[6] and Zierhoffer,[7] are especially worthy of mention.

* Reprinted from *Tijdschrift voor Economische en Sociale Geografie* 53 (January 1962), 1–7, by permission of the publishers.

However, these earlier formulations were based on certain critical ratios, for example, the average area per dwelling or the number of settlements in the commune, and generally no analysis was made of the actual linear distances separating the settlements within an area.[8] These attempts at quantitative analysis have therefore been criticised for their generality and for the fact that they are frequently insensitive to important variations in settlement pattern.[9]

In this study there is outlined a new approach to the problem of expressing the character of settlement patterns in mathematical terms. The approach is based upon modern statistical theory and the notions of probability. In contrast to earlier work in this field, greater emphasis is given to the actual distance separating settlements and the statistical techniques which are used in this study are in fact known as the *near-neighbour analysis*.

Statistical analysis of the *near-neighbour measure*, which is as the name suggests, a straight line measurement of the distance separating any phenomenon and its nearest neighbour in space, was originally developed by plant ecologists who were concerned with the distribution patterns of various plant species over the surface of the earth.[10] *Near-neighbour analysis* indicates the degree to which any observed distribution of points deviates from what might be expected if the points were distributed in a random manner within the same area. A random distribution of points is defined as a set of points on a given area for which 'any point has had the same chance of occurring on any sub-area as any other point; that any sub-area of specified size has had the same chance of receiving a point

Fig. 1. Theoretical settlement patterns

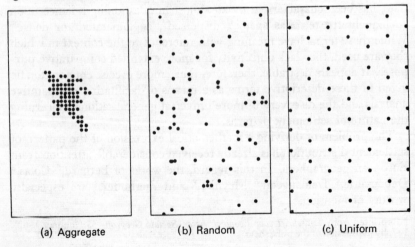

    (a) Aggregate   (b) Random   (c) Uniform

as any other sub-area of that size, and that the placement of each point has not been influenced by that of any other point'.[11] While this is essentially a mathematical concept, it is possible by use of a square grid with numbered intersections, and a random numbers table to construct an artificial random distribution (Fig. 1, b). From the laws of mathematical probability[12] it can then be demonstrated that the mean distance (rE) between each point and its nearest neighbour which could be expected in such a random distribution is equal to $\frac{1}{2} p^{-\frac{1}{2}}$, where p is the observed density of points in the area under consideration. The ratio of the observed mean distance (rA) to this expected value (rE), is termed the near-neighbour statistic (R). This ratio has a range in value from 0 when there is maximum aggregation of all the points at one location (Fig. 1, a), through 1 which represents a random distribution, up to $2 \cdot 15$[13] which is expressive of a pattern of maximum spacing analogous to the hexagonal arrangement discussed by Christaller and others[14] (Fig. 1, c). In this sense the statistic R provides a meaningful and precise expression of the distribution pattern of points within any area. Furthermore, the ratios for different areas can be compared directly with one another and the significance of the differences between them can be assessed by standard statistical procedures.[15] For any single area it is possible to test not only the significance of the departure of the observed mean distance (rA) from that expected in a random distribution (rE), but also the significance of the deviation of the observed mean distance from that which would be expected if the points within the area were either aggregated at one location or dispersed in a hexagonal pattern. In the first of these two hypothetical cases the expected value of rA would be zero while in the second it would be equal to $2^{\frac{1}{2}}/(3^{\frac{1}{4}} p^{\frac{1}{2}})$, where p is defined as before.[16]

In this study an attempt is made, using the techniques outlined above, to describe some of the empirical characteristics of the distribution of urban settlements in different areas of the United States. Whereas in the preceding discussion the emphasis has been on a set of points distributed in space, the focal point of attention now becomes a number of urban places which are distributed over the surface of the earth. It is assumed that within each area selected for study, there is an equal chance that an urban settlement will be located on any one unit area of ground as on any other area, and conversely, that every location has an equal chance of receiving an urban centre. Location theory suggests that these assumptions are quite unrealistic but as a theoretical norm or model they have considerable value.

The sample areas for this study were chosen in such a way as to ensure a representative cross-section of as many of the physical and economic regions within the United States as was practicable. The locations of the twenty areas which were selected are shown in Fig. 2. Within each area the term 'urban settlement' was taken to include all settlements listed in the United States Census[17] together with any smaller communities shown on the United States Department of Commerce Transportation Maps,[18] and published road atlases.[19]

For each area a series of straight line measurements were taken between the urban centres and their respective nearest neighbours.[20] There was no consideration given to the population size of the towns concerned,

Fig. 2. Location of sample areas

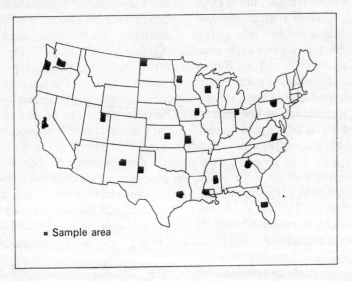

■ Sample area

since the emphasis was upon urban settlement as an attributal phenomenon, and while it is highly desirable that the variable, population size, should eventually be incorporated into the analysis, for the time being it is disregarded.

In many cases the nearest neighbour of a given town lay outside of the sample area. The distances to these neighbours were measured and included in the computations, but no town lying outside of the sample area was ever used as a centre of measurement. In addition, it was often the case that two towns within an area, were located closer to one another than they were to any other town, in which case the same distance was measured twice.

The obtained values of the *near-neighbour statistic R*, are presented in

Table 1: Near-neighbour statistics

Sample area	Number of towns	Density of towns per square mile	Mean observed distance (miles) rA	Expected mean distance in random distribution (miles) rE	Near-neighbour statistic R	Nature of pattern
California	96	0·0243	3·46	3·21	1·08	Random
Florida	64	0·0200	3·32	3·53	0·94	"
Georgia	132	0·0350	3·52	2·67	1·32	Approaching uniform
Iowa	82	0·0307	3·86	2·85	1·35	"
Kansas	51	0·0166	5·16	3·88	1·33	"
Louisiana	140	0·0437	2·57	2·39	1·08	Random
Minnesota	55	0·0169	5·32	3·85	1·38	Approaching uniform
Mississippi	104	0·0280	3·84	2·99	1·28	"
Missouri	80	0·0219	4·67	3·38	1·38	"
New Mexico	23	0·0065	6·82	6·20	1·10	Random
North Dakota	28	0·0082	6·13	5·52	1·11	"
Ohio	131	0·0512	2·80	2·21	1·27	Approaching uniform
Oregon	128	0·0317	2·86	2·81	1·02	Random
Pennsylvania	177	0·0466	2·82	2·32	1·22	Approaching uniform
Texas (N.W.)	38	0·0104	6·03	4·90	1·23	"
Texas (S.E.)	61	0·0182	4·29	3·70	1·16	"
Utah	20	0·0061	4·49	6·40	0·70	Aggregated
Virginia	122	0·0363	3·20	2·62	1·22	Approaching uniform
Washington	32	0·0073	4·14	5·85	0·71	Aggregated
Wisconsin	97	0·0299	3·58	2·89	1·24	Approaching uniform

Table 1. Intuitively it was expected that these values would vary in magnitude from one area to another, for it would seem as though variations in the physical geography, the economic base, transportation facilities, and land occupance history are likely to influence the spacing of urban settlements in any area. An examination of Table 1 reveals that the expected range in value for the near-neighbour statistic R did occur, and it is apparent that the tendencies towards aggregated, random, and uniform spacing of towns vary considerably throughout the country.

Fig. 3. Aggregated patterns

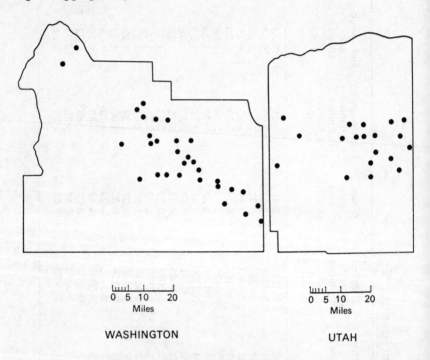

WASHINGTON   UTAH

On the one hand, the most marked tendency towards an aggregated settlement pattern appears in two of the areas within the western Cordillera system, namely Washington and Utah, for which the R values are 0·71 and 0·70 respectively. These low values here reflect an almost linear arrangement of pairs of towns along major rivers, the Yakima River in Washington and the Duchesne River and its tributaries in Utah (Fig. 3). In each case settlement is associated with irrigated 'oases' while the greater part of both areas remains virtually uninhabited. With such an arrangement of pairs of settlements the observed mean distance between towns and their nearest neighbours tends towards zero, and as a result the obtained value of R approaches that which would be characteristic of a more aggregated grouping.

At the other extreme, a tendency towards uniform spacing was apparent in twelve of the areas studied, most notably in Minnesota and Missouri ($R = 1\cdot38$), and in Iowa ($R = 1\cdot35$). At the same time however, additional statistical tests concerning the magnitude of the rA values revealed that in no area could the distribution of towns be described as a truly uniform one (Table 2). Nevertheless, the fact that the tendency towards uniform spacing is most marked in the Midwestern states of Minnesota, Missouri, and Iowa (Fig. 4), emphasises the descriptive value of the near-neighbour statistic R, since the general uniformity of relief, the method of original subdivision of the land based upon the

Table 2: Tests for uniform spacing

Area	Density of towns per square mile	Mean observed distance rA (miles)	Expected mean distance in uniform distribution of given density ru	Difference between rA and ru significant?
California	0·0243	3·46	6·90	Yes
Florida	0·0200	3·32	7·59	,,
Georgia	0·0350	3·52	5·74	,,
Iowa	0·0307	3·86	6·13	,,
Kansas	0·0166	5·16	8·34	,,
Louisiana	0·0437	2·57	5·13	,,
Minnesota	0·0169	5·32	8·27	,,
Mississippi	0·0280	3·84	6·42	,,
Missouri	0·0219	4·67	7·27	,,
New Mexico	0·0065	6·82	13·28	,,
North Dakota	0·0082	6·13	11·86	,,
Ohio	0·0512	2·80	4·75	,,
Oregon	0·0317	2·86	6·03	,,
Pennsylvania	0·0466	2·82	4·98	,,
Texas (NW)	0·0104	6·03	10·55	,,
Texas (SE)	0·0182	4·29	7·97	,,
Utah	0·0061	4·49	13·74	,,
Virginia	0·0363	3·20	5·64	,,
Washington	0·0073	4·14	12·57	,,
Wisconsin	0·0299	3·58	6·22	,,

Fig. 4. Tendency towards uniform spacing

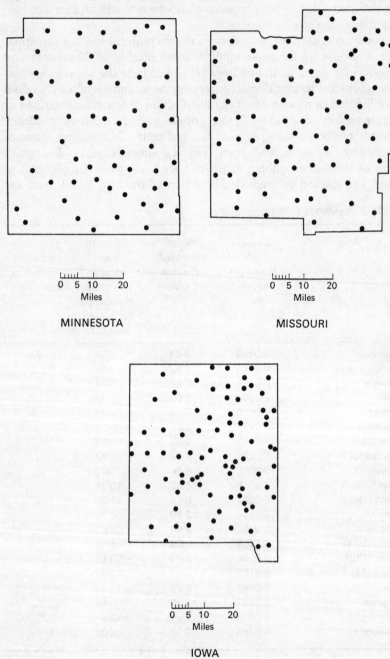

0 5 10   20
Miles

MINNESOTA

0 5 10   20
Miles

MISSOURI

0 5 10   20
Miles

IOWA

quarter section, the rectangular road pattern, and the generally even spread of population associated with a relatively intensive feed-grain–livestock economy, are characteristic features of these areas which would favour a more even spacing of towns. That even in these areas there is not apparent a more marked tendency towards a hexagonal arrangement of towns can in part be attributed to adverse physical features such as the glacial lake strewn surfaces of Minnesota; to the linear and dendritic patterns associated with the transportation routes of rivers, highways or railways; to original site features such as river fords, power sites, forestry

Fig. 5. Settlements and road networks

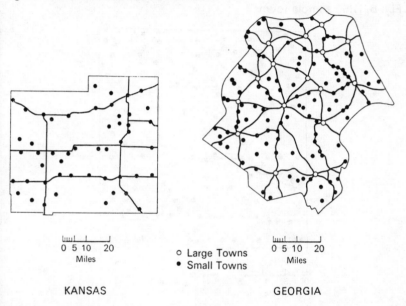

0 5 10   20
Miles

○ Large Towns
● Small Towns

0 5 10   20
Miles

KANSAS

GEORGIA

and mining centres, and finally to mere chance. The pattern of settlements in Wisconsin ($R = 1\cdot24$) appears to reflect the importance of these factors to an even greater extent, for in this area the tendency towards uniform spacing is even less pronounced than in the other Midwestern areas, notwithstanding the fact that it is very akin to these same areas in its broad physical, economic and social characteristics.

Elsewhere throughout the United States the tendency towards a uniform spacing of settlements is most marked in Kansas and Georgia and is of varying importance in a further six areas. Kansas might well be considered to be part of the Midwest although in terms of climate and landuse it is significantly different from the other Midwestern areas. A general east–west linearity in the arrangement of many of the towns within this area reflects the direction of the major transportation routes which traverse the area (Fig. 5). A similar control of settlement patterns by transportation networks is apparent in the Mississippi area and on the Staked Plains of northwestern Texas. In both of these areas a predominantly rectangular pattern of major highways is reflected in the relatively close spacing of towns along these routes while in the interstitial areas towns are spaced further apart. These conflicting patterns within the areas have tended to lower the obtained values of R. By contrast, in Georgia the pattern of transportation routes is in very close agreement with the

Fig. 6. Ohio sample towns

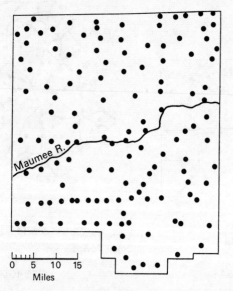

arrangement characteristics of an hexagonal pattern of settlements (Fig. 5). Many of the larger towns for example, appear to be associated with the intersection of five or six radial transportation routes. However, the comparatively low value of R is attributable to the irregular spacing of numerous small settlements along and between the major highways. Considerations such as these emphasise the desirability of incorporating the population-size variable into the analysis. In many areas the tendency towards either aggregation or uniformity would undoubtedly be more pronounced if the distribution patterns of only certain size towns were to be analysed. A further inadequacy of the study design is pointed up by a consideration of the pattern of settlements in Ohio (Fig. 6). In the northwestern half of this area, that is to the north and northwest of the Maumee River, the pattern of settlements appears more uniform than it does to the south of the river where there is considerable linearity in the arrangement of the settlements. Possibly this is related to the fact that in the northwest the terrain is slightly more hilly in association with old morainic deposits, whereas to the south and southeast, a lacustrine plain surface predominates. Considerable care should obviously be exercised in the choice of sample areas, since as in this case, two distinct patterns within an area may tend to contradict one another and thereby render the statistical results largely meaningless.

In the remaining areas of southeastern Texas, Virginia, and Pennsylvania, in which the tendency towards a uniform spacing of settlements is also statistically significant, the results are more difficult to interpret. In each case the observed mean distance (rA) is greatly exceeded by that which would be expected of a uniform distribution. In Pennsylvania this discrepancy stems in part from the fact that there were many closely spaced settlements in the northeast–southwest trending valleys, while the ridges and interfluves were frequently devoid of settlements. Similarly, on the Virginia Piedmont and the Texas Coastal Prairies, a close spacing of settlements along the major transportation routes with wide areas of intervening territory in which nucleated settlements are few in number, resulted in comparatively low values for the observed mean distance.

What of the six areas in which the distribution of settlements is apparently random (Table 1)? These anomalies are easily explained away in terms of the mathematics of the near neighbour measure. For example, the comparatively low value of R for North Dakota is a function of, on the one hand, the low density of towns per square mile which accounts for a large value of rE, and on the other hand a large value of rA resulting from the fact that there are only a few widely spaced towns within the area (Fig. 7). However, the more important consideration is whether or not a random distribution of settlements has any real geographic significance. In the North Dakota area for example, the critical fact appears to be that the settlements are located along three major transportation axes which have an approximate east–west orientation, rather than that the distribution is statistically random. Indeed, the concept of randomness with respect to settlement patterns might well be disregarded, except for the fact that the value of $R = 1$ is a convenient and useful origin from which to measure the tendencies towards an aggregated or uniform spacing of settlements. As the value of R decreases and approaches zero so the tendency towards an aggregation of settlements might be presumed to be greater, and conversely as the value of R

Fig. 7. Random pattern

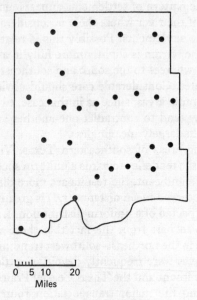

0 5 10   20
Miles

NORTH DAKOTA

increases from one then the tendency towards a uniform spacing of settlements becomes more pronounced.

The discussion up to this point has been focused upon the validity of the near-neighbour statistic as a descriptive statistic of the manner in which urban settlements are distributed over portions of the earth's surface. Considerable emphasis has been given to the interpretation of the various obtained values of R, and it is evident that the statistic is sufficiently sensitive in character to point up the differences which do exist between various distribution patterns. Whether or not the hypothetical norms of aggregation, randomness, and uniform spacing are accepted as meaningful reference points, the near neighbour statistic provides a logically acceptable and precise expression of the character of a distribution pattern of settlements. Furthermore, inasmuch as the statistic ranges in value from 0 to 2·15, within which limits any value is possible, it is logically consistent to consider the near-neighbour statistic as a continuous variable over this range. Accepting this to be the case, then a number of powerful sophisticated statistical techniques, such as correlation and regression analysis, can be brought to bear on the more fundamental and important problem of providing an explanation of the variation in the magnitude of the obtained values of R. Some tentative hypotheses relevant to this problem have already been suggested in this study, but the degree to which these hypotheses are valid with respect to all of the areas has yet to be determined. While an extended analysis along these lines falls outside of the scope of this paper, it might be noted that the value of R appears to be related in a positive direction with the variables *percentage of an area in cropland, percentage of land area in farms*, and *percentage of total population classed as rural farm*.[21] That is to say, the tendency towards a uniform spacing of settlements appears to be more pronounced in those areas in which the amount of cropland is high, or the percentage of total area in farms is high or finally the percentage of the total population classed as rural farm population is high. Conversely, the tendency towards an aggregation of settlements will be greater as the magnitude of these same variables decreases. It should be stressed that the amount of explained variation in the values of R which is accounted for by the relationship of these variables is not particularly high, and there are obviously a number of additional relevant variables which must be incorporated into the analysis before a satisfactory level of explanation is achieved. The problem awaits further investigation.

Notes and references

[1] See for example: GARLAND, J. ed. *The North American Midwest*, New York, Wiley, 1955, pp. 28–39.

Also MCCARTY, H. H. *The Geographic Basis of American Economic Life*, New York, Harper, 1940. In his discussion of the Great Plains area, for example, McCarty states (p. 237): 'Cities and towns are widely spaced, since their frequency necessarily varies with the density of the open-country population'.

[2] BERNARD, J. 'Une formule pour la cartographie de l'habitat rural avec application au department de l'Yonne', *C.r. du Congrés Internat. de Géog.* Paris, 1931, vol. 3, pp. 108–17.

[3] COLAS, M. R. 'Repartition de l'habitat rural', *Bull. de l'Assoc. Geog. Francais* (1945), pp. 51–6.

[4] DEBOUVERIE, A. H. 'Une methode à base numerique pour la cartographie de l'habitat, specialement applicable à la Belgique', *Bull. de la Soc. Belge d'Etudes Géog.* 13 (1943) 146–96.

[5] DEMANGEON, A. 'Une carte de l'habitat', *Ann. Géog.* 42 (1933) 225–32.

[6] MEYNIER, A. 'L'habitat rural dans les Ségalas', *C.r. Rendu du Congrès internat. de Géog*, Paris, 1931, vol. 3, pp. 99–102.

[7] ZIERHOFFER, A. 'Sur une formula servant á exprimer la dispersion et la concentration absolue de l'habitat rural', *C.r. du Congrès internat. de Géog.*, Varsovie, 1934, vol. 3, pp. 410–15.

[8] In a sense this judgment is not entirely correct. For example, ZIERHOFFER considered dwellings to be dispersed if more than 150 to 200 metres separated them.

DEBOUVERIE, in his study of Belgium, regarded the distance of 100 metres between dwellings as the limit of dispersion. However, no attempt was ever made to analyse these distances and to provide an explanation for the variation in them. In effect, the distance between dwellings (or towns) was always regarded as a constant and not as a variable.

[9] See HOUSTON, J. M. *A Social Geography of Europe*, London, Duckworth, 1953, pp. 81–5; TRICART, J. *Cours de Géographie Humaine*, vol. 1, *L'Habitat Rural*, Paris, Centre de Documentation Universitaire, 1959, pp. 72–5.

[10] See CLARK, P. J., and EVANS, F. C. 'Distance to nearest neighbour as a measure of spatial relationships in populations', *Ecology* 35:4 (1954) 445–53.

[11] *Ibid.*, p. 446.

[12] The derivation of the rE values involves consideration of the Poisson exponential function. The mathematical derivation of the formulae used in this study is presented in CLARK and EVANS, *op. cit.*, pp. 451–2.

[13] It is true that the mean distance between nearest neighbours is maximised in a hexagonal distribution where each point has six equidistant nearest neighbours. In this case it can be shown that the maximum value for rA is $2^{\frac{1}{2}}/(3^{\frac{1}{2}} p^{\frac{1}{2}})$ and that $R = 2 \cdot 15$.

[14] CHRISTALLER, W. *Die zentralen Orte in Süddeutschland*, Jena, 1933.

LÖSCH, A. *Die raumliche Ordnung der Wirtschaft*, Jena, 1944. BRUSH, J. E. 'The hierarchy of central places in southwestern Wisconsin', *Geogr. Rev.* 43 (1953) 380–402.

[15] An analysis of variance is sufficient. For the necessary transformations see CLARK and EVANS, *op. cit.*, p. 452.

[16] *Ibid.*

[17] U.S. Bureau of the Census. Seventeenth Decennial Census of the United States: *Census of Population*, 1950, vol. 1, *Number of Inhabitants*. Washington, Government Printing Office, 1952.

[18] United States Department of Commerce, United States Transportation Maps. Washington, Government Printing Office, 1938–49.

[19] Principally *Road Atlas*, *Chicago*, Rand McNally and Company, 1959.

[20] The distances, measured in miles, represent the direct airline distances between the approximately geographic centres of the towns concerned.

[21] These tentative conclusions were presented in KING, L. J. 'Consideration of the spatial distribution of urban places in selected areas of the United States', unpublished manuscript, Department of Geography, State University of Iowa, 1958.

Connectivity of the Interstate Highway System*
William L. Garrison

A recent informal survey of two thousand motorists disclosed that less than two per cent knew what the National System of Interstate and Defense Highways or the Interstate Highway System was. Undoubtedly, this proportion does not apply to the readers of this paper. But readers may not be familiar with certain of the needs for research regarding the Interstate System, so a general discussion precedes presentation of the problem treated in this paper. The problem treated is introduced in the paragraph below. This is followed by the general discussion which gives some characteristics of the Interstate System and the relevance of the research problem. Analyses of the problem and evaluation of results follow.

Everyone knows that the success of an activity is conditioned by its relative location, among other things. The Interstate Highway System is inducing changes in the relative location of urban centres and, thus, the success of activities within these centres. Locations of cities relative to each other are changing, city tributary areas are shifting, and the relative location of sites within cities is changing. General notions stressing locations relative to markets and/or raw materials and in association with compatible activities are available in the literature. However, present concepts of transportation systems are not at this level of generality. Present concepts relate to particular places—such as, the head of navigation and break of bulk places—and lack the generality of notions from location theory. Thus, they are of little value for the problem of transportation-induced shifts in relative location. What concepts are appropriate? In this paper the Interstate System is treated as a graph and the usefulness of concepts from the theory of graphs is examined. Examination of the graph yields several measures which may be thought of as indices of connectiveness, status indices, accessibility indices, or indices of relative location. The paper is elementary, both in its use of graph theory and in the analysis of the Interstate System. It reports the results of a pilot study from which it is hoped that more incisive studies will be developed.

The paragraph above is incorrect in one respect. There are certain concepts of transportation systems in the programming literature which are at a high level of generality. The ordinary transportation problem of linear programming is a case in point. The transportation problem may

* Reprinted with minor omissions from *Papers and Proceedings of the Regional Science Association* 6 (1960), 121–37, by permission of the publishers.

be approached from the theory of graphs, of course. The search in this paper is for a level of approximation which is more elementary than those approximations using programming formats, but which is useful for the consideration of location problems.

The interstate system

The Interstate System comprises 41,000 miles of high-speed, low transportation cost, limited access facilities linking many of the major cities of the nation (Fig. 1). The concept of the Interstate System dates back a number of years prior to implementation in 1956.[1] Previous federal highway policy has resulted in the federal aid primary system of about a quarter of a million miles, the federal aid secondary system (the farm to market system), and certain national parks and forest roads. The result of this previous policy is a relatively fine-scale network linking urban centres of all classes with each other, and linking urban centres with their tributary areas. The Interstate System is more gross in scale—in a sense it lies on top of previous highway systems and it emphasises linkages within and between major cities.

Perhaps two things may be gleaned from this brief statement. First, the Interstate System may be thought of as a large city or metropolitan system of highways since it provides links between (and within) metropolitan areas. This represents a marked shift in federal policy because previous highway policy might be characterised as catering to rural areas and small urban centres. Another notion is that the Interstate System may be thought of as a new highway network. In many ways it is more comparable to networks of airline and railroad routes than present highway networks.

Magnitude of changes induced

How far-reaching will be the location shifts following construction of the Interstate Highway System? The writer is inclined to the view that these changes will be as significant as those induced by other major technological changes in transportation systems—railroad developments or paving of rural roads. Many do not share this strong an opinion and some discussion of points of view is appropriate.

It may be argued that the situation is very different today from what it was when other transportation networks, say railroads, were developed. The railroads opened up large areas to distant markets, especially in the western United States. Consequently, many new industries were developed which produced directly from resources and exported products long distances. Extensive wheat farming is an example of an industry

Fig. 1. The National System of Interstate Highways, 1957, comprising 41,000 miles of expressway facilities

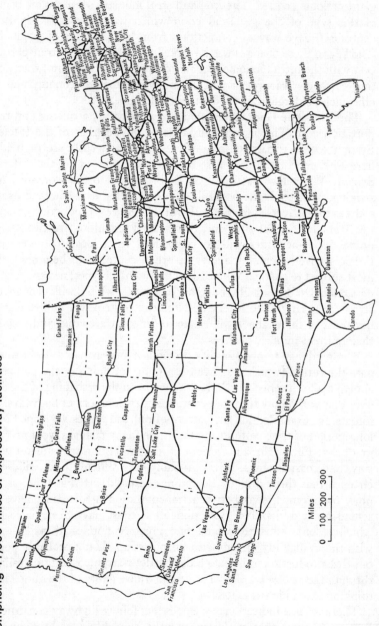

developed in this way. Also, railroads enabled centralisation of many manufacturing and service activities from small local establishments to giant national centres. The iron and steel industry serves as an example of this type of change. Production which was previously highly decentralised gave way to competition from large centres of production. The key to these changes was a marked reduction in unit transportation cost with the introduction of the railroad. With reduced unit transportation cost new resources could be brought into the economy and new efficiencies of large-scale production could be realised.

The Interstate Highway System is also markedly reducing unit transportation cost. This is especially true of the portions of the Interstate System within urban centres, where congestion costs are high.[2] It is here that one might look first for changes induced by the Interstate System. What new resources will be brought into the economy? Most striking, perhaps, is the possibility for upgrading to urban land uses resources formerly used for typically rural land uses. Production of amenities from residential sites and recreational amenities are two cases in point. What activities will be centralised from local to larger scale? Perhaps governmental activities in urban centres will be among those most subject to change. Wholesale activities of all types, newspapers, and department stores might be other activities which will change their structure greatly. The Interstate Highway System will induce changes, but most of the changes will relate to different activities and resources than railroad-induced changes.

The tendency to oversimplify previous experience and use it to evaluate the future (which we have been guilty of doing in the paragraphs above) makes it especially difficult to envision the reshaping of the economy that will follow from the continued development of highways. One forgets, for example, that the pattern of railroad routes developed over a long period of time, and during that time many changes went on rather gradually. First, railroads were built in competition with inland waterways and coastal routes. It was probably very difficult to see widespread changes that these original beginnings foretold. At that time, as even now, cost comparisons between transportation media must have presented great difficulties. How difficult it must have been to visualise which of our industries would find great economies of centralisation with the availability of railroad transportation. Many probably pointed out that production of buffalo hides hardly warranted building railroads through the arid West. To what extent are we guilty of the same kind of thinking about highways today?

There is some indication of changes that follow highway construction. It is well known that marked changes in rural life were brought about by paving of rural highways.[3] It is now necessary to predict marked changes in urban areas which will follow current developments of highways.

Other conditions

Highways alone are not enough to induce change, of course, just as railroads alone could not remake the face of America. The success of railroads depended upon markets for the products they hauled. Industrialisation of Europe and the growth and development of the United States were necessary conditions for the great changes brought about by railroads. Certain conditions are necessary if changes are to be induced by the Interstate System. Continued urbanisation and increasing demands for more leisure time at home, amenities, and services are conditions especially pertinent to the changes that will be induced by the Interstate System. Also, governmental conditions, such as the existence of FHA and transportation taxation policy, are important considerations in evaluating highway impact.

Some research questions

Decisions on the location of the System and its capacity largely have been made.[4] The Interstate System is limited to 41,000 miles and the general orientation of these routes is fixed. Decisions about capacity have been made. That is, certain operational methods for forecasting traffic are used to determine traffic demands and capacity is installed to meet these demands. However, much research on allocation of facilities is needed, in spite of the fact that many of the major decisions have been made. Methods of making capacity decisions on the Interstate System could be improved. Need for investment in highway facilities seems unlimited and many decisions bearing on location and capacity of facilities similar to those made for the Interstate System will be made in the future.

Certain problems of financing the Interstate System have been recognised. The U.S. Bureau of Public Roads is currently undertaking a highway cost allocation study designed to deal with these problems at the federal level.[5] Surely this study will not provide all the answers at the federal level, and there is need for work on state and local problems of financing. Also, questions of charges to properly allocate traffic among the several kinds of carriers arise when highway financing is reconsidered, as well as from pressures of problems arising in other sectors of the transportation industry.[6]

The relative location problem

Answering any one of the questions mentioned above requires some ability to speak intelligently about the influence of the Interstate System on activities. Answering questions of location and capacity obviously requires insights into effects on traffic by location shifts induced by the facility. Resolving questions of tax equity, financing, and the like requires ability to make intelligent estimates of location shifts. Thus, relative location is at the heart of these problems. The strategic position of some areas will be enhanced while that of others will be diminished when the highway improvements are made. Questions of how much change and where these changes will take place are inseparable.[7]

The Highway System as a graph

Notions from graph theory may be useful in evaluating the relative location problem. In the language of graph theory the Interstate Highway

Fig. 2.

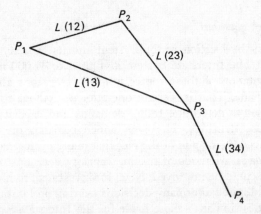

System is an ordinary graph with 325 edges terminating at 218 vertices. For convenience in this discussion, edges will be termed *routes*, vertices will be termed *places*, and the graph will be termed *highway system* or *network*. An example of a network is given by Fig. 2. Places are marked P_1, P_2, etc., and routes, $L(12)$, $L(23)$, etc. Properties which characterise ordinary graphs and, thus, transportation systems treated as ordinary graphs are:[8]

1. A network has a finite number of places.
2. Each route is a set consisting of two places.
3. Each route joins two different places.

4. At the most, only one route may join a pair of places.
5. No distinctions are made between the 'initial' and the 'terminal' places of routes; in other words, routes are two-way.

Identification of places

It was necessary to adopt operational definitions of a place on the I.H.S. All Standard Metropolitan Areas were recognised as places, provided they were on the System. 143 SMA's are on the System, 23 are not. Each intersection of three or more routes on the System was recognised as a place, regardless of whether or not it was occupied by an urban centre which met the size criteria. Also, all ends of routes were recognised as places, e.g., Sweetgrass, Montana. The definition of place was, then, partly topological and partly based on urban size criteria.

These definitions identify a *planar graph*—the intersection of any two routes on the graph is a place on the network. It was decided to use the topological definition of places because these ends of routes and, especially, intersections have locational assets, they are able to ship and receive from several directions. It is worth noting that many intersections on other transportation systems have not developed to the degree that the location at an intersection might seem to warrant. Complicating factors of tariff structures might have contributed to this. In the highway case there is an effect due to presence of demand on a highway which may be important in giving intersections an impetus for development. Heavy streams of traffic create demands for food, lodging and other goods and services, and these are not supplied by the facility itself. There are no dining rooms, staterooms, or swimming pools on the highway as there are on ships.

Consideration of intersections as major places introduces interesting problems which need to be investigated further. As the transportation network is filled in in an underdeveloped area, for example, intersections on the transportation system are created. These have the effect of introducing new places with strategic locations in the economy and shifting the relative location of places already developed (Fig. 3).

Measures of connectivity

Definitions:

A *path* is a collection of routes $P_1P_2, P_2P_3, \ldots, P_nP_m$, where all places are different from each other.
The *length* of a path is the number of routes in it.
The *distance* between two places is the length of the shortest path (or any one of the shortest paths) joining them.

Fig. 3. (a) Undeveloped area   (b) Developed area

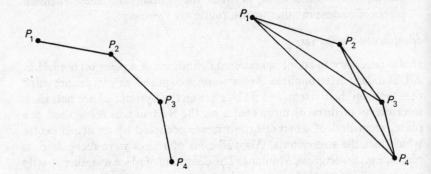

A number of measures have been suggested or may be directly inferred from the concepts of graph theory for measuring the relative cohesiveness of a network or the relative position of places on the network. One such concept is the *associated number* of a place. This number is the maximum of the distances from this place to all other places. In Fig. 2, the associated number of P_1 is 2; of P_3, 1. The *central place* of a network is that place whose associated number is a minimum. P_3 is the central place of Fig. 2. The maximum associated number indicates another characteristic of a network, the *diameter*.

Also, it is known that if there are m places in a network then the maximum possible number of routes, L^*, in the network is

$$L^* = \left[\frac{m(m-1)}{2} \right]$$

Prihar has suggested that the *degree of connectivity* of a network for which the number of places is known can be expressed:[9]

maximum connectivity $= L^* / \left[\dfrac{m(m-1)}{2} \right] = 1$

minimum connectivity $= L^* / (m-1)$

degree of connectivity $= L^* /$ observed number of routes

As Prihar suggests, these notions might be very useful in designing networks with several types of cost in mind. If unit over-the-road cost is relatively low and investment cost of facilities high, then the network might take the form of (a) in Fig. 3. If the reverse is true—investment cost low and over-the-road cost high—the network might take the form of (b) in Fig. 3.

Shimbel has suggested a measure of the *dispersion*, $D(X)$, of a network X, namely:[10]

$$D(X) = \sum_{i=1}^{n} \sum_{j=1}^{n} \text{distance } (ij)$$

He has also suggested a measure of the *accessibility* of the network to the ith place:

$$A(iX) = \sum_{j=1}^{n} \text{distance } (ij) \qquad i = 1, \ldots, n$$

Also,

$$\sum_{i=1}^{n} (iX) = D(X)$$

An ordinary network corresponds to a matrix $X = \{x_{ij}\}$ when:

$x_{ij} = 1$ if, and only if, a route exists between i and j

$x_{ij} = 0$ otherwise.

The matrix corresponding to (a) of Fig. 3 is:

$$X = \begin{matrix} 0 & 1 & 0 & 0 \\ 1 & 0 & 1 & 0 \\ 0 & 1 & 0 & 1 \\ 0 & 0 & 1 & 0 \end{matrix}$$

and the matrix corresponding to (b) is:

$$X = \begin{matrix} 0 & 1 & 1 & 1 \\ 1 & 0 & 1 & 1 \\ 1 & 1 & 0 & 1 \\ 1 & 1 & 1 & 0 \end{matrix}$$

Examination of the matrix corresponding to a network suggests methods of studying connectiveness. A glance at the ith row or column of the matrix indicates the number of routes associated with the ith place. Examination of the powers of the matrix is also useful. The matrix X^n contains elements indicating the number of ways the ith place may be reached from the jth in n steps. For example, the entry $x_{ij} = C$ indicates that there are C possible ways in the network for place j to be reached from place i in n steps. The sum over the jth column would indicate all of the ways available in n steps for place j to be reached from other places. A general notion of connectivity may be obtained from the matrix T where $T = X + X^2 + X^3 + \cdots + X^n$. Shimbel has termed the matrix X^n the *solution matrix*, in the case where powering of the matrix is carried until there are no elements having the value zero. n is the *solution time* of the system. Elements of this matrix show the numbers of ways to reach place j from place i in the n steps. Elements of the matrix T display this information for all routes and a summation across the columns or down the rows of T will produce a vector of numbers indicating what we might call the *accessibility* of each place on the system.

All of the above properties of a graph and associated matrices X^i and T may be proved by reference to definitions of matrix algebra. Consider, for example, the summation

$$x_{ik}^2 = \sum_{j=1}^{n} c_{ij} c_{jk}$$

The only terms which contribute to this summation are those where $c_{ij} = c_{jk} = 1$. When this is the case, there is a two length path between i and k via j.[11] By definition x_{ij}^2 is the element in the ith row and kth column of the matrix X^2.

Analyses

The regional subsystem formed by the Interstate System in a portion of the Southeast United States was selected for exploratory study. This subsystem is shown on the accompanying map (Fig. 4). The subsystem has 45 places and 64 routes. This particular subsystem was selected arbitrarily. The small size of the subsystem made computations relatively simple.

There are at least five types of analysis, not all of which have been made here, which might be applied to this subsystem, namely:

1. Analysis of the connection of the subsystem to the larger highway system.
2. Analysis of the subsystem as a whole.
3. Analysis of the position of particular places on the subsystem.
4. Analysis of details of the subsystem within each urban centre or place. A comparison of the within-city connections of the Interstate System will reveal marked differences from city to city.[12] One would expect, then, within-city differences from city to city resulting from the construction of the system.
5. Comparative analysis of different transportation graphs. These might be undertaken at any one of the four levels of analysis suggested above.

Fig. 4. A portion of the Interstate Highway System

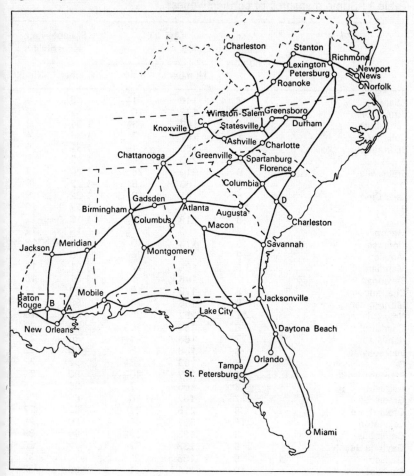

The regional subsystem

The following statements may be made about the regional subsystem:

1. Its connectivity is

$$L^* = \frac{45(45-1)}{2} = 1980$$

$$\text{connectivity} = \frac{L^*}{L} = \frac{1980}{64} = 30 \cdot 94$$

2. The diameter of the network is 12.

Table 1 : Some measures of connectiveness

Place	Associated number	A(i, X)		Shimbel-Katz accessibility	
		Number	Rank	Number	Rank
Atlanta	7	146	$1\frac{1}{2}$	1·88	1
Birmingham	8	173	10	1·37	2
Petersburg	9	189	$16\frac{1}{2}$	1·34	3
Columbia	7	157	3	1·35	4
Spartanburg	7	160	$4\frac{1}{2}$	1·31	5
A	10	213	$24\frac{1}{2}$	1·29	6
Statesville	9	214	26	1·24	7
D	7	168	8	1·22	8
Lake City	8	181	12	1·22	9
B	11	251	38	1·17	10
E	9	218	$29\frac{1}{2}$	1·16	11
Macon	7	160	$4\frac{1}{2}$	1·16	12
Florence	8	173	10	1·12	13
Mobile	9	213	$24\frac{1}{2}$	1·05	14
Meridian	9	199	22	1·01	15
Savannah	7	146	$1\frac{1}{2}$	1·01	16
Chattanooga	8	173	10	·99	17
Montgomery	9	196	20	·99	18
New Orleans	11	252	39	·96	19
Charlotte	8	189	$16\frac{1}{2}$	·96	20
Ashville	7	183	$13\frac{1}{2}$	·95	21
Jacksonville	8	188	15	·95	22
C	8	193	$18\frac{1}{2}$	·92	23
Stanton	11	257	$40\frac{1}{2}$	·90	24
Augusta	6	165	7	·86	25
Greenville	7	162	6	·86	26
Greensboro	9	215	27	·82	27
Lexington	11	257	$40\frac{1}{2}$	·80	28
Columbus	8	183	$13\frac{1}{2}$	·80	29
Daytona Beach	9	233	32	·72	30
Gadsen	9	198	21	·70	31
Durham	10	221	31	·68	32
Jackson	10	237	34	·67	33
Baton Rouge	12	293	44	·66	34
Winston-Salem	10	235	33	·65	35
Charleston	10	244	$36\frac{1}{2}$	·63	$36\frac{1}{2}$
Roanoke	10	244	$36\frac{1}{2}$	·63	$36\frac{1}{2}$
Knoxville	8	193	$18\frac{1}{2}$	·62	38
Newport News	11	259	42	·62	39
Tampa St Petersburg	9	217	28	·59	40
Norfolk	12	302	45	·55	41
Orlando	9	243	35	·52	42
Richmond	10	218	$29\frac{1}{2}$	·39	43
Charleston	8	212	23	·36	44
Miami	10	269	43	·27	45

3. The central places of the network are at Atlanta, Columbia, Spartan-
burg, D, Macon, Savannah, Ashville and Greenville.
4. The dispersion of the graph is

$$D(X) = \sum_{i=1}^{n} \sum_{j=1}^{n} \text{distance } (ij) = 9292$$

Evaluation of places on the subsystem

It was noted earlier that there were a number of ways the position of a
single place on the system might be evaluated. Examples of evaluation
of accessibility or status of places follow.

1. The associated number is one indication of how accessible places are
   to the network. Associated numbers were computed by determining
   the longest distance for each place. The result is given in Table 1. It
   must be remembered that distance by definition is the shortest path
   between two places.
2. The accessibility index, $A(iX)$, for places on the system is also given
   in Table 1. This may be thought of as the accessibility of places to the
   network.
3. An alternate method of measuring accessibility has been made following the method suggested by Shimbel and Katz.[13] The operational
   definition of the method is as follows:

Let X be the n by n matrix corresponding to the subsystem.

$$T = sX + s^2X^2 + s^3X^3 + \cdots + s^rX^r + \cdots$$

s is a scalar, $0 < s \leqslant 1$, measuring the effectiveness of a one-route connection, s^2 is the effectiveness of a path with two routes, s^r is the
effectiveness of an r length path. Using this measure, accessibility of
the ith place, a_i, is

$$a_i = \sum_{j=1}^{n} t_{ij} \qquad i = 1, \ldots, n$$

The relation

$$T + I = (I - sX)^{-1} = I + sX + s^2X^2 + s^3X^3 + \cdots$$

may be used to find T, provided s is selected in a proper manner.

The scalar used was $0 \cdot 3$ so each one-route path has the weight $0 \cdot 3$. Two-
route paths have the weight $0 \cdot 3 \times 0 \cdot 3 = 0 \cdot 09$. Three-route paths have the
weight $0 \cdot 3^3$. Results of this analysis are presented in Table 1.

115

Comparative analysis

There are a number of ways transportation systems may be compared. The operational question that is most difficult to answer is that of recognising the systems to be compared. A crude comparison of the Interstate System with the railroad network of the study area has been made by comparing the number of rays or routes at each place.[14] Only a partial analysis was made, using the data in Table 2. These results are quite interesting. For one thing, there are almost twice as many rays on the

Table 2: Comparison of selected cities

City	Railroad routes	Interstate routes	
		Expected†	Observed
Atlanta	9	4·8	6
Birmingham	9	4·8	5
Petersburg	5	2·7	3
Columbia	9	4·8	4
Spartanburg	6	3·2	4
Statesville	4	2·2	3
Lake City	5	2·7	4
Macon	6	3·2	3
Florence	5	2·7	3
Mobile	6	3·2	3
Meridian	6	3·2	3
Savannah	7	3·8	3
Chattanooga	6	3·2	4
Montgomery	8	4·3	3
New Orleans	8	4·3	3
Charlotte	7	3·8	3
Total	106	56·9	57

† Number expected if Interstate Routes were distributed in the same manner as railroad routes. The difference between the observed and expected distributions is not significant.

railroad system than there are on the Interstate System. The expected number of rays on the Interstate System (based on the distribution of rays on the railroad system) is quite like the observed number. However Atlanta would seem to be better served by the Interstate System than by the railroad network and New Orleans and Montgomery less well served. This leads to the tentative observation that in spite of the fact of the relatively sprawling character of the Interstate System, certain central places on the network are emphasised more than are central places on the railroad network. The reverse is also true. This is an interesting conclusion, but it is relatively specious at this state of the investigation.

Accomplishments

In this paper we have done no more than introduce the problem of the analysis of transportation networks and suggested some descriptive approaches via modern graph theory. Whether the approaches have merit remains an open question. There are two things in their favour, however. One is the relative simplicity of graph theory; another is the ability to look at the System as a whole or to look at individual parts of it in terms of the whole. There are alternate approaches that have the latter merit, but their application to problems of the scope of the Interstate System would require tremendous effort.[15]

At least two major inadequacies of the approach should be mentioned. For one, graph concepts are in no way normative. Whether or not some arrangement is good or bad, whether or not links should be added to the system, and like decision-making questions require empirical statements outside of the usual content of graph theory. Just what sort of relationships need to be specified and how they may be introduced is a subject for study. Also, the user of this method must make rather arbitrary decisions regarding the content of the graph. In the case of the Interstate System, the content of the graph is pretty much by definition. Even this is questionable, since there are routes constructed, under construction, or planned which are very similar in character to the Interstate System, but not integral parts of it. Evaluation of the railroad system in comparison to the Interstate System also required definition of a graph. Problems of definition, and perhaps a host of others, will become clearer as work continues.

Notes and references

[1] See U.S. Congress, House, *Interregional Highways*, 78th Cong., 2nd Sess., House Document 379; *Highway Needs of the National Defense*, 81st Cong., 1st Sess., House Document 249; and Federal Aid Highway Act of 1956, U.S., *70 Statutes at Large 374* (1956).

[2] Exact saving from freeway use is difficult to estimate. Including the value of time saved, passenger car savings are approximately 2 cents per vehicle mile and truck savings about 10 cents. See AMERICAN ASSOCIATION OF STATE HIGHWAY OFFICIALS, *Road User Benefit for Highway Improvement*, Washington, D.C.;

CITY OF LOS ANGELES, Street and Parkway Design Division, *A Study of Freeway System Benefits*, 1954; and JOSEPH, HYMAN, 'Automobile operating costs', *CATS Research News* 3 (13 Nov. 1959) 9ff.

[3] See, for example, LABATUT, JEAN, and LANE, WHEATON, eds. *Highways in our National Life, a symposium*, Princeton University Press, 1950.

[4] See references in note 1.

[5] The study is discussed in *Third Progress Report of the Highway Cost Allocation Study*, 86th Cong., 1st Sess., House Document 91.

[6] This problem has been discussed widely in the literature, e.g. *Highway Investment and Financing*, Bulletin 222, Highway Research Board (NAS–NRC Publication 682), Washington, D.C., 1959.

[7] These notions are elaborated in GARRISON, W. L., BERRY, B. J. L., MARBLE, D. F., MORRILL, R., and NYSTUEN, J. *Studies of Highway Development and Geographic Change*, Seattle, University of Washington Press, 1959.

[8] For bibliographies and expository discussions of graph theory see CARTWRIGHT, DORWIN. 'The potential contribution of graph theory to organisation theory', in *Modern Organisation Theory*, ed. Mason Haire, New York, Wiley, 1959.

HARARY, FRANK. 'Graph theoretic methods in the management sciences', *Management Science* 5 (1959) 387–403.

HARARY, FRANK, and NORMAN, ROBERT Z. *Graph Theory as a Mathematical Model in Social Science*, University of Michigan, Institute for Social Research, 1953.

Basic references are:

KÖNIG, DENIS. *Theorie der endlichen und unendlichen Graphen*, New York, Chelsea Publishing Company, 1950.

BERGE, CLAUDE. *Theorie des graphes et ses applications*, Paris, Dunod, 1958; chapters 8, 13, 14 and 20 are of special interest.

[9] PRIHAR, Z. 'Topological properties of telecommunication networks', *Proc. Institute of Radio Engineers* 44 (1956) 929–33.

[10] SHIMBEL, ALFONSO. 'Structure parameters of communication networks', *Bull. math. Biophys.* 15 (1953) 501–7.

[11] This method counts paths from j to j, e.g. in four steps one might follow the path P_1P_2, P_2P_3, P_3P_2, P_2P_1. In certain cases this may not be desired.

[12] Maps of the urban configurations of the Interstate System are in U.S. Dept. of Commerce, Bureau of Public Roads, *General Location of National System of Interstate Highways*, September 1955.

[13] SHIMBEL, *op. cit.*, and KATZ, W. 'A new status index derived from sociometric analysis', *Psychometrika* 18 (1953) 39–43.

[14] The count of railroad rays was made using ULLMAN, EDWARD L. *U.S. Railroads, classified according to Capacity and Relative Importance* (Map), New York, Simmons-Boardman Publishing Company, 1950.

[15] It might be useful, for example, to merge information on mathematical programming with information on highway networks as is done for electrical networks in DENNIS, J. B. *Mathematical Programming and Electrical Networks*, Technology Press of M.I.T. and Wiley, 1957.

Suggested practical exercises

Nearest neighbour analysis

Using graph paper, draw a square or rectangle of any convenient size to represent an area selected for survey. Insert a reasonable number of points (say twenty) within the area, clustering them all quite close together in one part of the area. Repeat this exercise using the same area and the same number of points twice more, once spacing the points randomly around the area and once trying to maximise the average distance between the points. Now calculate the R value for each of the three distributions using the formula

$$R = 2\bar{D}\sqrt{(N/A)}$$

where $\bar{D}$ = average of the observed distances between each point and its nearest neighbour

N = number of points

A = area of selected square or rectangle.

This formula is a simplified version of that suggested by King:

$$\frac{rA}{\frac{1}{2}p^{-\frac{1}{2}}}$$

where rA = the observed mean distance between points

p = density of points (N/A in the previous formula).

Having worked out a few experimental examples select various actual rural settlement patterns, using a square or rectangular survey area for ease of measurement, and compare their R values. Do the R values bear out the intuitive judgments that would be made about the extent to which the patterns are 'nucleated' or 'dispersed'? What problems of measurement arise and how might they be solved?

Network analysis

Select any reasonably simple network, for example, that formed by the A and B class roads of Anglesey. Define the 'places' on the network in topological terms, that is, by specifying that a place exists wherever a junction exists or a route terminates. The routes joining 'places' are the 'links'. Now transform the network into a diagram (like the London Underground map) making no attempt to draw the length of each link to scale but ensuring that all links are connected as in reality (see, for example, the illustration on p. 71 of Haggett's book*). Insert the correct road distance (measured off the actual map with a mapwheel) on each link.

It is now possible to measure the *connectivity* of the network and its *diameter* and *dispersion*. For each place defined, the *accessibility* and *associated number* can be measured. Similar measurements can be carried out for other networks of roughly similar complexity to see how they compare to that of Anglesey.

What might be the practical significance of some of these indices (for example, the degree of connectivity and the accessibility index)? How might the accessibility index be modified to a *potential* index (see the paper by Carrothers in Section 6 of this book)? For what purposes might such a potential index be important?

*See note 1 on page xvii.

4 Central place theory

The pattern made by the distribution of people on the earth's surface is something which is of fundamental relevance to almost any analysis of man and his behaviour. This pattern therefore is of significance to many other disciplines apart from human geography. But it is perhaps the geographer who has devoted most thought to population patterns, both from the point of view of measurement and of interpretation.

By and large, we think of population as being either 'rural' or 'urban'. This distinction was clearer in medieval Europe, when many towns were neatly ringed by a wall, than it is today. It is true that for administrative purposes every square foot of land in Britain is either rural or urban, depending on whether it forms part of a rural or an urban local government unit. But this classification is misleading for some purposes since it means that many quite large villages are 'rural'. Alternatively we could try to differentiate between urban and rural on grounds of population density. We could say that above a certain figure of population per square mile, the area in question is urban. But what figure are we to adopt? There is unlikely to be worldwide agreement, since parts of an area like the outer 'urban' fringe of London may well have a lower population density than certain 'rural' areas in India. Nor can we say that a town exists when a certain population figure is exceeded because, as in the case of population density, problems arise in arriving at an agreed figure. (The number actually specified varies a great deal from country to country.)[1]

This problem of how to define what is meant by 'urban' is raised here because Central Place Theory, to which the papers in this section relate, does not attempt to define urban and rural population in the terms already suggested. It deals instead with 'central places' and their 'regions' or hinterlands. A *central place* is a settlement that provides one or more services for people living outside it. Because this relationship between settlement nodes and the areas they serve is a worldwide one, it provides a framework by which settlement systems all over the world may be studied. The services referred to can range from a letterbox existing in a small hamlet up to a famous brain surgeon working in a national capital whose 'region' may be the entire world because people travel from all over the world to use his services. Between these two extremes exist a whole range, or *hierarchy*, of functions. In ascending order of importance this hierarchy would include (to take seven examples from many hundreds): a small general store, a public house, a ladies' hairdresser, a hardware shop, a secondary school, a department store and an opera house. This list is arranged in a progression from 'low order' to 'high order' goods or services and the significance of this is that normally (but not always) wherever a 'high order' function occurs in a central place then one or more of each of the 'lower order' functions also occurs in the same place. Thus any centre (whether town, village or even suburban shopping parade) that has a hardware shop is also likely to have all the lower order goods listed before it. Similarly, any large regional centre is likely to have all seven functions listed.

Another important feature of the list should be noticed. The population required to support each function tends to increase as one goes higher up the hierarchy. Whereas a small general store may exist with a 'market'of, say, two hundred regular users, a hardware shop may require perhaps one thousand. A secondary school may require five thousand regular 'users' (assuming that it is built for five hundred pupils between eleven and eighteen and that people between these ages constitute 10 per cent of the local population). The number of people required to support a function is called the *threshold population* and if this is not maintained the function may cease to operate. This can occur either when the local population decreases (which may cause a village shop to close in an area subject to rural depopulation) or when changes in taste decree that a smaller percentage of the population use the function (which partly explains the recent closure of many cinemas). Conversely as local population, or more accurately local user population, increases above the threshold the function will tend to make larger profits. This may continue until a population approaching twice the threshold is reached, by which time someone will have realised that he may well be able to profit by offering the same function. Competition, or even possibly cooperation, then occurs between the two purveyors of the function.

Threshold populations for the different functions vary because our needs conform to a pattern. Some things, such as food, newspapers, petrol and cigarettes, are needed very frequently. Others, such as furniture, are needed less frequently, while really high order functions, such as an opera house, may be visited only once a year. In the latter case to be sure of filling an opera house seating one thousand people every weeknight a threshold population of about 300,000 is needed. If, following a wave of enthusiasm for opera, people tend to average six visits to the opera per year, a threshold population of 50,000 will be sufficient to support the opera house. The expected frequency of use can therefore be seen to be an important aspect of threshold population and some functions, for example funeral directors, may need an enormous threshold population, because individuals use them very infrequently. Others, such as tobacconists (and schools), can exist on a smaller threshold population, because a sizeable and predictable number of people use them daily.

Having considered these fundamental, but not too difficult, ideas we can return to the problem with which we started. How can we build up a theory, or a set of explanatory statements, which will account for the way in which central places of widely differing sizes have come to be distributed as they are in the landscape? At this point our thinking, while still being based on common sense and simple ideas about our needs, becomes spatial and involves some simple geometrical ideas.

We can begin by assuming in some mythical region a population entirely engaged in agriculture. Each family is completely self-sufficient and therefore indulges in no trade. For the sake of simplicity we can assume that the land is of a fertility that does not vary spatially and that the culture is so egalitarian that each family farms a plot of standard size. Thus the population density does not vary spatially either. One of the farmers, having an inventive turn of mind, discovers how to make an implement that will increase crop yields. After a while he realises that he can stop farming and make a living by exchanging this implement for food produced by others. He becomes the first central place in the region because people come to him with food and trade it for an implement. He begins to employ people and other buildings are added around his farm to house his employees. So far the central place has an entirely industrial function but as more and more people live there, all dependent on exchanging a manufactured good for food from the farming areas, other functions are bound to arise. There must be book-keepers to keep the records and storekeepers to look after the stocks of machinery awaiting exchange. At a later stage other implements will be invented and the economy will have to devise some money token representing value because trading in actual commodities rapidly becomes very unwieldy as the number of commodities increases above the original two (the implement and food). Banking, retailing, credit and insurance all evolve in due course. As the regional culture grows in sophistication, political and educational institutions, repositories for works of art, and places for recreation will all become necessary and will be added. From an early stage in this process of accretion of new services, people will come from outside the manufacturing centre to make use of the functions it provides so that as well as being an industrial centre it will have become a service centre. In this simple outline of events most of the essential elements of urbanisation are present. There could be a great deal of variation in the detail. For example, the first centre could have been oriented to trade between producers of different crops rather than to manufacturing. But the key ideas of functional interdependence between central place and surrounding region, an increase in the variety of central function offered and an increasing percentage of the population not making their living from farming are all evident, as they have been historically in urbanisation.

The geographer has a very specific interest in this process. He is concerned to examine the principles that seem to govern the *location* of each new function as it is invented or emerges. There are many principles involved but we will think only of three at this stage. One relates to the idea of *threshold population*. As each function is added, a certain number of people are required to support it. This normally means that they must be able to reach it from where they live. Movement always costs the individual something. It will therefore be easier to attract a threshold population to a function, whether it is a theatre, a shop, or a museum, if the function is located in an existing population centre. Here people are already living at a higher density than they are in the farming areas. Therefore the aggregate distance that has to be travelled to bring, say, one hundred people to a shop every day is less if it is located in some existing centre than it would be if the shop were opened in a rural area.

The second principle also leads to the choice of existing central places as the location for new functions. Some functions are closely interdependent. The shops need to be near the factories producing the goods they sell. The bankers need to be near the manufacturers so that they can discuss business affairs more easily. The government needs to be near the bankers and the manufacturers so that they can coordinate activities more effectively. In fact there are savings to be made by all these institutions if they locate near the other institutions with which close contact is necessary. These savings are called *external economies* because they stem from factors outside the institution concerned and, in the cases mentioned, they are the result simply of building in one place rather than another; in making wise use of the existing spatial pattern of people and institutions.

These two principles alone do not give any indication about which particular central places, in a given region, will tend to attract new functions or how the pattern made by centres providing a particular function will evolve. To illustrate this we need to consider a third principle, that of *spatial competition*. Let us imagine a region in which central places of a more or less equal size are already established and are regularly spaced at a distance of about twenty miles from each other. In this region the people have traditionally solved the problem of storing their money by the rather crude expedient of stuffing it up the chimney in a sock. One day someone develops the idea of opening a bank where people can deposit money which is surplus to their immediate requirements. This spare money can, of course, be put to profitable use by the banker. The people are now faced with the choice of adopting the new method of storage, thus presumably gaining in safety and making some money in interest, or of keeping to the old method and avoiding the cost and inconvenience of the periodic journeys to the bank (which, for reasons already outlined, will be located in one of the central places). Let us assume that above a certain journey distance, say five miles, the cost of journeys to the bank outweighs the advantages of the banking method. The bank can therefore attract as customers only those living in the central place plus those in the neighbouring countryside up to a radius of five miles from the bank (see Fig. 1).

Figs. 1–4. ' Colonisation ' of a region by bankers

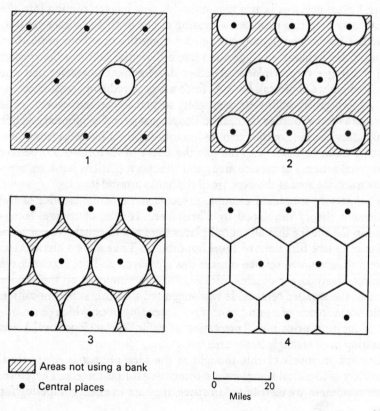

////// Areas not using a bank

● Central places

0   20
Miles

As the banker is seen to prosper and grow rich, other people set up in the same business. They will each choose a central place and, to avoid unnecessary competition from other banks, each will choose a different central place until all central places have a bank (Fig. 2). Now, as the development of the transport network reduces the cost of movement and as the banks acquire greater expertise and reduce costs by using computers (this is, after all, a mythical region), consumers become willing to travel more than five miles to use a bank. As soon as it becomes worth travelling ten miles, the situation shown in Fig. 3 is reached. Very soon the people living in the shaded areas will want to use a bank, and if they all go to the nearest one each bank will be serving a hexagonal area as shown in Fig. 4. Now the whole region has been effectively 'colonised' by bankers.

This situation can continue to develop in a number of ways. For example it is likely that smaller central places, if they have not done so already, will begin to grow up at those points where three service areas meet. These are the points from which the cost of reaching existing central place services is at a maximum. A new banker coming into the region may help this process by locating at one of these smaller centres. Whether he does so or not will depend upon the threshold population required for banking and upon the size differential between the smaller and the larger central places. Another development might be that one bank, which we could call bank X, finds a way of reducing costs substantially (perhaps by selling its computer) so that it becomes worth while to make a longer journey to reach it. People just over the boundary of this bank's service area are thus tempted to transfer their business from their existing bank to bank X. This has the effect of distorting the perfect hexagonal scheme of service areas and the more efficient bank enlarges its own service area at the expense of the banks around it.

This greatly simplified example presents some of the essence of the settlement theory developed by Christaller.[2] It was, of course, recognised in the theory that all central places were not of equal size nor were all central place functions of equal importance. Thus a great hierarchical system of hexagonal service centres was envisaged and the service areas of successively larger centres were seen as superimposed on the service areas of the smaller centres. It was suggested that this superimposition could occur in one of a number of ways depending upon which of a number of locating principles ('marketing', 'traffic' or 'sociopolitical') was operating most strongly in the area.

Implicit in much of this thought is the idea of *spatial competition*. Providers of identical functions are competing for customers. Therefore, since customers are distributed in space, they are in effect competing for space. New functions will tend to locate at points which are as far away as possible from existing functions of the same type. As one provider increases the space he serves so he decreases the space served by his immediate competitors. As people become more mobile, and as some providers become much larger and more attractive in their prices and range of services than others, then the smaller providers of that function may cease to operate altogether. This situation can be seen quite clearly as increasing numbers of rural dwellers acquire cars which may lead them to transfer some of their custom from the local village shop to a supermarket in some nearby town. (It should be noted, in passing, that there are important exceptions to some of these general statements. Sometimes, particularly within a town, certain functions such as antique shops tend to cluster together rather than space themselves as far apart as possible. The reader may care to theorise about the factors which might bring this situation about.)

On the basis of the theoretical structure that has been discussed, we are able to make a number of predictions about the pattern of settlement to be expected in reality. We could predict a functional hierarchy of central places since at any given point in time some central places would include functions not yet included by others. Also it would be likely that the larger central places would not be clustered in one part of the region but would be regularly spaced all over it. Additionally we would expect towns of a given importance in the hierarchy to be spaced at a roughly constant distance apart. It also follows, since the number of towns in each size class decreases as one goes up the size hierarchy, that larger towns should tend to be spaced further apart than smaller towns. To what extent are all these expectations borne out in reality?

The answer is that in many cases, perhaps most, the actual pattern differs considerably from that expected on the basis of the theory. This is partly because central place theory relates only to one activity of towns; their servicing function to surrounding regions. But, as we know, towns grow for a variety of reasons apart from this. They may grow because they are situated on a resource of some kind which occurs only in a limited area. 'Resource' here might mean a mineral of use for manufacturing (for example, coal), a scenic or climatic factor of use for recreation (for example, a coastline or a reliably warm summer), or a strategic location for transhipment or distribution (for example, a deepwater estuary). All these factors might confer upon the limited area in question advantages which would lead to a rate of urban growth in excess of that to be expected solely from the demand for central services generated by the immediate tributary region. This helps to explain why two such large cities as Liverpool and Manchester exist within a few miles of each other. It is therefore important to remember that central place theory does not set out to give a comprehensive explanation of the size and spacing of towns. It is not a complete theory of settlement. It aims to give some explanation of the intensity and spacing of *service* activity, and to give some insight into the ways in which service centres have evolved and are changing.

A second factor that distorts the perfect hexagonal scheme is the variations that occur in population density. For the sake of simplicity, we assumed in our example that population was spread all over the region at a constant density. This is unlikely to occur in reality, since factors upon which population density depends, for example soil fertility and climate, vary from place to place. In a relatively densely populated rural area, the threshold population necessary to support a central function occupies a smaller area of land than would be the case in a sparsely populated area. Since it is obviously threshold *population*, not threshold *area*, that determines whether a function will exist, then it is more useful to think in terms of *population space*, not actual space, when analysing central place systems. Maps drawn in population space are those where given areas on the map are made proportional to the population of those areas on the ground. Such maps are sometimes drawn at election times. The area of each constituency on the map is made proportional to the number of voters it contains and from this map one can tell at a glance the political significance of each constituency. Space distortions of this sort, which are considered again in Section 5, can help us a great deal to improve our comprehension of the spacing and size of service centres.

There is one other important shortcoming of central place theory that should be considered. The theory includes the assumption that to reach any given function the rural dweller will go always to the nearest possible centre which offers it. In other words it suggests that for each commodity, adjacent tributary regions are mutually exclusive and that there is no zone of overlap in which people go sometimes to one centre and sometimes to another. From our own common knowledge we know this to be untrue, since any one of a large number of reasons may induce us to go further than we need for a commodity or service. Once we accept that this is true it becomes less pressing to think in terms of hexagonal tributary areas, since the prime reason for suggesting hexagons was that they fitted together without overlapping. A more realistic approach to the problem of defining service areas is suggested by Huff in the paper in this section.

Despite the various criticisms that have been advanced, central place theory is a very thought-provoking set of ideas, even in the simplified form in which it has been presented here. Clearly we cannot expect it to produce a complete explanation of the present size and spacing of central places, since so many important explanatory factors are necessarily omitted. It is however a theory that contains certain vitally important concepts, such as the interdependence of town and region, the hierarchy of functions and centres, threshold population, and spatial competition. A great deal of research has been built on these central ideas and in at least one region, the newly reclaimed Dutch polders, new service centres have been located in accordance with the principles embodied in the theory.

Two of the papers in this section relate directly to classical central place theory. The paper by *Ullman*, although it does not contain a formal exposition of the theory, has been included because it was one of the earliest statements of Christaller's central place ideas to appear in English. Ullman refers to some of Christaller's findings, including the fairly close correspondence between the actual average distances apart of centres of various size classes and the distances to be expected from applying the $\sqrt{3}$ rule. He draws attention to the problems of measuring the 'centrality' of a central place and rightly points out that it is more important to think of central services performed rather than simply of population size. Christaller adopted the rate of telephone ownership as a readily accessible index of the servicing activity of a centre. This has obvious drawbacks and nowadays, by drawing upon such sources as the Census of Distribution,[3] we can use rather more accurate indices such as the amount of retail business carried on in a centre in relation to its size. If the amount of business done per head of population in the town is very high this may indicate that people are coming in from outside to shop. By further calculation it may be possible to determine the extent to which this is happening. Another index of centrality would be the number of people coming into the town over a given time period. The difficulty here, apart from the expense of measurement, is that we would not know what proportion were coming in to use the town's shops or services and how much each person was spending. Ullman also points out that, in reality, tributary regions are likely to be distorted out of a circular or hexagonal shape because of the effect of communication lines. Here again it depends upon the way in which we measure distance. If we measure in terms of miles, it is quite likely that we will end up with cigar-shaped hinterlands, but if time is used as an index of distance, the hinterland may become more circular in the transformed map.

A final very important point made by Ullman is that it is quite wrong to think of the central place system as static or fixed. It is in a constant state of change. A new road leading into a town from a certain direction will probably enlarge the hinterland in that direction because it will enlarge the area from which the town may conveniently be reached. Similarly a sudden large increase in the functional strength of one town, say a big new shopping development, will have an effect on the business done in all the nearby towns with which it is competing for customers. Many other circumstances can arise which change the relative standing and accessibility of central places and that is why it is essential to think of the system as an evolving system and to be constantly aware that a change in one element is bound to lead to changes in others.

The paper by *Berry and Garrison* marked a significant step forward in central place studies. Although short, it is a fairly demanding paper. To understand it fully some basic knowledge of standard statistical techniques is required, although even without this understanding much can be gained from the paper. The work assumes a fairly good knowledge of some of the specialist terms used by social scientists, such as 'taxonomy', 'attribute' and 'variate'. It will also be necessary to know the difference between a discrete and a continuous variable. But these problems can be solved without much trouble with the aid of a good dictionary.

If classical central place theory were exactly correct, central places, when ranked in order of size, would produce a 'stepped' size hierarchy not a continuous one. In other words, all towns would fall into one of a limited number of size classes. A simplified explanation of this expectation is that the hexagonal service areas are all of one of a limited number of sizes because they are all based on a set of fundamental hexagons of equal size. If, as pure theory sets out, there is a constant relationship between the size of a service area and its central place, then all the central places must be of a limited number of sizes and the population size of centres when they are ranked in size order, will not vary continuously from, say, one hundred to one million. In reality, towns of all population sizes appear to exist, although we do speak instinctively of hamlets, villages, towns and cities as if settlements of four size classes could be differentiated. It is curious how often, when the population size of each town in a region or country is graphed in size order (this is called a rank-size graph), 'plateaux' appear on the curve. This indicates that towns of certain population size ranges are comparatively frequent and those of other sizes rare or non-existent.

Berry and Garrison were concerned to investigate whether the thirty-three central places in a county in the State of Washington, U.S.A. seemed to fit into recognisable class groupings or whether they formed a continuous unstepped hierarchy (as maintained by Vining in his comments on the work of Brush). They attempted this by analysing the hierarchy of functions offered by the towns to see whether the centres fell into recognisable groupings according to functional significance. They identified a hierarchy of fifty-two central functions in the form of variates and fifteen in the form of attributes. In the case of the variates (that is, functions such as food shops that could be present in varying numbers) they carried out a regression analysis between the two variables, population size and functional strength, and by this means determined the threshold population for each function. In the case of the attributes (that is, functions such as a telephone exchange that were either present in a town or were not) they used a less well known statistical device which indicates the degree of correlation between an attribute and a variable (in this case population size).

The spread of threshold population values was then examined, using techniques which derive from linear nearest neighbour analysis,[4] to determine whether the distribution of these values was random or grouped in any way. The definition of a group in this context is that every member of the group should be closer to some other member of the same group than to any other point. It was found that some evidence of grouping was present and the variable central functions were arranged in three groups (see Table 2) on the strength of the gaps that appeared in the threshold population between Elementary Schools and Physicians and between Frozen Food Lockers and Sheet Metal Works. Central places of Class C had a nearly complete range of group 1, 2, and 3 type functions, Class B centres has virtually complete 1, a good range of 2, and a few 3, while Class A centres had a fair range of 1, and a sprinkling of 2, and 3 functions. It is important to note that the central places are arranged along the top of Table 2 in order of *functional* importance, not population size. Lake Stevens, for example, has a relatively high population but very limited functional importance. East Stanwood is the precise reverse. Anomalies of this sort always provide a temptation to carry out additional research and at the end of the paper Berry and Garrison suggest reasons for certain inconsistencies. A very similar analysis, based on the functional attributes, yielded similar results (Table 3). Lake Stevens was again an anomaly and in addition it can be seen that one attribute, general stores, is negatively related to population. This means that it is an attribute that is less likely to occur in larger centres than smaller. This accords with common sense because larger centres include a range of specialised shops and general stores tend not to be necessary.

A final analysis, shown in Fig. 2, indicates that when the total number of activities in each centre is plotted against population size three interesting results emerge. First, there is a rough positive relationship between population size and functional importance. Second, four centres are very deficient in services in relation to their size. And third, three fairly distinct groups emerge when the towns are analysed according to total number of activities or functions. These groupings are indicated by dotted lines and called A, B and C, thus providing the bases for the grouping of centres under these letters in Tables 2 and 3. Another curious feature not mentioned by the authors of the paper, is that there is a distinct break in the hierarchy of town population values. No town exists with a population between 974 and 1600, although there is a good spread of values on either side of this break. This could be a small piece of contributory evidence to support the idea that a stepped hierarchy of town sizes exists.

The third paper in the section, that by *Huff*, has no explicit connection with central place theory and in fact comes from a journal which is not in the least 'academic'. It has been included because it deals with the problem of hinterland delimitation, which has always been of interest to geographers. Huff writes in terms of 'firms', 'trading areas' and 'consumers', whereas geographers usually think of towns, hinterlands and population, but this difference of terminology should not preclude an understanding of the important principle that Huff is trying to establish.

Classical central place theory speaks of a hierarchy of central places each with a tributary region which is seen in the form of a hexagon so that it will not overlap with contiguous regions belonging to another centre of the same status. Huff questions this (though he never actually refers to the theory). He looks first at the original formulation by Reilly which aimed to estimate the proportion of business drawn to each of two towns from a town situated between them. He then refers to the refinement developed by Converse who devised a formula for predicting the 'breaking point' on the road between city A and city B. The breaking point is the point at which one is equally likely to travel to A or to B for goods and services. Clearly this point must be on the hinterland boundary or 'watershed' between the two centres and by linking the breaking points on all the roads leading out of a centre some sort of hinterland delimitation has been achieved.

Huff points out several shortcomings of this approach and suggests an alternative model which does not depend on establishing any specific breaking point but allows movement to take place from any point in the region to any other point. This accords with common sense (which is a necessity in any good model) since we know that although we usually go to the nearest big town to buy new shoes we may sometimes go much further to a larger town for this purpose. This may be either because we want to use other services, which the larger town alone provides, on the same trip, or because we want to see a wider range of shoes, or for any one of a dozen other reasons. The results of Huff's model are therefore expressed in terms of probabilities. For example, the probability of shopping in town A may be 0·99 (out of 1·00) if we live within one half-mile of it, or 0·70 if we live a little further away, or 0·05 if we live some way away and nearer to town B. By expressing these values in the form of contours around the town, and perhaps by superimposing similar contours from neighbouring towns, we get a far more realistic picture of the 'pull' of each of the towns in the region than if we spoke only in terms of breaking points and non-overlapping tributary regions. The model, as suggested by Huff also abandons the assumption made by Reilly (and many other people over the past forty years) that the likelihood of making a shopping journey is inversely related to the square of the distance to the shopping centre (see the paper by Carrothers in Section 6 for a fuller discussion of this point). In the present model the power to which the distance value is raised is simply denoted by the term λ, and it is suggested that further work is required to determine a value that will be realistic in view of the specific problem involved. For example, it is likely that the degree to which distance will act as a disincentive when deciding whether to make a shopping trip will vary according to such factors as the age of the shopper, whether or not he has a car, the commodity required, and so on.

Huff concludes that a trading area, or urban hinterland, is not a fixed and finite area capable of accurate delimitation with a line. It is in the nature of a gradient with values that decrease outwards from the centre. These values represent the likelihood that people living in the surrounding area will go to shop in the centre. The gradient will be steeper in some directions (for example in the direction of another nearby large town) than in others. This important idea, which is clearly at variance with some of the basic assumptions of central place theory, deserves careful consideration. As Huff points out, it is based on the individual's view of his possible range of action in space. It therefore does not depend on the artificially based suppositions of geographers and others that each town has a hinterland that can be meaningfully defined simply by drawing a line around it.

Notes and references

[1] See the useful discussion on the problem of defining a town in JONES, E. *Towns and Cities*, Oxford University Press, 1966, chap. 1.
[2] For a full discussion of these principles, and of the basic ideas of Central Place Theory generally, see CHRISTALLER, W. *Central Places in Southern Germany*,

trans. C. W. Baskin, Prentice-Hall, 1966, esp. 1. B. This translation of Christaller's book, which was first published in German in 1933, has been invaluable in bringing Christaller's fundamental thinking about settlement patterns to the attention of those who do not read German.

[3] An essential source of data for any analysis of the service function of British central places, BOARD OF TRADE, *Report on the Census of Distribution and Other Services, 1961*, H.M.S.O., 1963–4.

[4] For further reading on this technique see the list of references at the end of the paper by L. J. King in Section 3.

FURTHER READING

The literature on central place theory is enormous and varies a great deal in difficulty. For reasonably simple introductory statements of the theory, including the modifications suggested by Lösch, see:

JOHNSON, J. H. *Urban Geography*, Pergamon Press, 1967, pp. 94–102.

BERRY, B. J. L. *Geography of Market Centres and Retail Distribution*, Prentice-Hall, 1967, chap. 3.

HAGGETT, P. *Locational Analysis in Human Geography*, Arnold, 1965, chap. 5.I.
   An equally good statement is contained in:

BUNGE, W. *Theoretical Geography*, C.W.K. Gleerup, Lund, Sweden, rev. edn., 1966, chap. 6.

For a very full annotated bibliography of central place studies see:

BERRY, B. J. L., and PRED, A. *Central Place Studies*, Regional Science Research Institute, Philadelphia, 1965.

For a statement of central place theory and other settlement theories see:

GARNER, B. J. 'Models of urban geography and settlement location', chap. 9 in *Socio-economic Models in Geography*, ed. R. J. Chorley and P. Haggett, University Paperbacks, 1967.

A theory of location for cities*
Edward Ullman

Many studies have shown that cities are not scattered over the earth illogically, but a general theory of location has been lacking. The orderly spacing of towns as service centres forms a basis for a settlement/distribution theory. Service centres range in size from hamlets performing a few simple functions up to large cities providing specialised services for a large tributary region composed of the service areas of smaller towns. Thus, in an entirely uniform land the larger the town, the larger its tributary area should be. On the basis of a South German 'norm' of areal organisation Christaller has worked out deductively the central place theory for distribution of settlements. He sets up typical settlement sizes, determines the normal number of towns in each class, as well as the spacing of the centres, and the area and population of their tributary areas. The theory applies better to agricultural areas than to industrial districts. It is not static but changes to fit changes in underlying conditions, particularly transportation. The system also varies from place to place in the world in line with population density, type of agriculture, governmental organisation, and many other factors. These underlying regional differences make possible comparisons between central place systems in the United States and elsewhere. After further refinement some form of the theory should provide a logical framework for study of existing distributions and perhaps for planning optimum spacing of new settlements.

I

Periodically in the past century the location and distribution of cities and settlements have been studied. Important contributions have been made by individuals in many disciplines. Partly because of the diversity and uncoordinated nature of the attack and partly because of the complexities and variables involved, a systematic theory has been slow to evolve, in contrast to the advances in the field of industrial location.[1]

The first theoretical statement of modern importance was von Thünen's *Der isolierte Staat*, initially published in 1826, wherein he postulated an entirely uniform land surface and showed that under ideal conditions a city would develop in the centre of this land area and concentric rings of land use would develop around the central city. In 1841 Kohl investigated the relation between cities and the natural and cultural environment, paying particular attention to the effect of transport routes on the location of urban centres.[2] In 1894 Cooley admirably demonstrated the channelising influence that transportation routes, particularly

* Reprinted from *The American Journal of Sociology* 46 (1941), 853–64, by permission of the publishers.

rail, would have on the location and development of trade centres.[3] He also called attention to break in transportation as a city-builder just as Ratzel had earlier. In 1927 Haig sought to determine why there was such a large concentration of population and manufacturing in the largest cities.[4] Since concentration occurs where assembly of material is cheapest, all business functions, except extraction and transportation, ideally should be located in cities where transportation is least costly. Exceptions are provided by the processing of perishable goods, as in sugar centrals, and of large weight-losing commodities, as in smelters. Haig's theoretical treatment is of a different type from those just cited but should be included as an excellent example of a 'concentration' study.

In 1927 Bobeck[5] showed that German geographers since 1899, following Schlüter and others, had concerned themselves largely with the internal geography of cities, with the pattern of land use and forms within the urban limits, in contrast to the problem of location and support of cities. Such preoccupation with internal urban structure has also characterised the recent work of geographers in America and other countries. Bobeck insisted with reason that such studies, valuable though they were, constituted only half the field of urban geography and that there remained unanswered the fundamental geographical question: 'What are the causes for the existence, present size, and character of a city?' Since the publication of this article, a number of urban studies in Germany and some in other countries have dealt with such questions as the relations between city and country.[6]

II

A theoretical framework for study of the distribution of settlements is provided by the work of Walter Christaller.[7] The essence of the theory is that a certain amount of productive land supports an urban centre. The centre exists because essential services must be performed for the surrounding land. Thus the primary factor explaining Chicago is the productivity of the Middle West; location at the southern end of Lake Michigan is a secondary factor. If there were no Lake Michigan, the urban population of the Middle West would in all probability be just as large as it is now. Ideally, the city should be in the centre of a productive area.[8] The similarity of this concept to von Thünen's original proposition is evident.

Apparently many scholars have approached the scheme in their thinking.[9] Bobeck claims he presented the rudiments of such an explanation in 1927. The work of a number of American rural sociologists shows appreciation for some of Christaller's preliminary assumptions, even though done before or without knowledge of Christaller's work and performed with a different end in view. Galpin's epochal study of trade areas in Walworth County, Wisconsin, published in 1915, was the first contribution. Since then important studies bearing on the problem have been made by others.[10] These studies are confined primarily to smaller trade centres but give a wealth of information on distribution of settlements which independently substantiates many of Christaller's basic premises.

As a working hypothesis one assumes that normally the larger the city, the larger its tributary area. Thus there should be cities of varying size ranging from a small hamlet performing a few simple functions, such as providing a limited shopping and market centre for a small contiguous

Fig. 1. Theoretical shapes of tributary areas. Circles leave unserved spaces, hexagons do not. Small hexagons are service areas for smaller places, large hexagons (*dotted lines*) represent service areas for next higher-rank places

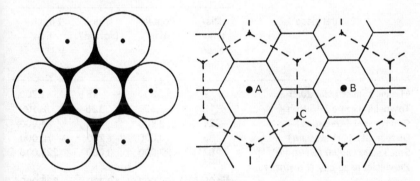

area, up to a large city with a large tributary area composed of the service areas of many smaller towns and providing more complex services, such as wholesaling, large-scale banking, specialised retailing, and the like. Services performed purely for a surrounding area are termed 'central' functions by Christaller, and the settlements performing them 'central' places. An industry using raw materials imported from outside the local region and shipping its products out of the local area would not constitute a central service.

Ideally, each central place would have a circular tributary area, as in von Thünen's proposition, and the city would be in the centre. However, if three or more tangent circles are inscribed in an area, unserved spaces will exist; the best theoretical shapes are hexagons, the closest geometrical figures to circles which will completely fill an area (Fig. 1).[11]

Christaller has recognised typical-size settlements, computed their average population, their distance apart, and the size and population of their tributary areas in accordance with his hexagonal theory as Table 1 shows. He also states that the number of central places follows a norm from largest to smallest in the following order: 1:2:6:18:54, etc.[12]

All these figures are computed on the basis of South Germany, but Christaller claims them to be typical for most of Germany and western Europe. The settlements are classified on the basis of spacing each larger unit in a hexagon of next order size, so that the distance between similar centres in the table increases by the $\sqrt{3}$ over the preceding smaller category (in Fig. 1, e.g., the distance from A to B is $\sqrt{3}$ times the distance from A to C). The initial distance figure of 7 km between the smallest centres is chosen because 4–5 km, approximately the distance one

Table 1

Central place	Towns		Tributary Areas	
	Distance apart (km)	Population	Size (sq. km)	Population
Market hamlet (*Marktort*)	7	800	45	2,700
Township centre (*Amtsort*)	12	1,500	135	8,100
County seat (*Kreisstadt*)	21	3,500	400	24,000
District city (*Bezirksstadt*)	36	9,000	1,200	75,000
Small state capital (*Gaustadt*)	62	27,000	3,600	225,000
Provincial head city (*Provinzhauptstadt*)	108	90,000	10,800	675,000
Regional capital city (*Landeshauptstadt*)	186	300,000	32,400	2,025,000

can walk in one hour, appears to be a normal service area limit for the smallest centres. Thus, in a hexagonal scheme, these centres are about 7 km apart. Christaller's maps indicate that such centres are spaced close to this norm in South Germany. In the larger categories the norms for distance apart and size of centres appear to be true averages; but variations from the norm are the rule, although wide discrepancies are not common in the eastern portion of South Germany, which is less highly industrialised than the Rhine-Ruhr areas in the west. The number of central places of each rank varies rather widely from the normal order of expectancy.

The theoretical ideal appears to be most nearly approached in poor, thinly settled farm districts—areas which are most nearly self-contained. In some other sections of Germany industrial concentration seems to be a more important explanation, although elements of the central-place type of distribution are present. Christaller points out that Cologne is really the commercial centre for the Ruhr industrial district even though it is outside the Ruhr area. Even in mountain areas centrality is a more important factor than topography in fixing the distribution of settlements. Christaller states that one cannot claim that a certain city is where it is because of a certain river—that would be tantamount to saying that if there were no rivers there would be no cities.

III

Population alone is not a true measure of the central importance of a city; a large mining, industrial, or other specialised-function town might have a small tributary area and exercise few central functions. In addition to population, therefore, Christaller uses an index based on number of telephones in proportion to the average number per thousand inhabitants in South Germany, weighted further by the telephone density of the local subregion. A rich area such as the Palatinate supports more telephones in proportion to population than a poor area in the Bavarian Alps; therefore, the same number of telephones in a Palatinate town would not give it the same central significance as in the Alps. He claims that telephones, since they are used for business, are a reliable index of centrality. Such a thesis would not be valid for most of the United States, where telephones are as common in homes as in commercial and professional quarters.

Some better measures of centrality could be devised, even if only the number of out-of-town telephone calls per town. Better still would be some measure of actual central service performed. It would be tedious and difficult to compute the amount, or percentage, of business in each town drawn from outside the city, but some short cuts might be devised. If one knew the average number of customers required to support certain specialised functions in various regions, then the excess of these functions over the normal required for the urban population would be an index of centrality.[13] In several states rural sociologists and others have computed the average number of certain functions for towns of a given size. With one or two exceptions only small towns have been analysed. Retail trade has received most attention, but professional and other services have also been examined. These studies do not tell us actually what population supports each service, since the services are supported both by town and by surrounding rural population, but they do provide norms of function expectancy which would be just as useful.[14]

A suggestive indicator of centrality is provided by the maps which Dickinson has made for *per capita* wholesale sales of cities in the United States.[15] On this basis centres are distributed rather evenly in accordance with regional population density. Schlier has computed the centrality of cities in Germany on the basis of census returns for 'central' occupations.[16] Refinement of some of our census returns is desirable before this can be done entirely satisfactorily in the United States, but the method is probably the most promising in prospect.

Another measure of centrality would be the number of automobiles entering a town, making sure that suburban movements were not included. Figures could be secured if the state-wide highway planning surveys in forty-six states were extended to gather such statistics.

IV

The central place scheme may be distorted by local factors, primarily industrial concentration or main transport routes. Christaller notes that transportation is not an areally operating principle, as the supplying of central goods implies, but is a linearly working factor. In many cases central places are strung at short intervals along an important transport route, and their tributary areas do not approximate the ideal circular or hexagonal shape but are elongated at right angles to the main transport line.[17] In some areas the reverse of this normal expectancy is true. In most of Illinois, maps depicting tributary areas show them to be elongated parallel to the main transport routes, not at right angles to them.[18] The combination of nearly uniform land and competitive railways peculiar to the state results in main railways running nearly parallel and close to one another between major centres.

In highly industrialised areas the central place scheme is generally so distorted by industrial concentration in response to resources and transportation that it may be said to have little significance as an explanation for urban location and distribution, although some features of a central place scheme may be present, as in the case of Cologne and the Ruhr.

In addition to distortion, the type of scheme prevailing in various regions is susceptible to many influences. Productivity of the soil,[19] type of agriculture and intensity of cultivation, topography, governmental organisation, are all obvious modifiers. In the United States, for example, what is the effect on distribution of settlements caused by the sectional layout of the land and the regular size of counties in many states?

In parts of Latin America many centres are known as 'Sunday towns'; their chief functions appear to be purely social, to act as religious and recreational centres for holidays—hence the name 'Sunday town'.[20] Here social rather than economic services are the primary support of towns, and we should accordingly expect a system of central places with fewer and smaller centres, because fewer functions are performed and people can travel farther more readily than commodities. These underlying differences do not destroy the value of the theory; rather they provide variations of interest to study for themselves and for purposes of comparison with other regions.

The system of central places is not static or fixed; rather it is subject to change and development with changing conditions.[21] Improvements in transportation have had noticeable effects. The provision of good automobile roads alters buying and marketing practices, appears to make the smallest centres smaller and the larger centres larger, and generally alters trade areas.[22] Since good roads are spread more uniformly over the land than railways, their provision seems to make the distribution of centres correspond more closely to the normal scheme.[23]

Christaller may be guilty of claiming too great an application of his scheme. His criteria for determining typical-size settlements and their normal number apparently do not fit actual frequency counts of settlements in many almost uniform regions as well as some less rigidly deductive norms.[24]

Bobeck in a later article claims that Christaller's proof is unsatisfactory.[25] He states that two-thirds of the population of Germany and England live in cities and that only one-third of these cities in Germany are real central places. The bulk are primarily industrial towns, or villages inhabited solely by farmers. He also declares that exceptions in the rest of the world are common, such as the purely rural districts of the Tonkin Delta of Indo-China, cities based on energetic entrepreneurial activity, as some Italian cities, and world commercial ports such as London, Rotterdam, and Singapore. Many of these objections are valid; one wishes that Christaller had better quantitative data and were less vague in places. Bobeck admits, however, that the central place theory has value and applies in some areas.

The central place theory probably provides as valid an interpretation of settlement distribution over the land as the concentric zone theory does for land use within cities. Neither theory is to be thought of as a rigid framework fitting all location facts at a given moment. Some, expecting too much, would jettison the concentric zone theory; others, realising that it is an investigative hypothesis of merit, regard it as a useful tool for comparative analysis.

V

Even in the closely articulated national economy of the United States there are strong forces at work to produce a central place distribution of settlements. It is true that products under our national economy are characteristically shipped from producing areas through local shipping-points directly to consuming centres which are often remote. However, the distribution of goods or imports brought into an area is characteristically carried on through brokerage, wholesale and retail channels in central cities.[26] This graduated division of functions supports a central place framework of settlements. Many non-industrial regions of relatively uniform land surface have cities distributed so evenly over the land that some sort of central place theory appears to be the prime explanation.[27] It should be worth while to study this distribution and compare it with other areas.[28] In New England, on the other hand, where cities are primarily industrial centres based on distant raw materials and extra-regional markets, instead of the land's supporting the city the reverse is more nearly true: the city supports the countryside by providing a market for farm products, and thus infertile rural areas are kept from being even more deserted than they are now.

The forces making for concentration at certain places and the inevitable rise of cities at these favoured places have been emphasised by geographers and other scholars. The phenomenal growth of industry and world trade in the last hundred years and the concomitant growth of cities justify this emphasis but have perhaps unintentionally caused the intimate connection between a city and its surrounding area partially to be overlooked. Explanation in terms of concentration is most important for industrial districts but does not provide a complete areal theory for distribution of settlements. Furthermore, there is evidence that 'of late . . . the rapid growth of the larger cities has reflected their increasing importance as commercial and service centres rather than as industrial centres'.[29] Some form of the central place theory should provide the most realistic key to the distribution of settlements where there is no marked concentration—in agricultural areas where explanation has been most difficult in the past. For all areas the system may well furnish a theoretical norm from which deviations may be measured.[30] It might also be an aid in planning the development of new areas. If the theory is kept in mind by workers in academic and planning fields as more studies are made, its validity may be tested and its structure refined in accordance with regional differences.

Notes and references

[1] Cf. PALANDER, TORD, *Beiträge zur Standortstheorie*, Uppsala, 1935; or HOOVER, E. M., jnr, *Location Theory and the Shoe and Leather Industries*, Cambridge, Mass., 1937.

[2] KOHL, J. G. *Der Verkehr und die Ansiedlungen der Menschen in ihrer Abhängikeit von der Gestaltung der Erdoberfläche*, 2nd edn., Leipzig, 1850.

[3] COOLEY, C. H. 'The theory of transportation', *Publications of the American Economic Association*, 9 (May 1894) 1–148.

[4] HAIG, R. M. 'Toward an understanding of the metropolis: some speculations regarding the economic basis of urban concentration', *Q. J. Econ.* 40 (1926) 179–208.

[5] BOBECK, HANS, 'Grundfragen der Stadt Geographie', *Geogr. Anz.* 28 (1927) 213–24.

[6] A section of the International Geographical Congress at Amsterdam in 1938 dealt with 'Functional relations between city and country'. The papers are published in vol. 2 of the *comptes rendus*, Leiden, E. J. Brill, 1938. A recent American study is HARRIS, C. D. *Salt Lake City: a regional capital* (Ph.D. dissertation), University of Chicago, 1940. Pertinent also is DICKINSON, R. E. 'The metropolitan regions of the United States', *Geogr. Rev.* 24 (1934) 278–91.

[7] *Die zentralen Orte in Süddeutschland*, Jena, 1935; also a paper (no title) in *C.r. du Congrès internat. de Géogr.*, Amsterdam, vol. 2 (1938) 123–37.

[8] This does not deny the importance of 'gateway' centres such as Omaha and Kansas City, cities located between contrasting areas in order to secure exchange benefits. The logical growth of cities at such locations does not destroy the theory to be presented; cf. R. D. MCKENZIE's excellent discussion in *The Metropolitan Community*, New York, 1933, pp. 4ff.

[9] Cf. Petrie's statement about ancient Egypt and Mesopotamia: 'It has been noticed before how remarkably similar the distances are between the early nome capitals of the Delta (twenty-one miles on an average) and the early cities of Mesopotamia (averaging twenty miles apart). Some physical cause seems to limit the primitive rule in this way. Is it not the limit of central storage of grain, which is the essential form of early capital? Supplies could be centralised up to ten miles away; beyond that the cost of transport made it better worth while to have a nearer centre, (PETRIE, W. M. FLINDERS, *Social Life in Ancient Egypt*, London, 1923; reissued 1932, pp. 3–4).

[10] GALPIN, C. J. *Social Anatomy of an Agricultural Community*, University of Wisconsin Agricultural Experiment Station Research Bull. 34, 1915, and the restudy by KOLB, J. H., and POLSON, R. A. *Trends in Town–Country Relations*, University of Wisconsin Agric. Exp. Stn Res. Bull. 117, 1933; MELVIN, B. L. *Village Service Agencies of New York State*, 1925, Cornell University Agric. Exp. Stn Bull. 493, 1929; and *Rural Population of New York, 1855–1925*, Cornell University Agric. Exp. Stn Memoir 116, 1928; SANDERSON, DWIGHT *The Rural Community*, New York, 1932, esp. pp. 488–514, which contains references to many studies by Sanderson and his associates; ZIMMERMAN, CARLE C. *Farm Trade Centers in Minnesota, 1905–29*, University of Minnesota Agric. Exp. Stn Bull. 269, 1930; SMITH, T. LYNN, *Farm Trade Centers in Louisiana 1905 to 1931*, Louisiana State University Bull. 234, 1933; LANDIS, PAUL H. *South*

Dakota Town–Country Trade Relations, 1901–1931, South Dakota Agric. Exp. Stn Bull. 274, 1932, and *The Growth and Decline of South Dakota Trade Centers, 1901–1933*, Bull. 279, 1938, and *Washington Farm Trade Centers, 1900–1935*, State College of Washington Agric. Exp. Stn Bull. 360, 1938.

Other studies are listed in subsequent notes.

[11] See LÖSCH, A. 'The nature of the economic regions', *Southern Economic Journal*, 5 (1938) 73. GALPIN, *op. cit.*, thought in terms of six tributary-area circles around each centre, see also KOLB and POLSON, *op. cit.*, pp. 30–41.

[12] Barnes and Robinson present some interesting maps showing the average distance apart of farmhouses in the driftless area of the Middle West and in southern Ontario. Farmhouses might well be regarded as the smallest settlement units in a central-place scheme, although they might not be in the same numbered sequence. See BARNES, JAMES A., and ROBINSON, A. H. 'A new method for the representation of dispersed rural population', *Geogrl. Rev.* 30 (1940) 134–7.

[13] In Iowa, e.g., almost all towns of more than 450 inhabitants have banks, half of the towns of 250–300, and 20 per cent of the towns of 100–150 (according to calculations made by the author from population estimates in *Rand McNally's Commercial Atlas* for 1937).

[14] See particularly the thorough study by MELVIN, B. L. *Village Service Agencies, New York State 1925*; HOFFER, C. R. *A Study of Town–Country Relationships*, Michigan Agric. Exp. Stn Special Bull. 181, 1928 (data on number of retail stores and professions per town); PRICE, H. B., and HOFFER, C. R. *Services of Rural Trade Centers in Distribution of Farm Supplies*, Minnesota Agric. Exp. Stn Bull. 249, 1938; REILLY, WILLIAM J. *Methods for the Study of Retail Relationships*, Bureau of Business Research Monographs, no. 4, University of Texas Bull. 2944, 1929, p. 26; KOLB, J. H. *Service Institutions of Town and Country*, Wisconsin Agric. Exp. Stn Res. Bull. 66, 1925 (town size in relation to support of institutions); SMITH, *op. cit.*, pp. 32–40; LANDIS, PAUL H. *South Dakota Town-Country Trade Relations, 1901–1931*, p. 20 (population per business enterprise) and pp. 24–5 (functions per town size); ZIMMERMAN, *op. cit.*, pp. 16 and 51ff.

For a criticism of population estimates of unincorporated hamlets used in many of these studies, see TREWARTHA, GLENN T. 'The unincorporated hamlet: an analysis of data sources' (paper presented 28 December at Baton Rouge meetings, Association of American Geographers, reprinted in *Rural Sociology* 6 (1941) 35–42).

[15] DICKINSON, *op. cit.*, pp. 280–1.

[16] SCHLIER, OTTO. 'Die zentralen Orte des Deutschen Reichs', *Zeitschrift der Gesellschaft für Erdkunde zu Berlin* (1937), pp. 161–70. See also map constructed from Schlier's figures in R. E. DICKINSON's valuable article, 'The economic regions of Germany', *Geogrl. Rev.* 28 (1938) 619. For use of census figures in the United States see HARRIS, *op. cit.*, pp. 3–12.

[17] For an illustration of this type of tributary area in the ridge and valley section of east Tennessee see MILLER, H. V. 'Effects of reservoir construction on local economic units', *Econ. Geogr.* 15 (1939) 242–9.

[18] See, e.g., *Marketing Atlas of the United States*, New York, International Magazine Co., or *A Study of Natural Areas of Trade in the United States*, Washington D.C., U.S. National Recovery Administration, 1935.

[19] Cf. the emphasis of Sombart, Adam Smith, and other economists on the necessity of surplus produce of land in order to support cities. Fertile land ordinarily produces more surplus and consequently more urban population, although 'the town . . . may not always derive its whole subsistence from the country in its neighbourhood' (SMITH, ADAM, *The Wealth of Nations* [Modern Library edn., New York, 1937] p. 357; SOMBART, WERNER, *Der moderne Kapitalismus* [zweite, neugearbeitete Auflage; Munich and Leipzig 1916] vol. 1, 130–1).

[20] For an account of such settlements in Brazil see DEFFONTAINES, PIERRE, 'Rapports fonctionnels entre les agglomérations urbaines et rurales: un example en pays de colonisation, le Brésil', *C.r. du Congrès internat. de Géog.*, Amsterdam, vol. 2 (1938) 139–44.

[21] The effect of booms, droughts, and other factors on trade-centre distribution by decades are brought out in Landis's studies for South Dakota and Washington. Zimmerman and Smith also show the changing character of trade-centre distribution (see n. 10 of this paper for references). Melvin calls attention to a 'village population shift lag'; in periods of depressed agriculture villages in New York declined in population approximately a decade after the surrounding rural population had decreased (MELVIN, *Rural Population of New York, 1855–1925*, p. 120).

[22] Most studies indicate that only the very smallest hamlets (under 250 population) and crossroads stores have declined in size or number. The larger small places have held their own (see LANDIS for Washington, *op. cit.*, p. 37, and his *South Dakota Town-Country Trade Relations 1901–1931*, pp. 34–36). ZIMMERMAN in 1930 (*op. cit.*, p. 41) notes that crossroads stores are disappearing and are being replaced by small villages. He states further: 'It is evident that claims of substantial correlation between the appearance and growth of the larger trading center and the disappearance of the primary center are more or less unfounded. Although there are minor relationships, the main change has been a division of labor between the two types of centers rather than the complete obliteration of the smaller in favor of the larger' (p. 32).

For further evidences of effect of automobile on small centres see MITCHELL, R. v. *Trends in Rural Retailing in Illinois 1926 to 1938*, University of Illinois Bureau of Business Res. Bull., Ser. 59, 1939, pp. 31ff., and SANDERSON, *op cit.*, p. 564, as well as other studies cited above.

[23] SMITH (*op. cit.*, p. 54) states: 'There has been a tendency for centers of various sizes to distribute themselves more uniformly with regard to the area, population, and resources of the state. Or the changes seem to be in the direction of a more efficient pattern of rural organisation. This redistribution of centers in conjunction with improved methods of communication and transportation has placed each family in frequent contact with several trade centers. . . .'

In contrast, MELVIN (*Rural Population of New York, 1855–1925*, p. 90), writing about New York State before the automobile had had much effect, states: 'In 1870 the villages . . . were rather evenly scattered over the entire state where they had been located earlier in response to particular local needs. By 1920, however, the villages had become distributed more along routes of travel and transportation and in the vicinity of cities.'

[24] This statement is made on the basis of frequency counts by the author for several midwestern states (cf. also SCHLIER, *op. cit.*, pp. 165–9, for Germany).

[25] BOBECK, HANS, 'Über einige functionelle Stadttypen und ihre Beziehungen zum Lande', *C.r. du Congrès internat. de Géog.*, Amsterdam, vol. 2 (1938) 88.
[26] HARRIS, *op. cit.*, p. 87.
[27] For a confirmation of this see the column diagram on p. 73 of LÖSCH (*op. cit.*), which shows the minimum distances between towns in Iowa of three different size classes. The maps of trade-centre distribution in the works of Zimmerman, Smith, and Landis (cited earlier) also show an even spacing of centres.
[28] The following table gives the average community area for 140 villages in the United States in 1930. In the table notice throughout that (1) the larger the village, the larger its tributary area in each region and (2) the sparser the rural population density, the larger the village tributary area for each size class (contrast mid-Atlantic with Far West, etc.).

Region	Community area in square miles		
	Small villages (250–1,000 pop.)	Medium villages (1,000–1,750 pop.)	Large villages (1,750–2,500 pop.)
Mid-Atlantic	43	46	87
South	77	111	146
Middle West	81	113	148
Far West		365	223

Although 140 is only a sample of the number of villages in the country, the figures are significant because the service areas were carefully and uniformly delimited in the field for all villages (BRUNNER, E. de S., and KOLB, J. D. *Rural Social Trends*, New York, 1933, p. 95; see also BRUNNER, E. de S., HUGHES, G. S., and PATTEN, M. *American Agricultural Villages*, New York, 1927, chap. 2).

In New York 26 square miles was found to be the average area per village in 1920. Village refers to any settlement under 2,500 population. Nearness to cities, type of agriculture, and routes of travel are cited as the three most important factors influencing density of villages. Since areas near cities are suburbanised in some cases, as around New York City, the village density in these districts is correspondingly high. Some urban counties with smaller cities (Rochester, Syracuse, and Niagara Falls) have few suburbs, and consequently the villages are farther apart than in many agricultural counties (MELVIN, *Rural Population of New York, 1855–1925*, pp. 88–9; table on p. 89 shows number of square miles per village in each New York county).

In sample areas of New York State the average distance from a village of 250 or under to another of the same size or larger is about 3 miles; for the 250–749 class it is 3–5 miles; for the 750–1,240 class, 5–7 miles (MELVIN, *Village Service Agencies*, New York, 1925, p. 102; in the table on p. 103 the distance averages cited above are shown to be very near the modes).

Kolb makes some interesting suggestions as to the distances between centres. He shows that spacing is closer in central Wisconsin than in Kansas, which is more sparsely settled; see KOLB, J. H. *Service Relations of Town and Country*, Wisconsin Agric. Exp. Stn Res. Bull. 58 (1923); see pp. 7–8 for theoretical graphs.

In Iowa, 'the dominant factor determining the *size* of convenience-goods areas is distance' (*Second State Iowa Planning Board Report*, Des Moines, April, 1935, p. 198). This report contains fertile suggestions on trade areas for Iowa towns. Valuable detailed reports on retail trade areas for some Iowa counties have also been made by the same agency.

[29] U.S. National Resources Committee, *Our Cities—Their Role in the National Economy: Report of the Urbanism Committee*, Washington: Government Printing Office, 1937, p. 37.

[30] Some form of the central-place concept might well be used to advantage in interpreting the distribution of outlying business districts in cities; cf. PROUD-FOOT, MALCOLM J. 'The selection of a business site', *Journal of Land and Public Utility Economics* 14 (1938), esp. 373ff.

The functional bases of the central place hierarchy*
Brian J. L. Berry and William L. Garrison

It is obvious that urban centres differ, each from others. On the intuitive
level one notion of difference is that of classes of urban centres. The
wealth of descriptive terms available illustrates this notion: hamlet, village, town, city, metropolis, and the like. The present study is concerned
with this problem of the differentiation of centres into broad classes. In
particular it provides original and urgent evidence that a system of urban
centre classes exists of the type identified on an intuitive level above.

There are several reasons for producing evidence of a system of classes
(hereafter termed the hierarchical class-system) at this time. A considerable body of theory relating to city size, function, and arrangement has
accumulated. One of the implications of this theory is that there exists
a hierarchical class-system.[1] Ample evidence is available that other
implications of this theory are valid, namely, that larger centres are
functionally more complex than smaller centres, with this increasing functional complexity being accompanied by increasing size of the urban
complementary region,[2] and that by virtue of the differential provision
of central functions there is interdependence between urban centres in
the provision of central goods and services.[3] On the other hand there has
been no satisfactory evidence provided that would suggest that a hierarchical class-system of centres does indeed exist.

Despite many attempts at the assignment of towns to classes or grades[4]
the converse has seemed to be more likely. The *a priori* methods used by
most of the studies have led to serious doubts as to whether a class system
is present in other than arbitrary form, and to the alternate idea that
perhaps instead of a class system there only exists differentiation along
a continuum.[5] Vining, for example, has written about the single best-
known empirical study of the central place hierarchy, that of John E.
Brush:[6]

> There is no evidence ... that exactly three natural partitions may be
> observed in this array of numbers of establishments ... the terms
> hamlet, village, and town are convenient modes of expression; but
> they do not refer to structurally distinct natural entities. ... Clearly,
> it is arbitrary to divide the array into three partitions rather than into
> a greater or lesser number; and similarly arbitrary is the determina-
> tion of where to put the dividing points separating the different classes

* Reprinted from *Economic Geography* 34 (1958), 145–54, by permission of the publishers.

or types. Having drawn the lines, one may list certain kinds of activities which are typically found within each of the designated classes of center, . . . , not all members of a class will contain all the activities listed and most of the communities within a class will contain activities not listed. (This) . . . is not an independently derived basis for a classification of communities by type. Rather it is itself derived from a previous partitioning of an array which appears as something similar to an arrangement of observations that have been made upon a continuous variable.[7]

These criticisms of Brush's study may well be valid. That he used an arbitrary division and then proved what he had in fact assumed is without question (this criticism applies to more studies of central places than is generally realised).[8] The ensuing discussion serves to disprove the implication which Vining drew from this fact, that central places are differentiated along a continuum rather than in a class system.

The finding of a hierarchical class system verifies implications of theory and thus performs one classic function of empirical research in the accretion of knowledge. In the present case the need for the performance of this classic function is quite pressing because other theories are available to explain characteristics of systems of cities.[9] To the extent that verification is provided for previously unverified schemes, the present study increases the attractiveness of these schemes versus more recent schemes which do not include hierarchical concepts. It might be added that the present study provides examples of taxonomic methods for the empirical study of the hierarchical class system and these methods may be found useful in ensuing studies; it was designed as a *critical study* which may be checked in the study area (Snohomish County, Washington) and which is capable of being reproduced by the methods provided in other areas and at levels of the central place hierarchy other than the universe of small centres considered in the present case.

The hierarchical concept

The hierarchical class system implication is an integral part of the spatial model of central places developed by Walther Christaller,[10] the generic base and single most important statement of central place theory. The model states that central places belong to one or another of class subsets. Each class possesses specific groups of central functions and is characterised by a discrete population level of its centres. Note that (1) classes are arranged one to another in a hierarchy such that the central places of functionally more complex classes possess all the groups of functions of less complex classes plus a group of functions differentiating them from the central places of less complex classes, (2) discrete population levels of the central places of each class are thought to arise because the income which supports the population of a central place is brought into the centre by the activities which provide goods and services for surrounding consumers. Since the central places of each class possess discrete groups of activities they also tend to have discrete population levels.

An observed hierarchy of central places

Evidence is provided here that a hierarchy of central places does exist. In Snohomish County, Washington, the area in which the present study was undertaken, it was found that centres could be arranged into three types, called A, B, and C (Table 1). These three types were defined on

Table 1: Classes of central places and associated groupings of central functions in Snohomish County, Washington

| Central functions | Classes of central places | | |
	A*	B	C
Variates			
Group 1_1	p	f	f
Group 2_1	—	p	f
Group 3_1	—	s	f
Attributes			
General store	p	—	—
Group 1_2	s	p	f
Group 2_2	—	p	f
Group 3_2	—	s	p

s-some; p-partial range; f-full range

* A Class A centre, for example, provides a partial range of the functions of group 1_1, a few of the functions of group 1_2, and most, although not all, of the centres will have general stores

the basis of the presence of urban functions 1_1, 1_2, . . . , etc., in varying degrees. In other words, in Snohomish County it was found to be possible to treat central places taxonomically and derive centre types A, B, and C (say, hamlets, villages and towns, respectively) on a functional basis. It was shown that these centre types differ more one type from another than they differ within types.

The data utilised involved thirty-three of the smaller central places of the county (Fig. 1). Since the present study was in the interest of expediency limited to small central places, excluded from the field survey was the largest centre in the county, Everett. Several of the smaller communities on the northern and southern margins of the county were also

Fig. 1. Locational features of the study area

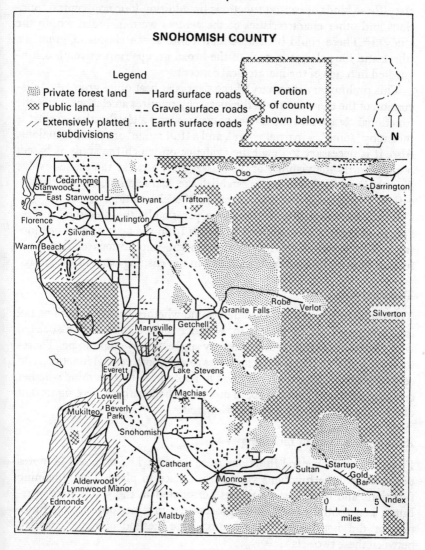

excluded. Reasons for the exclusion of these centres, an elaboration of the data used in the study, and relevant maps of the travel patterns of the rural residents to the central places are available elsewhere.[11]

Of the thirty-three centres studied, twenty were of class A, which contains the lowest complex of central functions; nine were of class B; and four were of class C, which contains the most complex grouping of functions. In these centres considered *in toto* it was possible to recognise sixty-three kinds of central functions (in addition four non-central functions and other characteristics of the centres were included within the study).[12] These could be differentiated into seven classes of functions (three and four classes in each of the broad groups respectively), distinguished in terms of the hierarchical concept.

This preliminary summary of the data is at best quite gross. Any discussion of the exact nature of the hierarchy requires an elaboration of the functional classes and the classes of centres, and a clarification of what is meant by 'some', a 'partial range', and a 'full range' of central functions. Also, it is necessary to detail the evidence on which the study is based, both to verify the viability of the classes and, because the classes evolve directly from the evidence, to establish the characteristics of the classification. The ensuing discussion provides this elaboration.

It will be noted that in the above paragraphs the hierarchical class system of centres was assumed to follow from the class system of functions. The assumption is derived from the implications of theory. A further note on this notion is included in the ensuing parts of the study.

The analysis

The problem before us was to determine whether central functions fall into groups of classes, and, if so, whether these classes were associated with classes of central places, as theory suggests they ought to be. Therefore, the initial step in the research was to rank both central functions and central places. The second step was to apply tests to determine whether groupings occurred, and, if so, to discover whether there were significant differences between the groupings isolated.

Ranking the central functions

Fifty-two of the central functions were variates, i.e., numbers of stores performing these functions varied from place to place. The remaining functions and other characteristics considered in the study were attributes, i.e., central places either possessed a unit performing this function or did not possess such a unit. The method of ranking varied between these two sets.

Variates

Previous empirical studies indicated that relationships exist between the population of a central place and the number of units of any function which that place possesses and this is, of course, clear from common knowledge.[13] Christaller suggested that through the working of the income mechanism the population of a centre was a function of the number of types of central goods and services the central place provided.[14] Hence it was specified that the population of a centre is a function of the number of stores of each type. Fifty-two scatter diagrams were prepared with population, P, and number of stores, N, as parameters to determine the relationships between P and N for each function. Each of the diagrams had thirty-three points, one for each of the thirty-three central places. Best fitting curves of the exponential growth series $P = A(B^N)$ where A and B are the parameters to be estimated were fitted to each of the scatters using standard least squares techniques, after logarithmic conversion.

Given these fifty-two best relationships it was then possible to rank the central functions on the basis of the threshold population of the centre which was necessary for the first complete store to appear, that is, by the value of P where $N = 1$ (Table 2).

Attributes

Relationships between the fifteen attributes and the populations of the centres in which they appear were determined by calculating the point biserial coefficient of correlation between each of the activities and the population of the centres. Activities were then ranked in ascending order of these coefficients, r_{pb}, since it was observed that higher correlations were associated with occurrence in larger centres (Table 3).[15]

The measurement of groupings between ranked activities

Given the ranks of central functions it was then possible to employ tests to determine whether there were associated groups among them. The tests used again varied between the two sets of central functions.

Variates

Threshold sizes were treated as points upon the population size continuum. Using the techniques developed by P. J. Clark, this distribution of points was tested for randomness by using a χ^2 (chi-square) test for significant differences between expected and observed reflexive relationships.[16] The tests showed that the observed distribution of points was nonrandom at the 0·95 level of significance, and this observed distribution was nonrandom in a grouped rather than a 'more even than random' manner.

Table 2 : The functional bases of classes of central places in Snohomish County : variates

	Threshold population	B-value	A																					B								C			
			Vedot	Silverton	Trafton	Florence	Getchell	Robe	Bryant	Cedarhome	Oso	Maltby	Cathcart	Machias	Index	Warm Beach	Startup	Gold Bar	Silvana	Lowell	Beverly Park	Lake Stevens	Alderwood Manor	Granite Falls	Darrington	Mukilteo	Sultan	Lynnwood	East Stanwood	Stanwood	Edmonds	Monroe	Arlington	Snohomish	Marysville
Population			20	15	25	300	25	50	150	100	200	700	175	200	220	314	300	325	300	1600	725	2586	600	600	974	900	850	500	390	720	2996	1684	1915	3494	2460
Number of activities			1	2	2	2	3	3	3	4	4	4	5	5	6	6	8	9	10	12	13	16	22	25	25	28	34	36	38	42	42	56	59	62	64
1₁ Filling stations	196	1·35	1	1	1	1	1	1	1	1	1	1	2	2	1	1	1	1	1	1	1	3	4	4	3	6	6	9	4	4	7	8	6	3	9
Food stores	254	1·74				1	1		1	1	2	1	1	1	1	2	2	2	1	1	1	2	3	3	2	3	3	9	3	4	6	6	5	6	5
Churches	265	1·29		1	1		1	1	1	1	1		1	1	2	2	1	2	2	2	1	2	3	3	2	1	3	3	3	8	8	6	9	6	5
Restaurants	276	1·33						1		1		2		1		1	2	4	2	2	2	2	2	2	2	2	4	3	2	3	5	9	6	17	14
Taverns	282	1·65									1		1	1	1	1	4	1	1	1	1	1	1	2	1	2	3	6	5	5	5	6	5	5	2
Elementary schools	322	1·67								1		1				1		1	1		1	2	1	1	3	1	1	3	3	1	1	2	4	6	6
Physicians	380	1·42																				3					1	1	2	5	5	3	10	5	3
Real estate agencies	384	1·40																				2	2	1	2	1	1	6	2	2	4	2	3	6	6
Appliance stores	385	1·46								1						2			1			2	1	1	2	1	1	1	2	2	2	1	4	10	2
Barber shops	386	2·39									1					1						1	1	1	2	1	1	1	1	1	2	4	3	4	4
Auto dealers	398	1·35																					2		1	1	1	2	4	2	2	3	10	3	2
Insurance agencies	409	1·32						1	1														1	1	1	1	2	1	2	1		4	4	10	10
Bulk oil distributors	419	1·56																				2	1	1	1	1	1	1	1	2		2	5	5	6
Dentists	426	1·57																				1		1	1	1	2	1	3	3		3	4	5	1
Motels	430	1·56												1								1			1	1	5	1	1	1		2	1	2	6
Hardware stores	431	1·90																					2	1	1	1	3	1	1	1		2	3	6	2
Auto repair shops	435	1·72					1														1	1	1	2	1	2	1	1	2	4		4	1	2	4
Fuel dealers (coal, etc)	453	1·78			1								1					2				1	1	1	2		3	3	1	3		1	1	2	4

Function		
Drug stores	456	2·23
Beauticians	480	1·89
Auto parts dealers	488	1·94
Meeting halls	525	2·01
Animal feed stores	526	1·79
Lawyers	528	2·12
2₁ Furniture stores, etc	546	1·85
Variety stores: 5 and 10	549	2·30
Freight lines and storage	567	2·04
Veterinaries	579	1·97
Apparel stores	590	2·53
Lumber yards and Wood-working	598	2·49
Banks	610	2·05
Farm implement dealers	650	1·95
Electric repair shops	693	2·62
Florists	729	2·40
High schools	732	3·64
Dry cleaners	754	3·56
Local taxi services	762	2·89
Billiard hall and bowling alleys	789	2·56
Jewelry stores	827	3·26
Hotels	846	2·92
Shoe repair shops	896	2·45
Sporting goods stores	928	3·30
Frozen food lockers	938	2·99
Sheet metal works	1076	3·80
Department stores	1083	4·50
Optometrists	1140	3·88
Hospitals and clinics	1159	3·77
3₁ Undertakers	1214	4·19
Photographers	1243	4·56
Public accountants	1300	4·11
Laundries and laundromats	1307	4·66
Health practitioners	1424	4·55

Table 3: The functional bases of classes of central places in Snohomish County: Attributes

		1_2				2_2								3_2		
		General store	Feed mill	Post Office	Weekly newspaper	Telephone Exchange	Incorporated City	Movie Theater	Bakery	Electricity distribution	Water supply system	Sewage system	State liquor store	Public Library	Printing press	Used furniture dealer
	r_{pb}	.347	.265	.290	.458	.584	.615	.616	.619	.646	.646	.691	.691	.758	.759	
	Marysville		1	1	1	1	1	1	1	1	1	1	1	1	1	
C	Snohomish		1	1	1	1	1	1	1	1	1	1	1	1	1	1
	Arlington		1	1	1	1	1	1	1	1	1	1	1	1	1	
	Monroe		1	1	1	1	1	1	1	1	1	1	1	1		
	Edmonds							1		1	1	1	1	1	1	
	Stanwood				1	1	1	1		1	1	1		1		
	East Stanwood			1				1		1			1			
	Lynnwood			1						1	1	1	1			
B	Sultan		1	1	1	1	1				1	1	1	1		
	Mukilteo	1		1				1		1	1	1	1			
	Darrington			1		1	1	1								
	Granite Falls				1			1			1	1				
	Alderwood Manor		1	1								1		1		
	Lake Stevens	1												1		
	Beverly Park			1							1	1	1			
	Lowell			1							1	1	1			
	Silvana	1	1	1												
	Gold Bar			1												
	Startup			1												
	Warm Beach	1	1													
	Index	1	1													
	Machias	1														
	Cathcart	1														
A	Maltby	1														
	Oso	1														
	Cedarhome	1														
	Bryant	1														
	Robe															
	Getchell															
	Florence	1														
	Trafton	1														
	Silverton	1														
	Verlot	1														

Given this tendency for there to be grouping, and using Clark's criterion of a group—that every member of the group should be closer to some other member of the group than to any other point—three groups of central functions, 1_1, 2_1, and 3_1 were found to be present (Table 2).

Attributes

Tests of significant differences between the r_{pb}'s were made at the 0.95

Fig. 2. Classes of central places in Snohomish County

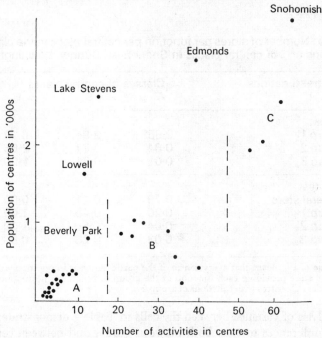

level of significance using standard techniques, and twelve of the attributes were found to fall into three groupings, 1_2, 2_2, and 3_2 with general stores existing as a class apart (Table 3).

Ranking and grouping the centres

The central places were represented as points on the continuum of functional complexity by the number of functions each possessed. Clark's test of randomness was then applied to this distribution of points and the chi-square test showed that the distribution of points was nonrandom and grouped. Using Clark's concept of a group, three groups of central places, here termed A, B, and C, could be distinguished (Fig. 2 and Tables 2 and 3).

The classes of central places

Given groups of central places defined on the basis of numbers of functions performed, and groups of functions, it remained to be determined whether the latter could be said to be significantly associated with the former. Tables 2 and 3 were constructed and, utilising the groupings, Table 4 derived. This table records the number of stores per function per central place.

Table 4: Number of stores per function per central place in the classes of functions and of central places in Snohomish County, Washington

| Central functions | Classes of central places | | |
	A	B	C
Variates:			
Group 1_1	0·65*	2·91	6·29
Group 2_1	0·04	0·77	2·65
Group 3_1	0·01	0·21	1·00
Attributes:			
General store	0·70	0·11	0·00
Group 1_2	0·20	0·45	1·00
Group 2_2	0·04	0·50	1·00
Group 3_2	0·03	0·28	0·88

* A value of 1·0 means that every centre of the particular class in question will tend to have one store providing each function of the group of functions in question (for example, class C centres with functions of group 2_2).

Analysis of variance between the cells in Table 4 demonstrated significant differences to exist both between groups and between centres at the 0·95 level of confidence. Therefore, variations between groups are greater than variations within groups. This confirms the differential nature of the groupings derived utilising the Clark techniques, and reveals the nature of the hierarchy of central places. As an extra step, it was found that general stores, the attribute existing as a group apart, were complementary with food stores (part of group 1_1), the coefficient of correlation being $-0·634$.

Findings

The data developed in constructing Tables 2, 3, and 4 can be generalised into the gross findings which were presented earlier in Table 1. It is apparent how the notion of classes of central places is defined with respect to the notion of functions. What is more, a technique has been provided whereby the hierarchical system may be isolated and identified, and the exact identification of an hierarchical system has been completed for Snohomish County. This is readily comprehended upon close examination of Tables 2 and 3.

It may also be shown that the three classes of towns tend towards discrete levels of population, as suggested by Christaller (Fig. 2). There are only four exceptions to the generalisation of levels in terms of population —Beverly Park, Lowell, Lake Stevens, and Edmonds. It is significant that these are centres which have experienced very rapid increases in population in recent years, becoming dormitories for the Seattle area. Their functional paucity may be attributed (a) to the timelag existing between population growth and the development of service industries, and (b) to the fact that, compared to other centres of their size, they serve relatively few people residing in immediately surrounding areas. As the timelag diminishes the centres can be expected to experience increasing functional complexity and possibly a rise in class status. But the dominant dormitory function suggests that some differential will persist *vis-à-vis* centres of comparable size in the country.

Notes and references

[1] CHRISTALLER, WALTHER, *Die zentralen Orte in Süddeutschland*, Jena, 1933, trans. C. Baskin at the Bureau of Population and Urban Research, University of Virginia, 1954; and LÖSCH, AUGUST, *Die räumliche Ordnung der Wirtschaft*, Jena, 1944, trans. W. H. Woglom and W. F. Stolper as *The Economics of Location*, New Haven, 1954.

The works of Christaller and Lösch are related in BERRY, B. J. L. 'Geographic aspects of the size and arrangement of urban centers', unpublished M.A. thesis, Department of Geography, University of Washington, 1956. See also ISARD, WALTER, *Location and Space Economy*, New York, 1956.

[2] REILLY, W. J. Methods of the Study of Retail Relationships, University of Texas Bull. 2944, 1929; *idem*, *The Law of Retail Gravitation*, New York, 1931.

[3] GALPIN, C. J. *Social Anatomy of an Agricultural Community*, University of Wisconsin Agric. Exp. Stn Res. Bull. 34, 1915. See also SMAILES, A. E. 'The urban hierarchy in England and Wales', *Geography*, 29 and 30 (1944) 41–51; *idem*, 'The urban mesh of England and Wales', *Institute of British Geographers*, *Trans. and Papers*, 1946, pp. 85–101.

[4] An extensive bibliography appears in BERRY, *op. cit*. Some of the better known works are: BRUSH, JOHN E. 'The hierarchy of central places in Southwestern Wisconsin', *Geogr. Rev.* 43 (1953) 380–402; BRACEY, H. E. 'Towns as rural service centres', *Inst. Brit. Geogr. Trans. and Papers* 19 (1953), 95–105; *idem*, 'A rural component of centrality applied to six southern counties of the United Kingdom', *Econ. Geogr.* 32 (1956) 38–50; GALPIN, *op. cit*.; GODLUND, SVEN, 'Bus

services, hinterlands and the location of urban settlements in Scania', *Lund Studies in Geography*, B: Human Geography 3 (1951); CARTER, H. 'Urban grades and spheres of influence in South-West Wales', *Scottish Geogr. Mag.* 71 (1955) 43–56; DICKINSON, R. E. 'The distribution and functions of the smaller urban settlements of East Anglia', *Geography*, 17 (1932) 19–31. Also see the very appropriate comments of CARTER, H. C. 'The urban hierarchy and historical geography: a consideration with reference to North-East Wales', *Geographic Studies* 3 (1956) 85–101.

⁵ VINING, RUTLEDGE, 'A description of certain spatial aspects of an economic system', *Economic Development and Cultural Change* 3 (1955) 147–95.

⁶ BRUSH, *op. cit.*

⁷ VINING, *op. cit.*, pp. 167–9.

⁸ See, for example, CARTER, *op. cit.*; SMAILES, *op. cit.*

⁹ See GARRISON, W. L., and BERRY, B. J. L. 'The distribution of city sizes', unpublished MS, Dept. of Geography, University of Washington, 1957; RASHEVSKY, N. *Mathematical Theory of Human Relations*, Bloomington, 1947; SIMON, H. A. 'On a class of skew distribution functions', *Biometrika* 42 (1955) 425–40.

¹⁰ CHRISTALLER, *op. cit.*

¹¹ GARRISON, W. L. *The Benefits of Rural Roads to Rural Property*, Seattle, 1956, pp. 35–6; and HENNES, R. G., WHEELER, B. O., and GARRISON, W. L. 'Washington State Highway impact studies', *Proceedings*, Highway Research Board, 1957.

¹² These four non-central functions or other characteristics of the centres are: whether the settlement is an incorporated city and whether it possesses a water supply system, a sewage disposal system, or an office of the electricity distribution system.

¹³ REILLY, *op. cit.*; HOFFER, C. R. *The Study of Town-Country Relations*, Michigan Agric. Exp. Stn Bull. 181, 1928.

¹⁴ CHRISTALLER, *op. cit.*

¹⁵ It is characteristic of the point biserial coefficient of correlation, a statistic designed for the correlation of attributes and variates, that as fewer attributes occur, and as they occur in conjunction with the higher values of the variates the correlation coefficient increases positively (compare Post Offices and State Liquor Stores); conversely, as fewer attributes occur, and in conjunction with the lower values of the variates, the correlation coefficient assures decreasing values (increasing negative values: compare Post Offices and General Stores).

¹⁶ These techniques consist of the examination of the reflexive relationships which exist between points on a line and the testing of these for significant differences with the expected random reflexive relationships calculated by Clark and Evans; see CLARK, P. J., and EVANS, F. C. 'Distance to nearest neighbor as a measure of spatial relations', *Ecology* 35 (1954) 445–53.

Defining and estimating a trading area*
David L. Huff

Market analysts have long speculated about the nature and scope of trading areas. Such speculations have been based primarily upon conclusions drawn from empirical studies.

However, except for the 'gravitationalists', few analysts, if any, have formulated their conclusions into propositions that are capable of being verified or refuted by empirical test. As a consequence, the conceptual properties of a trading area are extremely vague and perhaps in error. Furthermore, existing techniques for estimating trading areas are limited and subject to question.

The objectives of the present article are threefold: (1) to appraise the principal techniques used to delineate retail trading areas; (2) to enumerate significant conclusions derived from empirical studies using such techniques; and (3) to advance an alternative technique, believed to be better conceptually and superior predictively.

Estimating techniques

The methods employed to delineate trading areas, particularly retail trading areas, generally involve surveys or the use of empirically derived mathematical formulations.

Survey techniques

Typically, in the case of survey techniques, a sample of individuals representing either households or firms are interviewed at their places of origin or at the particular firm or centre for which the trading area is being estimated.

Such interviews are designed primarily to determine the kind or kinds of products that are purchased by each respondent, the frequency of patronage, and the home base location of each respondent. These data can then be used to prepare a map from which inferences can be drawn concerning the nature and scope of the trading area.

As a result of trading area studies using survey techniques, a number of important empirical regularities have been shown to exist:

1. The proportion of consumers patronising a given shopping area varies with distance from the shopping area.

*Reprinted from *Journal of Marketing* 28 (July 1964), 34–8, by permission of the publishers.

2. The proportion of consumers patronising various shopping areas varies with the breadth and depth of merchandise offered by each shopping area.
3. The distances that consumers travel to various shopping areas vary for different types of product purchases.
4. The 'pull' of any given shopping area is influenced by the proximity of competing shopping areas.

A number of market analysts have attempted to generalise about the nature and scope of trading areas by citing *specific* conclusions drawn from such empirical studies. For example, it is often maintained that the trading area for a certain size of retail facility offering a particular class of products will encompass a radial distance of some specified number of miles, of which the primary trading area will involve a certain proportion of the total area, etc., etc.

But generalisations of this kind may be subject to a great deal of error because of differences among regions with respect to transportation facilities, topographical features, population density, and the locations of competing firms.

Mathematical techniques

A few analysts have attempted to formalise some of the general conclusions drawn from empirical studies. They have expressed their ideas in terms of mathematical propositions that are capable of being tested empirically. The work that has been done in this area is limited primarily to the so-called 'retail gravitationalists'.

Notable among these is William J. Reilly who made a significant contribution by formalising a number of empirical observations concerning consumer shopping movements between cities.[1] The nature of his formal construct is shown below:

$$(1) \qquad \frac{B_a}{B_b} = \left(\frac{P_a}{P_b}\right) \left(\frac{D_b}{D_a}\right)^2$$

where B_a = the proportion of the retail business from an intermediate town attracted by city A;

B_b = the proportion of the retail business from an intermediate town attracted by city B;

P_a = the population of city A;

P_b = the population of city B;

D_a = the distance from the intermediate town to city A; and,

D_b = the distance from the intermediate town to city B.

The extensive empirical tests of Reilly's model that were made by P. D. Converse are also noteworthy.[2] In addition, Converse is to be credited for making a significant modification of Reilly's original formula.[3] This modification made it possible to calculate the approximate point between two competing cities where the trading influence of each was equal. As a consequence, a city's retail trading area could be delineated by simply calculating and connecting the breaking points between it and each of the competing cities in the region (see Fig. 1). The breaking point formula derived by Converse is:[4]

$$(2) \qquad D_b = \frac{D_{ab}}{1 + \sqrt{\dfrac{P_a}{P_b}}}$$

where D_b = the breaking point between city A and city B in miles from B;

D_{ab} = the distance separating city A from city B;

P_b = the population of city B; and

P_a = the population of city A.

Limitations. The significance of the pioneering efforts of both Reilly and Converse to provide a systematic basis for estimating retail trading areas cannot be denied. The variables employed, the functional relationships advanced, and the estimated parameters provide precise and meaningful hypotheses that can be tested empirically.

However, there are several important conceptual and operational limitations associated with the use of the 'Reilly-type' model.

Fig. 1. Estimating a trading area with the breaking point formula

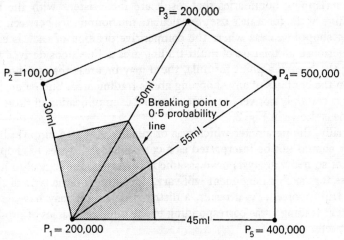

Calculation of breaking points:

$$D_2 = \frac{D_{12}}{1 + \sqrt{\dfrac{P_1}{P_2}}} = \frac{30}{1 + \sqrt{\dfrac{200,000}{100,000}}} = 12 \cdot 4$$

$$D_3 = \frac{D_{13}}{1 + \sqrt{\dfrac{P_1}{P_3}}} = \frac{50}{1 + \sqrt{\dfrac{200,000}{200,000}}} = 25 \cdot 0$$

$$D_4 = \frac{D_{14}}{1 + \sqrt{\dfrac{P_1}{P_4}}} = \frac{55}{1 + \sqrt{\dfrac{200,000}{500,000}}} = 33 \cdot 0$$

$$D_5 = \frac{D_{15}}{1 + \sqrt{\dfrac{P_1}{P_5}}} = \frac{45}{1 + \sqrt{\dfrac{200,000}{400,000}}} = 26 \cdot 3$$

First, the breaking point formula, as it now exists, is incapable of providing graduated estimates above or below the break-even position between two competing centres (see Fig. 1). As a consequence, it is impossible to calculate objectively the *total* demand for the product(s) or service(s) of a particular distribution centre.

Second, when the breaking point formula is used to delineate retail trading areas of several shopping areas within a given geographical area, the overlapping boundaries that result are inconsistent with the basic objective of the formula's use; to calculate the boundaries between competing shopping areas where the competitive position of each is equal. Furthermore, in the case of multi-trading area delineations derived from using the breaking point formula, there may be areas that are not even within the confines of any shopping area's trading area. Such a development is certainly not very realistic. A visual exemplification of these conditions is shown in Fig. 2.

Finally, the parameter which was originally estimated empirically by Reilly should not be interpreted as a constant for all types of shopping trips as so many analysts have assumed. It seems quite logical to hypothesise that such an exponent will vary, depending on the type of shopping trip involved. As a result, a distribution centre may have several different trading areas corresponding to the different classes of products that it sells.

Fig. 2. Estimating multiple trading areas with the breaking point formula

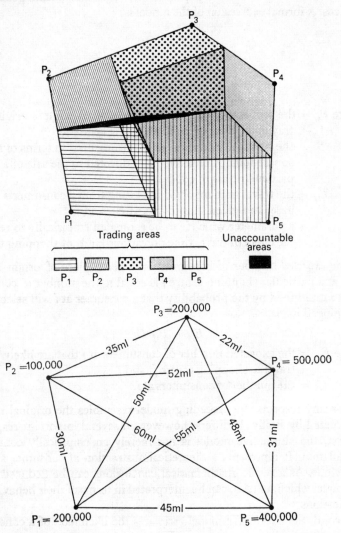

An alternative model

An alternative model will now be presented which overcomes the limitations described above.

The principal focus of the model is on the consumer rather than on the firm. It is, after all, the consumer who is the primary agent affecting the trading area of the firm. The model describes the process by which consumers choose from among acceptable alternatives, a particular distribution centre (a firm or group of firms) to obtain specific goods and services. A formal expression of the model is:

$$(3) \qquad P_{ij} = \frac{\dfrac{S_j}{T_{ij}^{\lambda}}}{\displaystyle\sum_{j=1}^{n} \dfrac{S_j}{T_{ij}^{\lambda}}}$$

where P_{ij} = the probability of a consumer at a given point of origin i travelling to a particular shopping centre j;

S_j = the size of a shopping centre j (measured in terms of the square footage of selling area devoted to the sale of a particular class of goods);

T_{ij} = the travel time involved in getting from a consumer's travel base i to a given shopping centre j; and

λ = a parameter which is to be estimated empirically to reflect the effect of travel time on various kinds of shopping trips.

The *expected* number of consumers at a given place of origin i that shop at a particular shopping centre j is equal to the number of consumers at i multiplied by the probability that a consumer at i will select j for shopping. That is,

$$(4) \qquad E_{ij} = P_{ij} \cdot C_i$$

where E_{ij} = the expected number of consumers at i that are likely to travel to shopping centre j; and

C_i = the number of consumers at i.

In many respects the preceding model resembles the original model formulated by Reilly. It differs, however, in several important respects.

First, the alternative model is not merely an empirically contrived formulation. It represents a theoretical abstraction of consumer spatial behaviour. As a result, mathematical conclusions can be deduced from the model which, in turn, can be interpreted in terms of their behavioural implications.[5]

Second, the alternative model estimates the likelihood of a consumer (P_{ij}) or the number of consumers (E_{ij}) patronising a particular shopping area by taking into consideration *all* potential shopping areas simultaneously.

Third, the parameter λ is not assumed to be to the second power. Rather, it is assumed to vary with different types of product classes. For example, in an initial pilot study λ was found to be 2·723 for shopping trips involving furniture and 3·191 for trips involving clothing purchases.[6]

The respective magnitudes of these estimates simply reflect the comparative amounts of time that consumers are willing to expend for each of these two product classes. The larger the estimated value of λ, the smaller will be the time expenditure. Similarly, the larger the estimated value of λ, the more restrictive will be the scope of the trading area.

Finally, equations (3) and (4) enable a retail trading area to be graduated in terms of demand gradients. These gradients are expressed as probability contours ranging from $P < 1$ to $P > 0$. An illustration of how

Fig. 3. A retail trading area portrayed in terms of probability contours. Source: David L. Huff, *Determination of Intra-urban Retail Trade Areas* (Los Angeles: University of California, Real Estate Research Program, 1962)

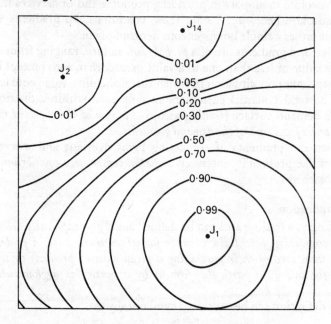

these contours look when mapped is illustrated in Fig. 3, in which a partial retail trading area has been calculated for shopping centre J_1.

If the retail trading areas of shopping centres J_2 and J_{14} had also been calculated and superimposed over the trading area of J_1, it would be seen that parts of each shopping centre's trading area envelop parts of the others. Furthermore, where these envelopments occur at intersections of contours having the same probability values, it would be possible to determine the breaking points between each of these competing centres.

General conclusions

The following general conclusions can now be drawn concerning the nature and scope of a trading area:

1. A trading area represents a *demand surface* containing potential customers for a specific product(s) or service(s) of a particular distribution centre.

2. A distribution centre may be a *single firm or an agglomeration of firms*.

3. A demand surface consists of a series of *demand gradients* or zones, reflecting varying customer-sales potentials. An exception to the condition of demand gradients would be in the rare case in which only one distribution centre existed in a unique geographical setting, thus representing an absolute monopoly in providing products and/or services that are of an absolute necessity. Under these conditions, no gradients would exist but rather a single homogeneous demand plane.

4. Demand gradients are of a *probabilistic* nature, ranging from a probability value of less than one to a value greater than zero (except in the complete monopoly situation in which the probability value equals one).

5. The total potential customers encompassed within a distribution centre's demand surface (trading area) is *the sum of the expected number of consumers from each of the demand gradients*.

6. Demand gradients of competing firms overlap; and where gradients of like probability intersect, *a spatial competitive equilibrium* position is reached.

Final definition

Accordingly, a trading area can be defined as: *A geographically delineated region, containing potential customers for whom there exists a probability greater than zero of their purchasing a given class of products or services offered for sale by a particular firm or by a particular agglomeration of firms.*

This definition can be expressed symbolically as:

$$(5) \qquad T_j = \sum_{i=1}^{n} (P_{ij} \cdot C_i)$$

where T_j = the trading area of a particular firm or agglomeration of firms j, that is, the total expected number of consumers within a given region who are likely to patronise j for a specific class of products or services;

P_{ij} = the probability of an individual consumer residing within a given gradient i shopping at j; and

C_i = the number of consumers residing within a given gradient i.

By comparison, the currently accepted definition of the term 'trading area', as expressed by the Committee on Definitions of the American Marketing Association, is: 'A district whose size is usually determined by the boundaries within which it is economical in terms of volume and cost for a marketing unit to sell and/or deliver a good or service.'[7] This definition provides little insight concerning the nature and scope of a trading area. Furthermore, this definition implies that a trading area does not encompass the entire region within which potential demand exists, but rather only that portion which a marketing unit finds it economical to sell and/or deliver a good or service.

It is obvious, however, that in order for a marketing unit to determine the specific region that it finds economical for distribution purposes, it first has to assess the demand in the entire potential trading area. In addition, no matter what cost variable is considered, for example, delivery or promotion, it is very likely that the cost of the service under consideration will not turn out to be a very satisfactory determinant of any precisely bounded trading area as suggested by the Committee's definition. Finally, this definition conveys the image that it is the marketing unit that determines the trading area rather than the consumer.

Notes and references

[1] REILLY, WILLIAM J. *Methods for Study of Retail Relationships*, University of Texas, Bureau of Business Research, Research Monographs 4 (1929).

[2] CONVERSE, P. D. *A Study of Retail Trade Areas in East Central Illinois*, University of Illinois, Bureau of Economic and Business Research, Business Studies 2, 1943; and *Consumer Buying Habits in Selected South Central Illinois*, University of Illinois, Bureau of Economic and Business Research, Business Studies 6, 1948.

[3] This modification as well as other changes that Converse made of Reilly's original model is well summarised in CONVERSE, P. D. 'New laws of retail gravitation', *Journal of Marketing* 14 (1949) 379–84.

[4] Converse did not demonstrate how he derived the breaking point formula from Reilly's equation. However, the proof of such a derivation is simply:

(i) $\dfrac{B_a}{B_b} = 1$

(v) $\dfrac{D_b}{D_{ab} - D_b} = \sqrt{\dfrac{P_b}{P_a}}$

(ii) $\left(\dfrac{P_a}{P_b}\right)\left(\dfrac{D_b}{D_a}\right)^2 = 1$

(vi) $\dfrac{D_{ab}}{D_b} - 1 = \sqrt{\dfrac{P_a}{P_b}}$

(iii) $\dfrac{D_b}{D_a} = \sqrt{\dfrac{P_b}{P_a}}$

(vii) $\dfrac{D_{ab}}{1 + \sqrt{\dfrac{P_a}{P_b}}} = D_b$

(iv) $D_a = D_{ab} - D_b$

[5] For a discussion of the theoretical aspects of the model see HUFF, D. L. 'A probabilistic analysis of consumer spatial behaviour', in *Emerging Concepts in Marketing*, ed. W. S. Decker, Chicago, American Marketing Association, 1963, pp. 444–50.

[6] HUFF, DAVID L. *Determination of Intra-urban Retail Trade Areas*, University of California, Real Estate Research Program, 1962.

[7] Committee on Definitions of the American Marketing Association, *Marketing Definitions: a glossary of marketing terms*, Chicago, American Marketing Association, 1960.

Suggested practical exercises

Central place theory

1. Survey the total needs for shops and services of various kinds* shown by all the households of the class over a period of, say, one week. This can be done by keeping a record of each shop type or service type visited by any member of all the households to which members of the class belong. List the shops and services in the order of frequency of need (probably grocers shops or perhaps newspaper/confectionist/tobacconist shops will be at the top of the list).

If a local shopping parade (either suburban or village) exists and if it has *n* shops are they the first *n* shops on the list?
What differences exist?
Why might this be?
If a shop closes down on the parade, is a different type of shop likely to open; if so, can you predict what type (on the basis of the list)?
Taking each shop or service in turn, what is the average of the distances from each household to its nearest shop or service of this type?
Do these average distances vary inversely with the frequency of use and if not why might they not?

2. Using a recent census, rank the cities, towns and villages of the county in the order of their population size. Plot a rank/size curve on a graph which has population size on the *y* axis and the rank (1st, 2nd, 3rd, etc.) on the *x* axis.

Does the relationship seem to be linear or exponential?

* The headings in Table 2 of the 1961 Census of Distribution could be used. The Census deals quite inadequately with service functions and a suitable list of services (for example launderettes, men's and ladies' hairdressers, dyers and cleaners, etc.) would have to be drawn up.

What form would it be expected to take on the basis of the scheme of overlapping hexagons?

Do any gaps appear in the hierarchy of population sizes?

Do any marked 'plateaux' appear on the curve?

The 'rank/size' rule* states that the nth town in a series of this sort should be $1/n$th the size of the largest town.

How closely does this relationship apply?

Might it be upset by a very large city situated just outside the county being analysed?

3. In relation to the paper by *Huff* in this section, see the practical exercise suggested at the end of Section 6, p. 281.

*See note 18 on page 40 for the full reference to the work in which Zipf sets out this rule.

5 Perceptions of space, distance and the environment

This section is concerned with the proposition that things are not what they seem. Or rather that, for certain important purposes, they *are* what they seem but that this is not the same thing as our maps and climatic data make them out to be. As was pointed out in Section 1, our interest as human geographers is in man as the actor in a partly manmade, partly natural spatial environment. His actions are conditioned by what he believes to exist. If they were conditioned by what actually and objectively does exist, no city would ever have been built where earthquake and flood could damage it, no explorer would ever choose the wrong route through a range of mountains, and no farmer would ever choose a combination of crops that did not perfectly suit the physical conditions of his farm and the economic conditions of the market. Life is lived on the basis of a set of expectations, some about future developments, some about present conditions which we only imperfectly appreciate, and some about past events that have been reported to us with less than perfect accuracy. The geographer tries to make sense and pattern from the events in a certain sphere of human behaviour. He should constantly be aware that the impressively accurate maps and climatic or economic data that he has been trained to use, while invaluable in themselves, do not always provide the key to human movement and behaviour. Our belief and perceptions about what the environment offers us is a more powerful explanation of what we do than is the environment as it exists in terms of cold objective fact.

This is particularly true in regions inhabited by people with a less advanced level of technology, or with certain cultural taboos. Whereas the highly trained agronomist, when confronted with the region, would prescribe a certain combination of crops to achieve the highest possible calorific return per acre, the peasant cultivator will probably choose a different crop or combination. He will be influenced by his traditions, by his less complete understanding both of the climate and of the range of possible crops, and possibly he will be constrained by taboos which might preclude certain crops or livestock. It is futile to try to explain the agricultural economy of the peasant cultivator in terms of what he should be doing according to more sophisticated appreciations of the local situation. Any such attempt would probably lead to the conclusion that the cultivator was wilfully and knowingly producing less than he could. This would be a total misunderstanding of the situation.

While, in a rather general way, geographers have probably been aware for some time of this vital difference between the *subjective* and the *objective* environments, it is only in the current decade that systematic attempts have been made to understand the process of perception and to measure the differences between the two types of environment.[1] As is often the case, we can gain by considering the experience of a neighbouring discipline. The historian Collingwood, writing in 1936 of the viewpoint of his great Italian predecessor Croce, maintained: 'It follows that the subject-matter of history is not the past as such, but the past for which we possess historical evidence.'[2] Implicit in this statement, and in much of Croce's thought, is the acceptance that there is no objective historical fact. What appears in history books is the historian's appreciation of events reported and interpreted by past historians or eye witnesses. Carr echoes this viewpoint: 'The element of interpretation enters into every fact of history.'[3] If we substitute 'geography' for 'history' in this quotation, the implications for the human geographer are obvious.

How sure can we be of the accuracy of certain geographical 'facts' and of their effects on our behaviour? Some of the facts of human and physical geography are presumably irrefutable. Everest is, according to recent estimates, 29,028 feet high. Canada exported so many tons of wheat in 1967. The centre of the town we live in is 1·67 miles from where we live. In themselves, these are all useful pieces of information. But are they the most important things to know if we are considering a crossing of the Himalayas, emigration to Canada, or a trip to the town centre? Our decision in each of these cases will depend upon less cut and dried considerations such as our expectations of the balance of difficulties and benefits in each case. For example, the 'pull' towards Canada may be conditioned chiefly by the 'image' of Canada propagated by travel company advertising which will no doubt include pictures of immaculate Mounties, sleek cars, ski-slopes, and lakeshore houses surrounded by coniferous woods. The exact and objective (although selected) socio-economic data available in the Canadian yearbook will be interesting but probably not decisive in deciding whether or not we migrate. Similarly our decision whether or not to go to the town centre for a shopping trip will depend hardly at all on the knowledge that it is 1·67 miles away. We are much more interested in what the journey will cost us, how long it will take, the spread of goods available there, and the average price level; all of which we shall probably have to estimate, quite inaccurately. This all points to the need to interpret human spatial behaviour, and the land use patterns this behaviour produces, in the light of what people *think* is there and not what is actually there (even assuming that the latter can be accurately determined). And of course this perception and interpretation of what the environment offers is bound to differ depending on our cultural background, our level of education, our tastes, our values system, and our age. The line of thought developed by Croce over fifty years ago[4] is of considerable relevance to human geographers. It is remarkable that only in the past ten years have systematic attempts been made to examine the implications of the idea that we act, to a large extent, according to our beliefs about the environment and not in relation to more objective information.

The material included in this section represents three ways in which our physical and spatial environment is either imperfectly perceived or else deliberately distorted for certain purposes. The extract from *Saarinen's* book deals with the Great Plains of the United States. This is an area which provides a classic case of misinterpretation of an environment whose essential features are difficult to gauge, except over a long period.[5] The penalties for the over-ambitious use of much of this area for intensive agriculture, rather than for extensive ranching, were enormous in terms of human misery. The area was first opened up for permanent white settlement in the seventies and eighties of the last century. This followed a period of fifty or sixty years when it had been regarded as the 'Great American Desert' on the basis of reports by a limited number of early explorers, most of whom crossed it in dry periods. When permanent settlement occurred, as opposed to the extensive cattle grazing which had been carried on by Texan ranchers during the middle years of the nineteenth century, the U.S. authorities were hopelessly optimistic about the size of holding necessary to produce a living for a family. Holdings were originally of the standard quarter-section size which had proved to be adequate in the more humid Midwest. Although subsequent legislation enlarged the amount of land granted to each farmer it was never enough to obviate the need for fairly intensive cultivation if the farmer wished to make a living. Intensive cultivation very soon led to drastic soil erosion during the latter decades of the nineteenth century and the social, economic and political results of this erosion were far reaching. They included migration on a very large scale from the Great Plains to California and elsewhere, and a whole climate of political thinking partly summed up in the Roosevelt 'New Deal' legislation of the 1930s. It is not too farfetched to relate these profound developments to a complete and expensive misunderstanding, both by individuals and by government authorities, of an environment whose essential characteristics are uncertainty and variability.

Saarinen was concerned to find out whether, in the light of this tradition of environmental misinterpretation, the present farmers of the Great Plains were clear about the nature of the climatic régime, especially in relation to the likelihood and severity of drought. He therefore chose six counties in four of the Great Plains states and interviewed nearly one hundred farmers. He chose counties that varied a great deal in the extent to which they are affected by drought. The choice of farmers to interview was made randomly and an approximately equal number were interviewed in each country. It was necessary to adopt some objective measure of the frequency and severity of drought to which the responses of farmers could be compared. Saarinen chose the Palmer Drought Index[6] as his objective measure, although at one point he comes near to undermining the logic of his study by remarking that the Palmer index makes a useful 'base-line' because the farmers' perception of current moisture conditions accords so well with it. Apart from this small flaw, the study seems to be methodologically very sound because Saarinen has gone into the field with a precisely determined set of hypotheses (most of which are set out at the head of each section of the chapter) and has designed his survey to collect information on these points only.

The results of this pioneer study, clearly carried out on very limited research resources, are interesting and suggestive. Saarinen found that farmers tended to estimate the present conditions in the light of the conditions of the previous month only, that they were optimistic in underestimating the frequency of drought and overestimating the number of good years and the crop yields to be expected, and that this optimism was to some extent differential by county. The farmers of some counties saw drought mostly in terms of crop yields; those in other counties saw it mostly in terms of rainfall. The relationship between drought experience and the perception of drought risk appears to be not too well established except that farmers aged over sixty-five were less perceptive than others. On the other hand, in Adams County, farmers well experienced in the area tended not to see the current dry spell as drought whereas less experienced farmers did. It also seems that farmers tend to have a clear recollection of the first drought they experienced on coming to the Great Plains, whether or not it was severe.

Although this study has some evident loopholes, and no doubt loses some of its impact by being taken out of the context of the book of which it forms part, it is a valuable piece of work. It examines a problem of environmental interpretation that is of the utmost interest both in view of the known history of man's use of the Great Plains and in view of the trends of study in human geography which show an increasing concern with the nature of man's understanding of objective reality.

The paper by *Thompson* deals with the way in which certain factors about a destination affect people's judgment about the distance to it. The paper is not particularly penetrating in approach but has the advantages of being short and fairly easy to comprehend. Although the work deals with shopping journeys and the estimation of distance to two different types of shop (a 'discount operation' being, roughly, a large cut-price shop) the principle which Thompson is trying to illustrate could apply to any sort of journey. This principle is that, consciously or subconsciously, we tend to underestimate (or overestimate to a lesser extent) the distance to more desirable destinations compared to less desirable destinations. In this way we probably rationalise, to ourselves and to others, our choice of action. This principle may be operating when we choose which shopping centre or place of entertainment to visit or when deciding whether or not to make a social visit to a certain location.

Thompson used simple ratios to indicate that in almost all cases people overestimated the time and distance to shops. But the significant thing about the results was that they consistently overestimated the distance to less desirable shops (the discount houses) more than to the more desirable shops (the department stores). Certain of the results were not statistically significant but those that were all showed the same trend. In a subsidiary analysis it was found that estimates of the distance and time to a given location made by people who used it regularly were less than those made by people who did not. Whether the latter group overestimated because they never went there, or never went there because they overestimated, is clearly an intriguing question for further research.

The conclusion drawn from this study is that it is sometimes misleading to try to interpret people's spatial behaviour in terms of objectively measured distances, whether they be in terms of miles or minutes. The nature of the destination 'colours' the distance estimation and people act in an environment made up of subjectively located destinations. In other words, we all carry around a rough map of places and distances in our head and we often act according to this map rather than to more objectively drawn maps.[7]

The paper by *Getis* deals not with our perception of space but with a method by which space may be distorted to predict the location of a certain feature of the urban landscape. The locations predicted are then compared to the actual locations. The method used involves the 'transformation'[8] of the map of an urban area from space measured in square miles to space measured in terms of the amount of money available for expenditure on food.

The study area chosen by Getis is part of the city of Tacoma in the State of Washington. Like most North American cities, Tacoma was laid out on the township/range settlement system which means that it can easily be divided into sections one quarter of a mile square and that the boundaries of these sections will often coincide with features such as main roads and residential blocks. This grid pattern, while it does not add to the beauty and interest of North American cities, certainly helps the urban geographer. It presents him with an urban unit (the city block) which is of regular shape and constant size and for which certain information, such as the approximate population, can sometimes be obtained.

Using published information, Getis built up the estimated expenditure available for grocery purchases for each of the forty eight 'cells' he chose. He then made the area of each cell proportional to the amount of grocery expenditure available, while at the same time keeping the same overall shape for his study area and maintaining correct contiguity of cells as far as possible. He then assumed, in view of the threshold spending power necessary to support a supermarket and the known total spending power, that twelve supermarkets would exist somewhere in his study area. Each should have a hexagonal service area of equal size (following the classic central place ideas of Christaller). By superimposing this hexagonal grid on his distorted map, then transferring the locations of the supermarkets back into the geographical space map, he determined the best theoretical location for each supermarket. The final step was to transfer his theoretically derived locations to the nearest area of land zoned for shops. He then compared the predicted locations with the twelve supermarkets that actually exist in this part of Tacoma and found that the average distance between predicted and actual locations was under three hundred yards. A similar analysis for certain complexes of grocery shops, rather than supermarkets, gave similar results.

Getis sets out some of the limitations of the study, notably that his method of superimposing the hexagons could be questioned, but these are of relatively minor importance compared to certain very real achievements which he does not mention. The first of these is that, methodologically, the work is very sound since it sets out with certain assumptions, some derived from common sense and some based on existing theory, and on these assumptions it tries to 'explain' a certain landscape feature by predicting where it should occur. It then compares the prediction with reality, notes the discrepancies and offers some explanation for them. This is an enormous methodological advance over the sort of study (of which there are many) which begins by plotting the distribution of a feature and ends sometimes at that point or sometimes by offering an 'explanation' which fits the facts of the particular case but which may not reflect the underlying principles working to produce the distribution.

From a practical point of view, the study could be used to locate a new supermarket as the total spending power grows in the area. Clearly certain areas (for example, the southwestern corner) are poorly served by supermarkets. Also, valuable clues might be obtained about the location of new facilities if the pattern of future population growth was spatially very uneven in the study area. It must be remembered that since retail facilities take some time to build they tend to reflect the needs of a past, not a present, distribution of population. If it were known in advance that a new residential development of given size were to be built, say, in zones 14–10 and 15–10 it would be possible to give some idea of where a new supermarket could best be located to serve the combined needs of the existing and the new population. In this sense the method is predictive since it can give some guidance about the best course to follow for any given future population distribution. Apart from these merits, the paper provides a reasonably intelligible introduction into the idea of map transformation and illustrates one situation where space should be measured in something other than square miles.

Notes and references

[1] An interesting statement of the problems involved is KIRK, W. 'Problems of geography', *Geography* (1963) 357–71.

[2] COLLINGWOOD, R. G. *The Idea of History*, Oxford University Press, 1956, p. 202.

[3] CARR, E. H. *What is History?* Penguin, 1964, p. 13.

[4] See Collingwood, *op. cit.*, pp. 190–204.

[5] Two classic accounts of man's use and misuse of the Great Plains are WEBB, W. P. *The Great Plains*, Grosset & Dunlap, 1931; KRAENZEL, C. F. *The Great Plains in Transition*, University of Oklahoma Press, 1955.

See also LEWIS, G. M. 'Changing emphasis in the description of the natural environment of the American Great Plains area', *Institute of British Geographers Publications* (1962) 75–90.

[6] The Palmer Drought Index provides a means of measuring the duration and severity of droughts and of comparing one drought with another over time. Positive values indicate wetter than normal conditions for the area and negative values drier than normal. The severity of dry conditions is indicated as follows:

Index value	Drought category
0	Normal conditions
-0.50 to -0.99	Incipient drought
-1.00 to -1.99	Mild drought
-2.00 to -2.99	Moderate drought
-3.00 to -3.99	Severe drought
-4.00 or less	Extreme drought

For further details see PALMER, W. C. 'Climatic variability and crop production' in *Weather and Our Food Supply*, Center for Agricultural and Economic Development, Ames, Iowa, 1964, p. 180.

[7] For a fascinating pioneer investigation of the way in which people perceive three very different urban environments see LYNCH, K. *The Image of the City*, M.I.T. Press, 1960.

[8] For a very interesting discussion of map transformations see BUNGE, W. *Theoretical Geography*, C. W. K. Gleerup, Lund, Sweden, rev. edn., 1966, chap. 2.

Perception of the drought hazard*

T. F. Saarinen

Awareness of the drought hazard

Preliminary reconnaisance work quickly established the fact that Great Plains wheat farmers speak frequently, animatedly, and in dry spells, almost exclusively about drought.[1] Before probing more fully the various

Fig. 1. Counties chosen for samples

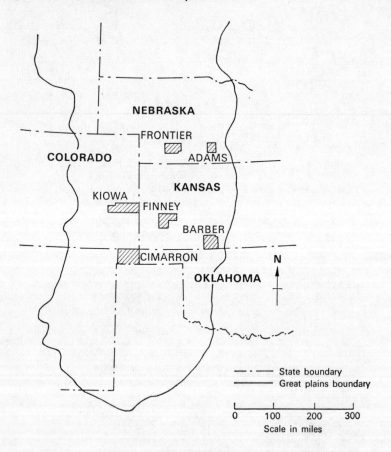

* This extract forms Chapter 4 of Saarinen's book *Perception of the Drought Hazard on the Great Plains* (1966). The study areas are shown in Fig. 1 and described in Table 1, both of which are taken from an earlier chapter. The extract is reprinted with the permission of the publishers, University of Chicago.

aspects of drought perception each farmer was asked the general question, 'What are the main advantages and disadvantages of this area?' Although they were not then aware that the main purpose of the interview was to examine the question of drought, eighty-one of the ninety-six interviewed (84 per cent) mentioned dryness or lack of moisture as a disadvantage. Usually it was the first, most emphatic, and often the only disadvantage mentioned. Table 2 shows the percentage in each area who mentioned dryness as a disadvantage.

Table 2: Percentage of farmers mentioning dryness as a disadvantage

County	Adams	Barber	Frontier	Finney	Cim-maron	Kiowa
%	71	87	67	94	86	100

Perception of present moisture conditions was also clear. However, there appears to be a tendency to judge present moisture conditions not only according to long term averages but also in terms of the immediately preceding conditions. Table 3 shows the farmers' answers to the question, 'Would you consider the past few months to have been average,

Table 3: Farmers' assessment of present moisture conditions

County	Adams	Barber	Frontier	Finney	Cim-maron	Kiowa
Much drier	0	0	8	11	1	12
Drier	4	0	7	5	4	5
Average	10	1	0	0	7	0
Wetter	3	14	0	0	2	0
Much Wetter	0	1	0	0	0	0
Don't know	0	0	0	1	0	0
	17	16	15	17	14	17
Palmer Index						
Time of interview	−·33	1·77	−1·57	−3·16	−2·54	−3·60
Previous month	1·63	1·60	−1·27	−3·61	−2·29	−3·73
Two months prior	1·12	−2·85	−·86	−3·38	−3·50	−3·54

[1] This became apparent during the several week period of preliminary reconnaisance work and pretesting during the summer of 1964. An example of a similar comment made in reference to Northwestern Oklahoma is 'Rain, the lack of it, or the possibility of it enters into nearly every person's daily thoughts and forms a topic of discussion and conversation', in *A Treasury of Western Folklore*, ed. B. A. Botkin, New York, Crown Publishers Inc., 1951, p. 85.

Table 1: Chief characteristics of counties chosen

County and state	Average annual ppt. (in in.)	Thornthwaite moisture index	Vegetation (Shantz)	Vegetation (Küchler)	Topography (Hammond)	Population density per sq. mile	Average size of farm (acres)	No. of years in area		Av. age	Av. ed.
								Farmer	Family		
Adams Nebraska	24·28	−9·24	Needle grass and slender wheatgrass	Bluestem prairie	Smooth plains 50—75% of gentle slope on upland	52	320·6	23·9	73·6	46·8	10·1
Barber Kansas	24·50	−16·20	Bluestem bunch grass	Bluestem grama prairie	Irregular plain 50—75% of gentle slope on upland	8	1,157·5	26·2	51·0	52·5	11·2
Frontier Nebraska	19·13	−19·16	Wiregrass	Wheat grass bluestem needle grass	Irregular plain 50—75% of gentle slope on upland	5	1,375·3	21·6	62·4	42·2	11·2
Finney Kansas	18·67	−24·44	Wiregrass	Grama Buffalo grass	Smooth plains 50—75% of gentle slope on upland	12	1,432·1	24·2	36·5	49·7	10·6
Cimarron Oklahoma	16·51	−27·25	Grama and Buffalo grass	Grama Buffalo grass	Smooth plains 50—75% of gentle slope on upland	3	1,960·4	22·7	41·1	44·0	11·7
Kiowa Colorado	13·64	−31·39	Grama and Buffalo grass	Grama Buffalo grass	Smooth plains 50—75% of gentle slope	1	4,289·9	21·0	32·9	47·5	10·5

wetter than usual, drier than usual, much wetter than usual, or much drier than usual?' In general the replies of the farmers to this question correspond quite closely to what might be expected when one considers the Palmer Drought Index for the time of the interview and the two months preceding. In Adams, Finney, Kiowa, and Barber Counties the perception of the farmers corresponds very closely with the Palmer Drought Index for the month of the interview. In Frontier County where conditions for the past two months were becoming progressively drier more of the farmers said, 'much drier than usual', than the mild drought conditions might indicate. In Cimarron County, Oklahoma, half of the farmers spoke of present moisture conditions as average and a couple even said wetter than average. Here there appears to be a tendency to estimate the present conditions by comparison with immediately preceding conditions rather than a longer range average. The result in the case of Cimarron County was for half of the farmers to describe present moisture conditions as average although the drought index indicated conditions of moderate droughts. Another possibility is that they were describing actual rainfall rather than moisture conditions in which case average and wetter than average would be reasonable. The fact that the farmers' perception of current moisture conditions agrees so well with the values of the Palmer Drought Index indicates that this index should be very useful as a base line for comparison with the farmers' perceptions of other aspects of the drought hazard.

Meteorological and perceived drought

Although Great Plains wheat farmers are aware of the drought hazard they appear to underestimate its frequency and to overestimate the number of very good years and the average crop yields in such years.

The farmers were asked to estimate the number of drought years they would experience if they were to live in their area for 100 years. The averages for each area are seen in Table 4 where they are compared to the

Table 4: Comparison of farmers' estimate of drought frequency with actual drought conditions in the past as indicated by Palmer Index

County	Adams	Barber	Fron-tier	Finney	Cimar-ron	Kiowa
Farmers' estimate drt yrs/100	17	16	19·9	28·6	34·8	34·9
% Time drought	42·4	46·9	41·6	47·2	48·7	47·2
% Mild drought and severer	32·8	39·6	32·0	37·0	39·8	34·8
% Moderate drought and severer	23·6	26·8	20·8	26·6	30·8	24·4
% Severe and extreme drought	15·7	13·8	11·2	15·4	18·4	13·4

actual frequency of drought months of each degree of severity according to the Palmer Index. These values were available on a month-by-month basis for each study area from January 1924 to the time of the interview. This corresponds to the period in which most of the farmers presently there gained their experience. Only ten of the ninety-six interviewed started before that date.

One could argue that the Palmer Index measures rainfall variability rather than drought *per se*. But it takes much more into account than simple variations in amount of precipitation. The close correspondence between the farmers' estimates of present moisture conditions and those of the index, and the fact that even Palmer's incipient drought is noticeable to the farmers in the most humid area suggests that it is valuable as a measure of drought. Further support is provided by the fact that in all areas the more perceptive farmers, according to all other information available, were the ones whose estimates of drought frequency corresponded most closely with the objective measure of the Palmer Drought Index.

There appears to be a clear progression from humid to arid areas in terms of the number of drought years expected in 100, or as it could be interpreted, the percentage of drought years. When the farmers' estimates are compared to the actual percentages of drought months it becomes apparent that all tend to underestimate the frequency of drought. Looking more closely at the two sets of figures reveals an interesting bias. The estimates of drought frequency in the most humid of the study areas (Adams and Barber Counties) correspond closely with the percentage of severe and extreme drought months. In more arid Frontier, Finney, and Cimarron Counties the farmers' figures seem to include the moderate droughts as well. In the most arid of all study areas the perceived percentage corresponds to the figure for all droughts from mild to extreme. This seems to indicate that as aridity increases the correspondence between perceived and meteorological drought becomes closer. It appears that all of the farmers tend to underestimate the frequency of drought and the degree to which it is underestimated increases with increasing humidity.

It is quite clear that meteorological drought is not what the farmers perceive except in the more arid areas. Probably on a very large scale there is, as Palmer assumes, an adjustment of the established economy of any area to the average climate of the area. But since the same crops are grown over a wide area, there are differences in the fineness of the adjustment. Thus in the most humid of the areas studied a near-normal operation may be possible with a considerable negative deviation from normal moisture conditions. However, in the drier areas even a slight

Table 5: Expectation and actuality of very good crops

County	Barber	Finney	Cim-maron	Kiowa
% Years expected	38	36·9	35	36
No. of bushels/acre	27·8	31·3	22·0	24·6

Actual yields in bushels/harvested acre*				
1963	15·0	19·0	7·0	7·0
1962	20·0	26·0	12·2	17·1
1961	30·0	31·0	20·2	22·0
1960	29·0	39·0	15·8	25·0
1959	20·0	21·0	19·5	18·0
1958	29·0	30·0	23·4	18·1
1957	16·0	31·0	15·3	13·4
1956	12·8	15·3	6·1	5·1
1955	5·6	14·3	7·4	6·0
1954	12·3	9·6	5·7	6·0
1953	10·9	8·5	5·2	6·0
1952	22·2	23·3	12·5	12·0
1951	13·1	11·8	6·0	9·0
1950	11·0	10·0	3·4	9·0
1949	12·0	12·4	13·4	12·0
1948	16·3	16·7	9·9	18·0
1947	17·5	23·7	16·3	22·0
1946	18·6	14·1	9·5	21·0
1945	15·2	19·9	7·9	13·0
1944	17·3	14·3	15·2	13·0
1943	14·0	13·6	10·0	18·0
1942	20·0	19·9	13·7	18·0
1941	15·0	14·9	11·6	8·0
1940	10·9	8·6	11·3	7·0
1939	16·3	5·4	7·3	5·0
1938	9·2	10·0	0	12·0
1937	10·8	3·8	0	—
1936	11·0	5·8	4·1	5·0
1935	8·0	3·0	0	7·0
No. of years actual yields exceeded or equalled expected yields	3	1	1	1

* The crop yield figures for each of the counties were obtained from the state offices of the U.S. Department of Agriculture, Statistical Reporting Service. It was assumed that the farmers' figures reflected yields per harvested acre. Had figures for yields per planted acre been used the farmers' estimates would appear even more optimistic.

deviation has a much greater impact and as a result might be more quickly perceived as drought. This may be the reason for the heightened perception of the farmers on the most arid margins.

The farmers appeared overoptimistic in replying to the question, 'how often do you expect a very good crop?' However, the questionnaire as originally set up provided no way of knowing whether the farmers were actually thinking of average rather than very good yields. To more precisely determine this the following additional question was asked in the final four study areas, 'What do you think of as a very good crop?' Table 5 compares the results of these two questions with the actual crop yields in each of the areas for the past twenty-nine years. This shows that the farmers were indeed thinking of a very good crop, in fact one larger than any but the most recent bumper crop in their particular area.[2] Clearly there is a tendency to overestimate both the frequency of occurrence of very good years and the yields in such years.

A measure of individual variation in perception of the drought risk

An indication of the individual farmer's perception of the drought hazard is provided by answers to the question, 'If you were to live here 100 years, how many drought years would you expect to have?' The percentage of drought months over the past forty years for each area was used as an objective standard of the actual drought risk. By comparing individual farmers' perception of the drought risk with this standard based on the Palmer Index, a measure was derived which takes into account the degree to which each individual's estimate deviates in either direction from the actual drought frequency over the past forty years. (Most underestimated but a few, especially in the arid areas, made overestimates.) This was used as a measure of their perception of the drought risk. The farmers were classified on a one to nine scale with larger numbers indicating greater deviation, hence less accurate perception.

The half dozen most and least perceptive farmers in each area according to this classification were selected. The same number of farmers was selected using deviations from the average frequency of drought years estimated by the farmers in each area. The individuals included in the most and least perceptive categories according to each standard were compared using field notes, other interview information, and intuitive

[2] Only in Barber County do the average yields for the county exceed more than once the yield that the farmers think of as a very good crop. In Barber County there is a very rapid transition in moisture conditions from east to west. Although the study area was chosen as representative of the county as a whole it may be that the averages have been pulled up somewhat by the greater yields in the more eastern portion of the county.

judgment. The results are listed in Table 6. Under the least and most perceptive columns is indicated the standard which most precisely selected that group for each county. In cases where both standards were equally discriminating this is indicated. In only one case did the classification based on the average expectation of drought in each area appear to be the more discriminating. In Frontier County it appeared to more accurately select the least perceptive group. In three other instances it was about equal to the other classification. In all other cases the classification based on deviations from drought frequencies as indicated by the Palmer Index seemed more appropriate. This tends to offer further sup-

Table 6: Comparison of area averages and Palmer percentages as standards for selection of most and least perceptive individuals

County	Most perceptive of drought risk	Least perceptive of risk
Adams	Palmer Index	Both Indexes equal
Barber	Palmer Index	Palmer Index
Frontier	Palmer Index	Area averages
Finney	Equal	Palmer Index
Cimarron	Palmer Index	Palmer Index
Kiowa	Equal	Palmer Index

port to the conclusion above regarding greater underestimation by those on the humid margins. It provided evidence that the individual farmers on the humid margins most likely to have good judgment according to all other indications were indeed those who tended to have higher estimates of the frequency of drought years. In some individual cases the measure may be misleading due to fortuitous guesses by some farmers but by and large it appears to discriminate along the dimension desired. The sample farmers were divided into two groups approximately equal in numbers, those more perceptive of the drought risk (47) and those less perceptive (43). They were so classified on the basis of how closely their estimate of the drought risk corresponded to that indicated by the Palmer Index. These two groups are used in subsequent sections of the study to provide a rough estimate of perception of the drought risk for comparison with other variables.

The role of aridity

Several variables reflecting various aspects of drought perception appear to vary with aridity, as measured by the Thornthwaite Moisture Index.

Table 7 contains a number of these, some of which have been previously mentioned. The number of drought years expected in 100 generally increases with aridity although not in a regular fashion. The six study areas divide into two groups. In the three most humid areas drought is expected just under one-fifth of the time while in the three most arid drought is estimated to occur close to one-third of the time. The percentage of very good years expected decreases as aridity increases. The only serious exception is Barber County, Kansas, whose farmers on the

Table 7: Aridity and selected aspects of drought perception

County	Thornthwaite moisture Index	Drought years/100	Chances of drought next year (%)	% Very good years expected
Adams	−9·24	17·0	24	69
Barber	−16·20	16·0	22	38
Frontier	−19·16	19·9	46	52
Finney	−24·44	28·6	48	46
Cimarron	−27·25	34·8	46	35
Kiowa	−31·39	34·9	74	36

average expected a very good crop only 38 per cent of the time. This is much lower than would be predicted on the basis of aridity. It may be due to the fact that continuous cropping is the rule in Barber County whereas in all the others some form of summer fallow is practised.

Some curious results came from the question, 'What are the chances of drought next year?' In general the farmers felt an increasing likelihood of drought next year with an increase in aridity. The two dry areas were similar, the drier ones were also close, but the two driest were different. Although both Cimarron County, Oklahoma and Kiowa County, Colorado, had been suffering severe drought for equivalent periods of time, the farmers in the former area gave much more optimistic answers. It is hypothesised that this difference was due to a series of small showers in November and early December which had a more marked effect on the morale of the Cimarron County farmers than on soil moisture conditions.

There appear to be differences in the way in which farmers from different areas define drought. They were asked the question, 'What do you think of as drought?' Table 8 outlines some of the elements considered and shows the percentage of farmers in the various areas who mentioned each in answering the question. A large proportion of the farmers define drought both in terms of crop yields and rainfall and often other elements were mentioned as well. It may be that all of them perceive drought where it most directly affects them. Usually for Great Plains farmers this would mean crop yields although pasture conditions

Table 8: Drought definitions: percentage mentioning each element

County	Adams	Barber	Frontier	Finney	Cimar-ron	Kiowa
Crop yields	76	80	80	65	67	47
Rainfall	34	56	60	82	74	82
Poor pasture	6	25	20	0	14	29
Heat	29	25	0	6	14	6
Wind	6	19	0	12	21	6
Others	6	0	7	0	7	12

would be most important in some types of operations, as can be seen in the larger percentages for Barber, Frontier, and Kiowa counties who define drought in terms of poor pasture. In the driest areas where even slight moisture deficiencies can readily be seen in smaller crop yields rainfall is more often used to define drought than in moister regions where the effect may not be quite so immediately apparent. Heat was mentioned as a factor mainly by those in the two most humid areas. Other ways of defining drought were in terms of economic effects on the community, subsoil moisture, and insect infestment.

The measure of perception of the drought hazard derived above was

Table 9: Aridity and perception of the drought risk (% of county farmers in each group)

County	More perceptive	Less perceptive
Adams	25	75
Barber	27	73
Frontier	50	50
Finney	62	38
Cimarron	69	31
Kiowa	82	18

applied to divide the farmers into two approximately equal groups, the more and less perceptive. Table 9 shows the percentage of farmers in each group according to areas. The percentage of farmers in the group more perceptive of the drought hazard increases with the degree of aridity.[3] Aridity is clearly an important factor in perception of the drought hazard.

The rôle of drought experience

Many questions arose in the attempt to develop an accurate index of drought experience for comparison of individual farmers in the six different study areas. The number of years each farmer had been farming would not be a good index of drought experience because it would not take into account differences in the number of drought years from area to area. The Palmer Index for past years in each area provided a measure of the number of months at each degree of drought severity. But would the experience of one month of mild drought have an equal effect on the humid and arid edges? How can the difference between a month of extreme drought and a month of mild or moderate drought be taken into

Table 10: Drought experience and perception of the drought risk

Drought experience (no. of months)	Low 0–72	Medium 88–143	High 174 & over	High (under 65)	High (65 & over)
Number of farmers	30	35	24	12	12
Average age	35·9	45·0	62·5	54·5	70·3
Average perception *	4·9	4·3	5·1	3·8	6·4

* The lower the number here the more accurate the perception.

account? Is one month of drought in the growing season equivalent to one month of drought at some other time of the year?

It was assumed that fluctuations in wheat yields roughly reflect the effect of drought though hail, rust, etc., also may be important. Several different measures were compared with wheat yields such as total number of drought months in the year, total number of drought months in the growing season, drought months during the fall, and total negative value of the Palmer Index for the year. None was clearly better than the others and all seemed to vary roughly as wheat yields. For the sake of simplicity and ease of calculation the total number of drought months experienced by each farmer was used as an index of drought experience. That is the total number of drought months in the area since the farmer started was used as a measure of his drought experience.

Comparison of drought experience with perception of the drought risk

[3] When the Thornthwaite Moisture Index is correlated with per cent more perceptive $r^2 = 0.94$.

is shown in Table 10. It is apparent that perception of the drought risk improves with increasing experience. However this does not seem to hold true for the very oldest farmers (those sixty-five years of age and older) who as a group appear to be much less perceptive despite their greater experience.[4] Perhaps the imminence of their retirement makes drought a less vital issue for them, or perhaps those who stay longest are those who steadfastly depreciate the hazard. To test this latter hypothesis a check was made of the fifteen farmers who failed to mention dryness as a disadvantage. Although the ratio of local people to newcomers for all areas is 56 to 40, thirteen of the fifteen who failed to mention dryness as a disadvantage came from the local area and only two from other more humid areas. This indicates that most of the newcomers do notice the drought conditions and that some of the local people

Table 11: Drought experience and estimate of chances of drought next year (%)

County	Adams	Barber	Frontier	Finney	Cimar- ron	Kiowa
Most experienced	24	35	50	40	40	57
Least experienced	33	22	37	55	54	60

tend to ignore the hazard, or take it for granted, or at least do not mention it.

When drought experience is compared with the farmers' estimates of the chances of drought next year, no clear relationship results. The half of the farmers in each area with the least experience were compared with the most experienced half after elimination of those sixty-five years of age and over. The results are shown in Table 11. In two cases the most experienced have a more pessimistic estimate than the less experienced, in three cases this is reversed, and in one case both groups provide similar estimates. The index of drought perception is derived from the farmers' estimate of the number of drought years per hundred as compared

[4] The oldest farmers are all in the group with the greatest amount of experience and were separated because their answers appeared so atypical. In addition there is a four year gap between the youngest member of the sixty-five and over group and the oldest member of the others in the very experienced group so factors due to old age may be removed. The division is unfortunate since this leaves the groups unequal in size. However they are best retained as such groups because between them are great gaps in amount of experience, i.e., the difference of over thirty months between the highest in the medium group and the lowest in the high group, and fourteen months between highest in low group and lowest in medium. Nowhere else are there such large gaps in the distribution.

with the actual drought frequency. Thus, it provides a measure of the accuracy of the farmers' assessment of the drought risk. Experience does seem to help in making such an estimate since the more experienced farmers in general appeared the more perceptive. However, experience does not seem to aid the farmers in the face of uncertainty, that is, in the task of estimating what the chances of drought are in a particular year. This is not entirely surprising since there is no clear consensus among experts on this point.

Remembrance of droughts past

To investigate how past droughts are remembered two questions were asked: (1) When was the last drought in this county? and (2) Have you experienced any others? If the answer to (2) was yes, an effort was made to elicit some comment as to when it was and what it was like.

Many difficulties prevent precise comparison of an objective standard of the number of droughts and the memories which farmers retain. The Palmer Index enables one to state the beginning and end of any particular drought with reasonable precision but farmers do not as clearly delimit them. Most often they label the drought according to the year in which it occurred. This can lead to confusion if there are several closely spaced droughts with one ending and another beginning within one year. It would be difficult to determine which one the farmer was referring to. To avoid the possibility of omitting droughts mentioned, ambiguous cases were classified in as many ways as seemed reasonable. For example, if the farmer said 1950 and there were two droughts touching that year, both would be included; or if he said 'the fifties', all droughts within that decade would be included. The result was that many minor droughts appeared to be more mentioned than the farmers might have meant. Only a rough classification was possible under the circumstances. Table 12 indicates only those droughts which were mentioned by at least half of the farmers present at the time of its occurrence. It can readily be seen that only the most recent and severe droughts are included. If the most recent ones are omitted, the remainder are all extreme droughts. Furthermore, all the extreme droughts are included but no droughts of lesser severity except the severe drought of September 1931 to July 1933 in Finney County, Kansas. This was included as part of the drought of the thirties.

As the droughts become more remote in time the exact years are not mentioned as often. Instead they are described as the drought of 'the thirties' or 'the fifties' or 'the early fifties'. These more general terms often include several droughts separated by short periods of moister conditions.

Table 13 shows the percentage of farmers in each area using such terms. The base used was the number of sample farmers in the area during the final year of the drought. In the case of 'the thirties' this resulted in percentages of over 100 since many farmers mentioned this period even though they were not then farming. This could possibly

Table 12: Droughts mentioned by at least one-half of farmers present at time of drought

County	Adams	Barber	Frontier	Finney	Cimar-ron	Kiowa
	'63–'64	'63–'64	'64	'62–'64	'62–'64	'63–'64
	(– ·88)*	(–3·50)	(–1·89)	(–4·18)	(–3·50)	(–3·78)
	'54–'57	'52–'57	'54–'57	'55–'57	'51–'57	'54–'57
	(–4·29)	(–5·59)	(–4·74)	(–4·75)	(–4·64)	(–5·35)
	'33–'41	'32–'38	'36–'41	'52–'55	'32–'38	'30–'38
	(–6·53)	(–4·27)	(–4·89)	(–4·18)	(–4·99)	(–5·09)
			'32–'35	'34–'39		
			(–5·61)	(–5·22)		
				'31–'33		
				(–3·25)		

* Maximum severity of the drought according to the Palmer Index is shown in brackets.

result from some combination of childhood memories and local tradition. It is interesting to note that the tendency to use such terms is most highly developed in the more arid areas. In Kiowa County, Colorado, almost one-quarter of the farmers were already applying the term 'the fifties' to the series of separate droughts which took place during that decade.

Table 13: Percentage of farmers using the terms ' The 50s ' and ' The 30s '

County	Adams	Barber	Frontier	Finney	Cimar-ron	Kiowa
' the 50s '	0	0	0	6	8	23
the 30s '	67	75	140	100	160	250

The majority of farmers in every study area spoke of the most recent drought as is indicated in Table 14. This is not particularly surprising since in all cases the most recent drought was currently being experienced or had just ended. Even in Adams County, Nebraska, whose recent drought would be labelled as incipient, 69 per cent of the farmers

Table 14: Percentage of farmers remembering most recent drought

County	Adams	Barber	Frontier	Finney	Cimar-ron	Kiowa
Drought category of most recent drought	Incipient	Severe	Mild	Extreme	Severe	Severe
Per cent remembering it	69	81	53	77	100	94

mentioned it. For the farmers in this area it was the driest spell since February 1957, and by contrast with the immediately preceding weather it was indeed dry. This is reflected in an analysis of those who included it and those who did not as shown in Table 15. The eleven who mentioned this recent drought in Adams County averaged fifteen years of farming experience and include all the farmers (5) who started farming since the last drought in the county. Those who failed to mention this drought averaged forty years of experience in the area. It may be that their backlog of much more serious drought experience would lead them to dismiss the present moisture conditions as a dry spell while those with less experience regard it as more significant because of their lack of preparation. It is interesting to see that even in the most humid area incipient drought is clearly perceived at least when it is preceded by a long period of much moister conditions. Why then do the farmers here tend to underestimate drought as they do? Is it that they see the effects but as long as they get by they tend to forget about them afterwards?

One exception to the above tendency to remember only most severe and recent droughts could be described as the factor of primacy. That is, farmers are likely to remember the first drought they experience even if it is not extreme or severe. Several times it was noted that one farmer might include a moderate drought which was not mentioned by any other person in his area. Closer examination usually revealed that the drought had occurred shortly after the individual started farming in that

Table 15: Number of years of experience of farmers mentioning and not mentioning recent incipient drought in Adams county

	Number	Average number of years in area	Standard deviation
Mentioned drought	12	14·9	11·7
Did not mention drought	5	40·6	16·6

area. Table 16 shows the percentage of farmers in each area who mentioned the first drought after their start in the area. A surprisingly high percentage results, considering the fact that this includes all droughts from incipient to extreme. It will be remembered that only the most severe droughts were mentioned by at least half of the farmers.

Table 16: Primacy in remembrance of droughts past

County	Adams	Barber	Frontier	Finney	Cimarron	Kiowa
% Remembering first drought	41	40	41	29	28	50

Type of operation and perception of the drought risk

Perception of the drought risk appears to vary with the type of operation. Table 17 indicates the number and percentage of each type of operator who would be included in the most and least perceptive group. The types of operations are arranged from those most highly dependent on grain to those most highly dependent on livestock. It can be seen that the percentage of farmers included in the most perceptive group goes down as livestock emphasis increases. Since a livestock enterprise can operate efficiently in a much drier area than an operation entirely dependent on grain, it may be that as the farmers become more diversified and

Table 17: Perception and type of operation

Type of operation	Most perceptive		Least perceptive	
	number	%	number	%
Straight grain	14	61	·9	39
Diversified (Grain emphasis)	16	57	12	43
Diversified (Half and half)	12	55	10	45
Diversified (Livestock emphasis)	4	31	9	69

less dependent on cash grain crops, they become less concerned with the vagaries of the weather and somewhat less perceptive of the drought risk.[5]

The preceding discussion in this chapter shows that in general Great

[5] Similar conclusions were arrived at independently by John Bennett in his current investigations in S.W. Saskatchewan, as indicated in a letter of 5 October 1965.

Plains wheat farmers are aware of the drought hazard and are able to accurately assess the moisture conditions of the moment. However, they tend to underestimate the frequency of drought years, and to be over-optimistic about the number of very good years and the size of crops in such years. All but the most recent, the most severe and longest droughts tend to be forgotten though individuals may recall the first one they experienced. Within the Great Plains there appear to be variations in perception of the drought risk. Those from the most arid areas, those with the most drought experience, and those whose operations are most vulnerable to variations in the weather have a more accurate perception of the drought risk.

New concept: subjective distance

Store impressions affect estimates of travel time*

Donald L. Thompson

Models concerned with the distribution of retail trade within any geographic area must include distance in some form as an independent
variable. Reilly's law is the best known effort in this direction, although
several other simple trading area models are to be found in marketing
literature.[1]

Authors who include distance in trading area models do so on the assumption that it is a planning variable of some importance in consumer
decision making. Distance, it is assumed, constitutes a 'friction' or inertia which tends to keep retail activities localised in any given area. And
actual distance is assumed to correspond with the consumer's *estimate* of
distance, convenience, and travel time.

Since consumers hesitate to undertake the costs and effort of overcom-
ing distance, market researchers conveniently 'explain' retail sales volume in terms of local base of demand, or they combine with this an adjustment factor to approximate any 'leakage' or 'escape' which might
take place between communities or clusters of population and establishments. Commonly, distance is used in the formulation of this escape
factor, either as a weight to resident population or as an independent
variable in a multiple regression.

Our purpose here is to evaluate how much distance really affects consumer decisions on where to shop. If no consistent pattern of consumer
'rationality' with respect to distance can be isolated, one can then question the usefulness of this factor as a simple input variable.

The 'Experiment'

Our research design can best be described as an 'experiment'; that is,
a conscious attempt was made to control as many outside factors as possible. Four San Francisco Bay area communities were isolated as each
having a large, established department store within the immediate vicinity of a large-scale discount operation. Investigators then defined survey areas on the basis of the following criteria:

1. The survey areas should be residential in nature, located at points

* Reprinted from *Journal of Retailing* 39 (Spring 1963) 1–6, by permission of the
publishers.

approximately equidistant from the department store and the discount house.

2. The road distances and the driving time from the survey areas to the two types of retail outlets also should be equal. The time standard adopted was the average of five trips by the investigator from the test areas to the destinations, driving at prevailing highway speeds during normal weekday traffic between the hours of 10 a.m. and 4 p.m.

3. A distance of one or two miles and driving time of approximately five minutes were the desired values, although geographic considerations forced some departure from this criterion.

4. There should be only one principal route available for the consumer to travel from his home to each of two types of retail outlets in his immediate vicinity.

5. This route should be sufficiently wide and have adequate access so that travel time would not differ appreciably according to the time of day or the day of the week under consideration.

6. The routes available primarily should be used by shoppers; they should not be major commuter arterials.

Localities surveyed

The following sites were selected as survey areas:

Albany, approximately equidistant from Capwell's Department Store in El Cerrito Plaza and the B.B.B. Discount Department Store in Berkeley.
San Francisco, at a point somewhat closer to the Emporium Department Store in Stonestown Shopping Centre than to the G.E.T. Discount House in Lakeshore Plaza.
San Rafael, approximately equidistant from Macy's in downtown San Rafael, and Mac's Discount Department Store.
Walnut Creek, approximately equidistant from Capwell's Department Store in the Broadway Centre and the C.B.S. Discount House at Four Corners.

Consumers in test areas were asked whether or not they patronised the retail outlets in question, and if so, to estimate the distance in miles from their residences to the two outlets. They were asked also to estimate the actual driving time spent in travel, not including time used to find a parking place. In San Rafael, consumers were asked, in addition, the distance and travel time via a freeway to a regional shopping centre somewhat farther away. In all cases the route was verified, and it was determined that the trip in question was a direct one, with no side journeys involved.

Table 1: Estimated vs. actual distances and driving times from survey areas to department store, discount house, and regional shopping centre (distance in miles; driving time in minutes)

	Albany*	San Francisco†	San Rafael‡	Walnut Creek§
Department Store				
Estimated distance	1·25	0·75	1·65	3·56
Actual distance	1·50	0·75	1·10	3·50
Ratio: Estimated/actual	0·83	1·00 ‖	1·49	1·02 ‖
Estimated driving time	5·50	3·45	6·07	8·42
Actual driving time	5·00	2·50	5·00	7·00
Ratio: Estimated/Actual	1·10	1·38	1·21	1·20
Discount House				
Estimated distance	1·68	1·46	1·67	3·65
Actual distance	1·50	1·25	1·10	3·50
Ratio: Estimated/Actual	1·12	1·17	1·52	1·04 ‖
Estimated driving time	6·41	6·77	6·86	9·44
Actual driving time	5·00	3·50	5·00	7·00
Ratio: Estimated/Actual	1·28	1·93	1·37	1·35
Regional Shopping Centre				
Estimated distance			5·46	
Actual distance			3·80	
Ratio: Estimated/Actual			1·44	
Estimated driving time			12·71	
Actual driving time			6·00	
Ratio: Estimated/Actual			2·12	
Ratio: *Discount house ratio / Department store ratio*				
Distance	1·35	1·17	1·02 ‖	1·02 ‖
Driving time	1·16	1·40	1·12	1·13
Ratio: *Regional shopping centre ratio / Department store ratio*				
Distance			0·97 ‖	
Driving time			1·75	
Ratio: *Regional shopping centre ratio / Discount house ratio*				
Distance			0·95 ‖	
Driving time			1·44	

* Time and distance measured from vicinity of Solano and Carmel Avenues (1950 San Francisco-Oakland Census Trace AC-1) to the B.B.B. discount house and Capwell's Department Store in El Cerrito Plaza.
† Time and distance measured from vicinity of Lagunitas and Beachmont Streets (1950 Census Tract (0—7)) to G.E.T. discount house in Lakeshore Plaza and the Emporium Department Store in Stonestown Shopping Centre.
‡ Time and distance measured from vicinity of LynCourt and Irving Avenues to MAC's discount house on Highway 101, Macy's in downtown San Rafael, and the J. C. Penney Store at Corte Madera Wye and Highway 101.
§ Time and distance measured from vicinity of Eccleston Avenue and Oak Park Boulevard to C.B.S. discount house at Four Corners and Capwell's Department Store in the Broadway Shopping Centre.
‖ Insignificant at 0·05 level.

Objectives

The objectives were:

1. To probe the extent to which suburban consumers, travelling by private automobile, are capable of evaluating distance and driving time in any consistent fashion.
2. To determine whether or not consumer evaluation of time and distance is affected by the character of the destination.

In other words, does the markedly different merchandising character of the department store versus the discount house have any effect on the consumers' evaluation of distance and travel time?

It was not possible to locate a residential area in San Francisco meeting the equidistance criterion. In order to render the San Francisco results comparable with the others, therefore, a series of ratios was computed. The first ratio divides the respondents' averages as to time or distance by the actual measured time or distance. A value of greater-than-one for this ratio indicates an upward bias of consumers in estimating the magnitudes involved. A second ratio was then computed, dividing the above ratio for the discount house by the corresponding ratio for the department store as destination. A value in excess of unity for this ratio indicates that consumers tended to overestimate the distance or driving time to the discount house proportionately more than they did the distance or driving time to the department store.

Obviously, any ratios immediately in the neighbourhood of 1·00 enjoy very little statistical significance, although the variance around such central tendency values may be of interest. Ratios near unity, therefore, indicate that consumer differences in estimation are in the aggregate equivalent to a statistical error term, tending to cancel out as the sample becomes large. Models using actual distance and driving time measures would, therefore, under such circumstances, be using an objective independent variable that correctly reflects the subjective evaluation of the consumers whose reactions are effectively captured by means of a mathematical function. This says nothing about the manner in which this variable should be handled in such models, but merely validates the appropriateness of its inclusion.

It is interesting to note from Table 1 that in 13 out of 16 cases the ratios are significantly greater than unity. This shows a general tendency on the part of the sample consumers to overestimate both the driving time and the distance travelled in the satisfaction of their retail needs. Furthermore, when one considers the ratio between the discount house ratio and the department store ratio (with the exception of distance for San Rafael and Walnut Creek), the latter ratios also are significantly greater than unity. One could suggest, therefore, that the sample consumers regarded the discount houses as being farther away from their residences in time and distance than the department store.

Consumers in the San Rafael survey area, as a rule, showed significant upward bias in evaluating the distance to the regional shopping centre at Corte Madera, and even greater upward bias in estimating the corresponding time, even though a high percentage of them traded there. Their relative upward bias in estimating the distance to the regional shopping centre closely approximated that evidenced in estimating the distance to the department store and the discount house. In their evaluation of driving time, however, they showed a greater tendency to overestimate than they did when the department store or the discount house was the destination (see the ratios of 1·75 and 1·44, respectively).

Subjective distance

This investigation poses some interesting questions on trading area analysis of consumer behaviour in general. Many authors have pointed out that approximately collocated retail outlets may support trading areas of different size and configuration.[2] This study suggests the further refinement that two retail outlets offering approximately the same merchandise lines—department stores and discount houses—may take on different geographic dimensions in the mind of the consumer. As a rule, the discount houses in the sample generally offered less consumer convenience and fewer services, and usually were more crowded and less desirable places to shop, than were the competing department stores. Apparently the impression made upon the consumer by the fewer conveniences offered in the discount house was further extended by him to influence his evaluation of the physical distance between his own home and the store. This subjective colouring of an objective fact is thus termed, 'the concept of subjective distance'.

In order to further amplify this concept, detailed information was collected in the San Rafael survey of consumers' estimates of time and distance to retail outlets where they did *not* shop; obviously, the location of these had to be sufficiently familiar to the consumers for an estimate to be made.

Twelve consumers who did not shop at Macy's estimated, on the average, that the store was 2·00 miles and 8·37 minutes driving time distant. The corresponding figures for 87 consumers shopping at Macy's were 1·60 miles and 5·75 minutes, respectively.[3] Fifteen consumers who did not shop at the discount house estimated that it was 1·75 miles away, with an average driving time of 8·03 minutes. On the other hand, 68 consumers shopping at the discount house estimated, on the average, 1·66 miles and 6·60 minutes driving time.

Despite the small samples involved, the results seem to reinforce the initial hypothesis—namely, that one's subjective feelings about a retail establishment affect his ability to evaluate its geographic position. In the San Rafael example, consumers stated they did *not* patronise the stores in question; therefore, there must have been some negative factor operating to divert patronage to competitors. A further extension of this negative 'image' could have led to the generally higher estimates, or the upwardly biased concepts of distance and driving time could have been part of a larger set of negative factors preventing patronage of the outlets in question.

Summary and conclusions

While the sample in this survey is relatively small in terms of absolute numbers—400 consumers in all—it nevertheless represents a high percentage of persons living in the vicinity of the specific points chosen as approximately equidistant from the two types of retail outlets in question. Further field survey effort is necessary to establish conclusively the relevance of the basic hypotheses suggested by this study.

First, objectively determined distance and driving time measures may not be entirely appropriate inputs for simple models designed to describe or explain geographic patterns of consumer purchasing behaviour. Appreciation is necessary of subjective aspects of distance and the varying interpretations of what, from the decision maker's standpoint, may be 'givens'. Then the idea of 'market outreach' or 'drawing area' may be restated in more flexible terms than might have been suggested in the past.[4]

Second, the convenience aspects of a retail store can be an important element in fixing its 'location' in the minds of consumers. If the discount houses in the survey areas are 'farther' away than department stores, other compelling and offsetting factors must be important in attracting consumers to their merchandise offerings.

Third, the general upward bias in estimation of driving time and distance indicates that shopping centres might well publicise these factors more than at present in an effort to broaden their market outreach. By publicising accessibility of a group of stores, the shopping centre might gain further at the expense of smaller, more scattered merchants whose exact location may not be as definitely fixed in the minds of consumers. In short, a 'convenient' location from the point of view of the developer is not necessarily as 'convenient' to the consumers on whom its profitability ultimately rests. Neat, often circular, market areas drawn on a map, therefore, may be very poor representations of geographic purchasing patterns dependent on the operation of highly variable elements of human behaviour.

Notes and references

[1] For example, CONVERSE, PAUL D. 'New laws of retail gravitation', *Journal of Marketing* 14 (1949) 379–84; FERBER, ROBERT, 'Variations in retail sales between cities', *Journal of Marketing* 22 (1958) 295–303; REILLY, W. J. *The Law of Retail Gravitation*, New York, Putnam's Sons, 1931.

[2] For example: BOWERS, W. A., and MITCHELL, W. L., jnr. *Hardware Distribution in the Gulf Southwest*, United States Department of Commerce, Bureau of Foreign and Domestic Commerce, Domestic Commerce series 52, Washington, U.S. Govt. Printing Office, 1931, p. 116; LÖSCH, A. *The Economics of Location*, Yale University Press, 1954, pp. 414–20.

[3] One woman regularly *walked* to both outlets in question, and while her results were not included, they seem to indicate the wide range of consumer rationality. Despite the fact that she followed the survey routes, she claimed a ten-minute, one-mile journey to the department store, and a thirty-minute, three-mile journey to the discount house. Repeated questions as to her route or side trips failed to shake her confidence in the above, highly inaccurate figures.

[4] For example, Reilly's law has been used to determine the breaking point between two retail establishments, substituting their floor space and the distance between them for population and road mileage respectively. See NELSON, RICHARD L. *The Selection of Retail Locations*, New York, F. W. Dodge Corporation, 1958, p. 149.

The determination of the location of retail activities with the use of a map transformation*

Arthur Getis

The hexagonal form of market areas as derived in the original statement of central place theory has been criticised in the geographic and economic literature. Much of this criticism rests on the idealised assumptions on which the theory is based. Isard's analysis penetratingly exposes how non-isotropic distributions distort the theoretical trade area pattern.[1] The purpose of this paper is to introduce a method by which the existence of irregularly shaped, but theoretically sound, trade areas may be ascertained. We are concerned primarily with the distribution of retail activities within urban areas. The test which is carried out demonstrates how, with the use of a technique of map transformation, scholars might better study such economic distributions. However, before the technique and the test are demonstrated a word must be said about the nature of retail store location.

The location of personal consumption expenditures and sales

Stores are spread unevenly in urban areas. Geographers in their quest for an explanation of store patterns have introduced implicitly in their analyses the effect of uneven population densities on store location. However, a more comprehensive indicator would be the distribution of the money that the population allocates for retail goods, rather than the distribution of the population itself. The problem, therefore, is to determine the effect of the distribution of consumer disposable income for retail goods on the location of retail stores.

For decades economists have been plagued with the problem of determining the mechanism responsible for consumption expenditures. If it were possible to predict how each consumer will act in the market place, the problem would be solved. Theories have been put forth and operational methods of analysis have been developed, but the problem of the psychology of individual consumer behaviour has not been solved. Most economic analyses are based on the assumption that man is a rational being, and that quantification is possible since maximisation of satisfaction or utility lends itself to standard methods of economic analysis. Economists have isolated certain important variables, such as price and income, which influence consumer demand. As geographers interested

* Reprinted from *Economic Geography* 39 (1963) 14–22, by permission of the publishers.

in spatial relations, we are concerned with how price and income act over space. The same problem of the psychology of consumer behaviour, however, inhibits the geographer in understanding consumer movements and, also, store location. Nevertheless, if geographers also assume that man is an economically rational being, it is possible to understand partially consumer movements and store location.

Consumption expenditures are spread unevenly over space. In a figurative way we can think of consumption expenditures as moving to stores for the purchase of retail goods. If there are known limitations on the distances people will travel for goods, then it is possible to delimit areas where stores might locate. It has been shown how far people have gone for the purchase of some retail goods.[2] Although distance alone does not determine where consumers purchase goods, nevertheless most retail stores cannot successfully locate in an area if the consumption expenditures available in that area are not sufficient for the store to operate at or above the threshold level of the firm. Therefore, it may be concluded that distance from consumption expenditures can be a determinant of store location only if the total consumption expenditures available in a market area for the goods offered by a given type of retail store are equal to or greater than the threshold requirement of that type of store.

The above discussion provides the necessary framework for the theoretical delimitation of market areas. Aggregates of consumer trip distances and consumption expenditures make it possible to begin to define trade areas. At the same time, threshold levels of firms are distinctly related to consumption expenditures available for the particular goods they offer, thereby connecting firms with definite market areas.

Map transformation of disposable income data

The method of map transformation of disposable income data has as its purpose the allocation of income available for retail goods to places in urban areas where stores might profitably locate. It is based on the premises that: (1) market areas exist for retail stores, as indicated in the preceding statement; (2) there is a minimum or no overlap of market areas; (3) consumption expenditure location has a direct bearing on the location of retail stores; (4) travel time or cost is the same for any unit distance from place to place; (5) rent or any other economic factor except consumption expenditures for goods supplied in retail stores has no bearing on the general location of the firm. A short description of the technique as it was applied to a city in the State of Washington follows.

On a population dot map of South Tacoma, Washington, a number of square-shaped, equal-area grid cells were drawn (Fig. 1). The consumption expenditures available for groceries (including produce and meat) were computed for each cell. The cells were then distorted according to a specified set of rules so that the new cells would be rectangular and in areal proportion to the computed consumption expenditures available for groceries in each of the original cells.

Fig. 1. Study area in test city

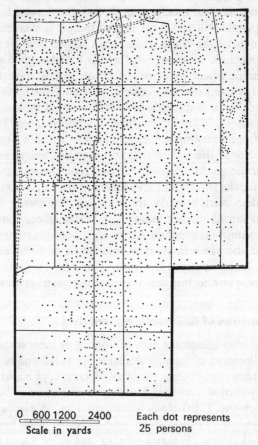

0   600 1200   2400   Each dot represents
    Scale in yards   25 persons

It was decided to allocate twelve supermarkets to the area of South Tacoma. These stores were positioned by means of: (1) superimposing an hexagonal market area pattern consisting of twelve hexagons on the distorted cell diagram, (2) plotting the centres of the hexagons on the distorted map, and (3) transferring the twelve centres of the distorted grid system to their proper positions on the original grid system. Finally, the twelve largest actual supermarkets and the twelve largest districts of grocery store sales were plotted on separate but identical maps using the original grid and containing the theoretical store locations. The theoretical pattern was then compared to the real pattern. A more detailed discussion of the technique follows.

Delimitation of the study area

The area of South Tacoma that was delimited (Fig. 1) has rather definite barriers to movement, especially for such short distance trips as those for groceries, on its edges. The north is bounded by a combination of a major United States highway, railroad right-of-ways, and industrial land. These three cover an area averaging a quarter of a mile in width. The eastern and southern boundaries are less well demarcated, but it is noted that the area becomes less and less densely populated in these two directions, with population falling off considerably within the study area. The western boundary is well defined by a north–south freeway which has been hindering movement in an east–west direction for the last six years (an existing topographic depression impeded movement before that time).

The city of Tacoma uses the township-range system for land location identification, thereby making it easy to divide the study area into grid cells of one-quarter mile dimension on each side, totalling forty-eight cells.[3] Information regarding the parts of cells in the north and east was included in the cells directly bordering them on the south and west respectively. The partial cells fell within the delimited area but their size and shape precluded their being considered separately.

Determination of income available for groceries

The population of each cell was determined by the use of a 1957 population dot map of the city. Income data for census tracts were taken from the 1950 census and adjusted to 1957 wage levels. For each census tract the consumption expenditures for groceries were computed by first dividing the population into income groups. The United States Census for 1950 allocates the families in each census tract to income groups. Next the amount of income allocated for groceries by each income group in each census tract was determined by consulting one of the many tables available which show how consumers apportion their income for various goods and services.[4] These expenditures were then transferred from the census tracts to the grid cells with the use of the population dot map. Housing data were used to estimate the areas within a census tract where the various income groups resided. Figure 2 shows the results of these calculations. As a check on the validity of these figures, the total sales of all grocery stores in the area were compared with the estimated consumption expenditures for groceries in the area. The results of this crude check were highly favourable.[5]

Fig. 2. Location of consumption expenditures available for groceries in study area (in thousands of dollars)

	10	11	12	13	14	15
10	235	321	611	449	462	496
11	543	663	764	472	612	400
12	457	827	940	535	264	1023
13	345	827	823	420	288	162
14	194	515	680	265	298	46
15	24	397	508	336	153	99
16	35	312	300	31		
17	43	251	263	169		
18	87	147	175	88		

The map distortion

Next the grid cells were distorted so that a unit of area anywhere on the distorted map would be equal to the estimated consumption expenditures for groceries (Fig. 3). Thus we note on Fig. 3 that cell 10-10 with consumption expenditures available for groceries of $235,000 is one-half the size of cell 10-14 with $462,000 available for groceries. The following rules were used in distorting the map:

1. Cells should be rectangular whenever possible.

2. All cells which are contiguous on the original map must also be contiguous on the distorted map.
3. The size and shape of the distorted map must be the same size and shape as the original map.

Fig. 3. Map distortion of consumption expenditures for groceries in study area

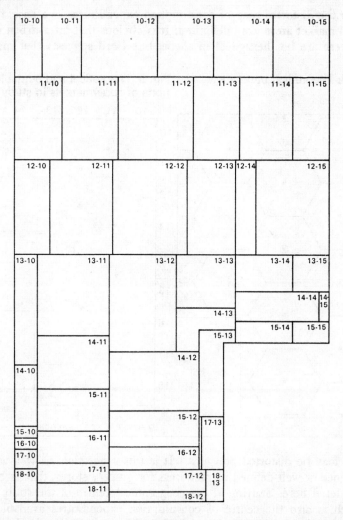

There are an infinite number of ways in which the map might have been distorted, but the method presented appears to be plausible. In effect what was done was to stretch or shrink the original cells within the

rigid boundaries of the area to sizes approximating the consumption expenditures available for groceries in each of the cells.[6] It should be pointed out that when the map is distorted so that consumption expenditures are spread evenly throughout the study area, the centre of consumption expenditures is also the geographical centre of the area.

Determining theoretical market areas

Using the distorted map of consumption expenditures as a base, theoretical market areas were delimited. It is obvious that intra-urban market areas are not hexagonal in shape, but Isard suggests that market

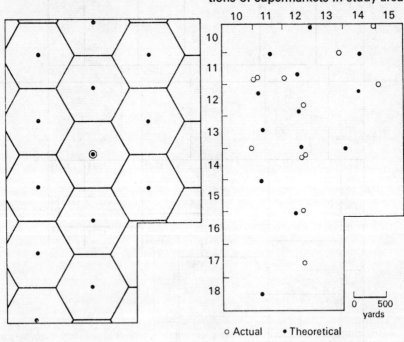

Fig. 4. Theoretical trade areas

Fig. 5. Theoretical and actual locations of supermarkets in study area

o Actual   • Theoretical

areas may be distorted polygons.[7] It is this suggestion, as well as the existence of well-defined market areas for grocery stores, that is being considered here. Starting at the geographical centre of the study area (which is also the centre of consumption expenditures available for groceries), hexagons were constructed so that as close to twelve hexagon centres could be included on the map as possible (Fig. 4).[8] The number twelve was not binding, since any number of hexagons could have been drawn, but was based on the fact that if only supermarkets supplied the consumers of this area with groceries, then probably twelve or less would be needed. The average sales of a supermarket are a little over $1,500,000, and computed consumption expenditures for groceries in the area are approximately $18,000,000.

Finally, the centres of the hexagons were transferred to the original map. The map of theoretical trade areas (Fig. 4) was superimposed on the distorted map of consumption expenditures (Fig. 3), and the position of the hexagon centres in the distorted cells noted. These centres were then relocated on the map of the study area (Figs 1 or 2). For example, a hexagon centre fell within the lower central portion of cell 10-11 on the distorted map of consumption expenditures. This was placed on a map of the study area in its same relative position in the lower central portion of cell 10-11 (Fig. 5). Distorted hexagons (six-sided polygons) were not drawn to represent the theoretical market areas. This was not necessary,

Fig. 6. Theoretical and actual locations of largest centres of grocery store sales in study area

Fig. 7. Theoretical locations adjusted to nearest commercially-zoned land, and actual locations of supermarkets in study area

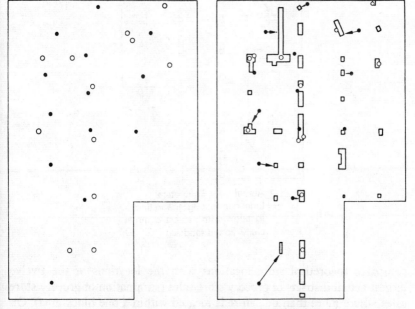

○ Actual   • Theoretical   ◄— Line connecting theoretical location with nearest commercially zoned land

for if twelve supermarkets are shown to exist in the study area at the theoretically derived locations, then the existence of their market areas, represented by distorted hexagons, would be implied.

Theoretical grocery store location and actual grocery store location

Figures 5–8 show the results of this method of theoretically determining grocery store locations. Figure 5 compares theoretical store locations with the locations of the twelve largest actual supermarkets, while Fig. 6

Fig. 8. Theoretical locations adjusted to nearest commercially-zoned land, and actual locations of largest centres of grocery store sales in study area

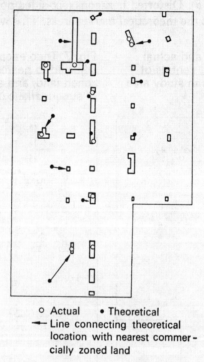

o Actual   • Theoretical
→ Line connecting theoretical
location with nearest commercially zoned land

compares theoretical store locations with the locations of the twelve largest actual districts of grocery store sales (summation of grocery store sales where more than one store is located within a one block area). On both maps the theoretical pattern and the actual patterns are rather similar. Measurements were made to determine the degree of similarity between the theoretical and actual patterns. The average distance of the theoretical locations from the actual locations is 345 yards for the case of the twelve largest supermarkets, and 328 yards for the case of the twelve largest centres of grocery store sales. These numbers were reduced to 282 and 249 yards when each theoretical location was adjusted to fall on the nearest commercially zoned land (Figs 7 and 8).[9] The 282 and the 249 yard figures approximate the distance of two city blocks. It should be noted that we are dealing with an area of over 12 square miles.

Limitations and conclusions

It is possible to conclude from the foregoing that by using map transformations of disposable income data a feasible solution to store location problems is available—that well-defined market areas for retail stores exist. This would be a hasty conclusion. There are a number of limitations on the confidence one may have in the methodology and the apparent conclusions.

First, the procedure was carried out for grocery stores only. Although grocery stores command more expenditures for retail goods than any other types of retail firm, and have a strong bearing on the location of shopping centres, one must be aware that this procedure, followed in the manner outlined above, would not yield as favourable results for most other types of firms. Nystuen has shown that the shortest and most frequent shopping trips are those for groceries. This fact leads one to believe that the market areas for grocery stores are rather definite and that monopolistic elements reflected in true convenience-type retail firms are operating for this type of establishment. The results of rather elaborate tests described elsewhere show that it would be most difficult to conclude that retail stores of any kind are truly monopolistically competitive.[10] For this reason we should be wary of applying this technique to other types of stores. However, an interesting possibility is related to the use of our knowledge of store linkages. If it should prove possible to theoretically locate grocery stores by use of this technique of map distortion, then our knowledge of store linkages (stores often seen in combination with one another) may be utilised to help explain the location of other types of retail firms.

A second limitation of the method is that a number of actual locations apparently are not 'explained'. 'Excuses' such as the inability to interpret partial six-sided polygons are readily available for this shortcoming in the technique, but it is felt at this stage in the development of thought concerning retail store location that 'excuses' are not called for. Certainly, this is a shortcoming in the technique; nevertheless, present research should point to refining explanations, and not toward subjective notions of 'explaining' the unexplained.

Third, the theory of the location of retail store activity includes notions of the rent-paying ability of retail firms.[11] The above analysis disregards rent. One might conclude from the above procedure that this factor may in fact be omitted when attempting an understanding of retail patterns, but again this would be a hasty conclusion. In determining the general location of stores, rents may be disregarded, but for a more refined, exacting study their inclusion would be necessary, since rents appear to have a direct bearing on the particular site chosen by the particular firm.

Fourth, although there is a rather limited number of patterns made from the centres of twelve equal-size hexagons that can be included on a map of the study area, still the hexagons might have been rotated somewhat differently, with a better or worse theoretical explanation resulting. Also, one might argue that the first hexagon constructed should have used some other originating point than the centre of the map, which is, of course, the centre of disposable income. If the theory were concerned directly with urban growth, then a starting point might be the location of the first grocery store established in the study area, or the first established supermarket of the twelve. The results obtained by using some other starting point than the one used might prove more favourable, but it is felt that the spirit of the theory would be violated since we are dealing with a static theory—a theory which is not concerned explicitly with change over time.

Finally, and probably most important, is the advisability of using this technique of a map transformation. Tobler, who clearly indicates the usefulness of map transformations for studying economic geography phenomena, warns the researcher to use this type of technique as an approximation method.[12] He points out that there are an infinite number of solutions; in the case presented the distorted rectangles could have been drawn in an infinite number of ways. However, it is felt that using the rules presented above, any researcher attempting the map transformation would arrive at a map not significantly different, in its general makeup, from the one presented.

The constraints limiting confidence in the above use of a map transformation indicate the need for designing a more comprehensive testing device. Nevertheless, the analysis did show that the map transformation is useful for the understanding of retail location, although it falls somewhat short, in this case, of accurately predicting the location of retail activities. A refinement of the technique might provide researchers with the needed comprehensive testing device.

Notes and references

[1] ISARD, WALTER, *Location and Space-Economy*, New York, 1956, pp. 254–87.

[2] NYSTUEN, JOHN D. in GARRISON, WILLIAM L. *et al.*, *Studies of Highway Development and Geographic Change*, Seattle, 1959, pp. 220–1.

[3] It would prove a more tedious undertaking to use as a test city one with an irregular street pattern or one using a more complicated land location identification system. It is suggested that researchers attempt using equal-sized areas whenever possible and practical, even though more work is involved. This system eliminates spatial bias and facilitates further research by such an efficient ordering of information.

[4] For example, see NELSON, RICHARD L. *The Selection of Retail Locations*, New York, 1958, p. 222.

[5] The author would like to express his indebtedness to the Tacoma City Planning Department for furnishing the retail store sales data. The estimated consumption expenditures for groceries in the study area are $18,356,151. The actual sales in the area were $17,105,713 for 1958. The difference is 5·2 per cent.

[6] The general form of this technique is demonstrated and analysed by TOBLER, WALDO R. in 'Map transformations of geographic space', unpublished Ph.D. dissertation, University of Washington, 1961, pp. 151–63.

[7] ISARD, *op. cit.*, pp. 271–3.

[8] Figures 4 through 8 contain thirteen theoretical supermarket locations. This is the smallest number of centres that can be included within the study area given the size of the hexagon and the requirement that the first hexagon be constructed from the geographic centre of the study area. The author rotated the hexagons with the geographic centre as the vertex. After each rotation of fifteen degrees of arc the number of hexagon centres falling within the study area was counted. Figure 4 shows the position of the hexagons when the smallest number (13) of centres appears within the borders of the study area.

[9] These figures were arrived at in the following manner: (1) For Figs 5 and 6, the distance from each theoretical supermarket location to the nearest actual location was listed. These distances were averaged. For each figure seven of the thirteen readings were below the mean. (2) For Figs 7 and 8, the distance from the adjusted theoretical supermarket location to the nearest actual location was listed; these distances were averaged. For Fig. 7, seven of the thirteen readings were below the mean, and, for Fig. 8, eight of them were below the mean.

[10] GETIS, ARTHUR, 'A theoretical and empirical inquiry into the spatial structure of retail activities', unpublished Ph.D. dissertation, University of Washington, 1961.

[11] For a review of some of these theories see GARRISON *et al.*, *op. cit.*, pp. 50–66.

[12] TOBLER, *op. cit.*, pp. 155–9.

Suggested practical exercise

The perception of distance

Draw a rough sketch map, centred on the present working location, which includes a number of local landmarks all situated within about one mile. Indicate roughly the direction and distance away that each of these is thought to be. Compare the distance and direction to each landmark drawn with the actual values from a suitable map (say, a 1:25000 sheet). No doubt some inaccuracies occur. Is there any systematic error? If so, can you think of some theory to explain it (for example, you may under-estimate distances to places you know well)?

Compare all the maps drawn by the class. Wide differences will occur. Can these be explained in any systematic way? What methods were adopted to decide upon the distances set out on the subjective maps? How many people thought mainly in terms of walking time, cycling time, bus fares, recollections of a map, etc?

Repeat the exercise for large towns within a distance of roughly fifty miles. What is the average of the distances guessed for each of the distant towns and how does this compare with reality? How can the discrepancies be explained?

6 Some predictive models

So far little use has been made of the word 'model' in this book. This is partly because it has been used a great deal elsewhere in recent geographical literature,[1] partly because for some people it conjures up frightening visions of pages of mathematical formulae, and partly because the need has not arisen. A model in this context is a simplified, and perhaps idealised, version of some aspect of reality. A toy train, a geomorphological tank, an aerial photograph, and a game of Monopoly are all models since each reproduces some, but not all, aspects of the reality it represents. Obviously these examples differ in their nature and aim. Some, the toy train, the tank and the game of Monopoly, are dynamic models in that they 'move' or 'work'. By contrast the aerial photograph is a static model since it tells us about reality at only one point in time.[2] All the models could be used to teach us something about the reality they portray, although some of them are more obviously designed for this purpose than others. While each model shares the quality of having been reduced from reality, the reduction is sometimes in both time and space (the game and the tank) and sometimes only in space (the toy train and the aerial photograph). In the reduction certain details are lost, although the model has in each case been so designed that it tries to reproduce the essential features of the reality and to omit those of minor importance. Nevertheless, a real danger remains that what has been omitted makes the model so different from the reality that the things we learn from it (for example, the speed at which a real train will come off the rails at a corner, or the ease with which one can become a property tycoon) may be seriously misleading. Despite this danger, which must constantly be borne in mind, models seem to be useful devices and they are often a positive pleasure to think about and play around with.

Most of what has been said applies with equal validity to the geographical models contained in this section. They are simplified abstractions from reality, devised to give us a fuller understanding of reality. Each model starts with a limited number of simple common-sense principles. These principles are combined in such a way that if we feed in certain information a prediction about reality will emerge. The models are therefore dynamic or working models, not static models, and in this respect they resemble the game of Monopoly rather than the aerial photograph. The validity of the prediction that is produced can be tested against reality in one of two ways. Either we can predict some outcome for the future and then wait to see if it occurs or we can take some information for, say, 1950 and 'predict' the position for 1960. The latter method is known as 'postdiction' and one of its advantages is that we do not have to wait to test the results, since 1960 has already occurred. If the postdictions are poor, we can refine the model until they become more accurate. If they are good, we can carry the prediction forward to 1970 with some confidence of the accuracy of the outcome.

It must be stressed that models of any type should be used critically. The predictions they produce (or the interpretations we make of them), can be inaccurate for a large number of reasons. The principles may be incorrectly perceived or the logic of the way in which they are combined may be wrong. The information we feed into the model may be too inaccurate. Our understanding of the meaning of the results may be seriously deficient. Any of these things, and a number of others, may produce quite erroneous appreciations of present or future events. In fact one of the essential things to keep in mind when using and assessing models is the extent to which the results seem reasonable. It is easy to be led astray by the results, perhaps to several places of decimals, produced by an elegantly formulated model which omits some common-sense but vital consideration.

One of the most useful yet simple models in geography is the *gravity model*. This seeks to predict the amount of human interaction of various sorts which will occur between two places. It is based on two simple principles. The first is that the likelihood of our making a journey to another place, normally a distant town, is positively related to the amount of activity occurring at that place. In other words, given that two towns of unequal size are equally distant, we are more likely to visit the larger one than the smaller. This clearly does not mean that we will *always* visit the larger one but simply that it is more likely that we shall, since almost by definition there is more there to visit. The second principle is that given two destinations of equal attractiveness situated at unequal distances, we are more likely to travel to the nearer town than to the farther. We shall not very often waste time and money on fares to visit the farther town if it offers us no more than the nearer. These two simple principles, generalised and refined in various ways, are the basic ideas in the gravity model of human interaction. It is a model which was borrowed by social scientists over one hundred years ago from the gravitational ideas of physical scientists. Although basically so simple it is still being used for a number of important practical purposes and there is no sign that its usefulness, or its capacity to develop in increasingly meaningful ways, is diminishing.

The paper by *Carrothers* provides a fairly full review of the development of the gravity model, and the closely related potential model, up to the mid-1950s. A great deal has happened to the idea since then and references to a number of more recent studies are listed at the end.[3] Carrothers reviews the first association of the physical gravity idea with problems of social analysis and mentions the early rules of migration formulated by Ravenstein. He then deals with Reilly's Law of Retail Gravitation (used in a recent important study concerning new shopping centres in northwest England)[4] and considers the idea that between any given set of regions there exists some 'energy' of interaction, the amount of which can be calculated. This has obvious implications for transport planning and the provision of routes between the regions. The concept of population potential is examined and it is pointed out that both gravity and potential values can be mapped as contours.

One important question that is given full consideration is the precise effect that distance is likely to have upon our decision whether or not to make a journey. If two equally attractive centres are at distances of five and ten miles from us, are we exactly twice as likely to go to the first as to the second? This would be the effect if each mile added to a journey reduced our enthusiasm for the journey by an equal amount. But perhaps each additional mile makes us more than proportionately less likely to make the journey. Or perhaps the fare for a two hundred mile journey is only 50 per cent more than for a one hundred mile journey. In both cases our propensity to make the journey will not have an exact inverse relationship with the distance measured in miles. In the latter case the likelihood of making the journey is dependent on the cost rather than the distance. In the former the distance may need to be weighted in some way, perhaps by raising it to a power the value of which will need to be determined by research work on observed journey patterns already carried out. The possibility that this distance exponent may vary depending upon the type of trip undertaken is discussed in the paper, together with the idea that the exponent may be related to the size of the destination.

The attractive force may similarly need to be expressed in terms more precise than sheer population. Some population clusters, because of the excellence of the services they provide, will have a greater propensity to attract interaction than others. Thus a large city may be more attractive than a smaller city by a factor that exceeds the ratio between their respective populations. An additional complication is raised by the idea of 'intervening opportunities'. Given that towns A and B are equally attractive to us and at equal distances from us, but that there are several interesting towns on the way to A and none on the way to B, are we more likely to end up at B or A? In practice this raises extremely difficult problems about what 'on the way' means, but it is nevertheless an important question to remember.

Carrothers is careful to point out the dangers of reasoning and predicting by analogy with the events of physical science. People are not molecules, but it is arguable that they share to some extent the property of being predictable in their aggregate behaviour, at least in the short term. The wise researcher, while using the very useful and stimulating ideas contained in the various formulations of the gravity model, will nevertheless always be ready to apply the test of common sense to his results and will be ready to juggle around with the formulation until it begins to produce results that look realistic. This is perfectly legitimate since the idea of a model is that it should represent reality. Any attempt to make the reverse apply is unlikely to lead to good predictions.

The paper by *Gould* uses Game Theory, a branch of mathematics, to predict the best possible choice of crops in an area of Ghana, given that the aim is to maximise crop yields. A second analysis in the paper deals with the problem of which strategy to adopt when selling cattle driven down from the north, given that the weather is unpredictable. Actually in both cases it is assumed that man is playing a game against the climate, which is assumed to have a vindictive nature since it is trying to minimise the farmers' returns. Certain simplifying assumptions have been made about reality in this model. For example in the first problem it has been accepted that the weather for any given year in this part of Ghana will be either wet or dry. The weather will not use intermediate strategies and the one which it will use is not predictable. The farmers have a choice of five possible crops and the average yield for each of the five crops for each of the two weather types is known from past experience. The problem is to decide upon a particular combination of crops to ensure that, no matter what the weather does, the farmers' returns from the land over a long period will not fall below a certain minimum figure.

This problem can most easily be solved graphically (see Fig. 3). The answer which results (a combination of hill rice and maize) can be understood at two levels. Intuitively, we can see that this answer looks reasonable because if the weather tends over the long term to be either wetter or drier then the farmers' overall yield will increase; it can never be reduced (since the solution is at the lowest point on the uppermost boundary of the composite line on the graph). The overall yield can never fall below that obtainable by planting a combination of 22·6 per cent hill rice and 77·4 per cent maize. For a more complete understanding of why this solution should ensure this result in terms of crop yield, it will be necessary to consult an introductory text on game theory or linear programming.[5]

The second problem of choice arises because cattle traders, driving their cattle down from the region of the Niger, have a choice of five possible markets in which to sell. It is assumed for this example that the climate tends to produce one of five weather types each year. This situation is interpreted as a game between two players. On the one hand there are the traders, who are naturally anxious to get the highest possible prices over a period whatever the weather does, and on the other hand there is the weather, which is rather unreasonably intent on minimising the farmers' cash returns. It is assumed that each player will play alternately and that the strategy each adopts will be decided upon in the knowledge of the other's previous move and with the aim of achieving the ends outlined above. The game, like time, is endless, but each pair of moves simulates the passing of one year. It can be seen from Fig. 8 of the paper that after a period of sixty years has passed two markets stand out as most advantageous for the traders. This result is radically changed (see Fig. 11) when a new pattern of prices is set out following the building of a new road between two of the markets. Thus the model allows the traders, in theory at any rate, to calculate the balance of advantages in the new situation and to choose their markets accordingly. As Gould points out, it would be possible to simulate all sorts of new conditions in a model of this sort, including the situation where information on prices and travel conditions early in a given year could be communicated back to farmers starting south later in the year.

The idea of playing games has frivolous connotations. But in this situation, where man is struggling to make rational decisions concerning the choice of crops and markets and where the safest assumption to make about the weather is that it will be as unhelpful as it can, any new research technique should be carefully examined. The problems of hunger in underdeveloped countries are so pressing, and the potential improvements in yields that can be brought about by a calculated choice of farming strategies so great, that game theory might well turn out to be a vitally important tool. The paper by Gould is almost unique in geographical literature in its use of this technique and it will repay careful consideration even if, as is quite likely, parts of it remain not fully understood until an introductory text on decision theory is consulted.

The paper by *Morrill* deals with certain aspects of ethnic distributions in North American cities. The problem of racial disharmony is perhaps the largest problem facing the world today, and in the big cities of the United States the confrontation between white and coloured elements has led to a disturbing train of events whose end it is difficult to foresee.

221

Morrill's paper does not pretend to examine in any depth the socio-logical and social psychological roots of racial prejudice. Instead it deals with the spatial pattern made by the distribution of Negro ghettos in various cities and concentrates on the processes by which ghettos expand into areas that were formerly occupied by white people. It attacks this problem by means of a *spatial diffusion model*. This seeks to represent in a simplified form as many as possible of the essential forces at work in the process of ghetto expansion and it combines these forces in such a way that postdictions are made about the areal extent of the ghetto at chosen points in time.

The paper begins with some useful general information concerning the movement of Negroes around the United States in recent decades. It also indicates some of the ways in which unfair discrimination is prac-tised against Negroes, both by individuals and by property interests. Morrill evidently believes that fear is the basis of this discrimination and it is no doubt due partly to this fear that white and Negro areas are so effectively separated in American cities. It is certainly a feature of all big cities in the United States that there is hardly any zone of transition between white and Negro areas and virtually no penetration of Negroes into white areas and vice versa.

The area covered by the ghetto is not static but expanding. Expansion is caused by a complex of factors including high rates of natural increase in Negro areas and high in-migration of Negroes and other minority groups from rural areas to the only areas of the city to which they can go: the low quality inner suburbs already occupied by people of their own race. The periphery of the ghetto is therefore being steadily pushed outwards as white people see the approach of Negro families to nearby blocks and move out. Morrill sees this steady expansion as a process of spatial diffusion and in the paper he has suggested a model which will represent the cardinal forces at work and which can be run to give some idea of the future speed and direction of expansion of the ghetto.

To make the model simulate reality as closely as possible, the rules under which it operates had to be carefully thought out. It is important to realise that it is from the framing and refinement of the rules, each of which must reflect an important principle operating in reality, that much of the benefit of using a model of this sort is derived. The real life pro-cesses at work include natural increase in the Negro areas, immigration into these areas by Negroes from outside the town, Negro movement outwards at the periphery of the ghetto (shorter movements being more probable than longer movements for a variety of reasons including the social impossibility of moving right out to a white suburb), and white resistance to Negro expansion. Apart from these, allowance should be made for the workings of chance or luck, just as it is in Monopoly and in many other games. Because of the inclusion of this chance factor, for which a random number table rather than a dice is used, the model is described as a *stochastic* (or Monte Carlo) diffusion model.[6] Models which make no provision for the operation of pure chance are termed *deterministic*.

The way in which Morrill has formulated his rules to reproduce these real life processes deserves careful and critical attention. Some rules, such as the growth rate by natural increase of 5 per cent every two years, can be taken straight from published data. Others, such as the way in which immigrants into the ghetto should be distributed between the various city blocks, must be devised in the light of what seems sensible. The likelihood that, in reality, movement out will probably be over a short distance is reproduced by means of a *migration probability field*. This is a simple device which can be visualised as a movable transparent grid with a chosen number of squares each of which is given a number of chances. The number of chances allocated to each square decreases with increasing distance from the central square of the grid. This central square is then placed over the point from which the movement out will take place and a number is chosen randomly from a range of numbers, each of which is represented somewhere on the grid. The square in which this randomly chosen number occurs, or rather the block in the city visible through the grid, thus becomes the potential recipient area of the out-migrant. Whether or not the move is made depends upon other rules governing the degree of white resistance to the move (if the block chosen in this way is in a white area) and the maximum population allowable in any block.

Obviously the actual rules adopted by Morrill are open to question. It is from this process of questioning, which must take place in the light of some reading about the actual situation, that perhaps the greatest teaching benefit from using this particular model could be obtained. By trying to single out the processes at work in the situation, and by trying to devise simple rules that reproduce the essence of these processes, we are getting near to the heart of analytical thinking. Criticism and refinement of the rules could perhaps take place at any level. We can all ask ourselves whether or not all the essential processes seem to have been reasonably embodied in the rules used. For example, a geographer at almost any stage of his training might have offered the suggestion that the effects of topography could have been allowed for in some way. This is not to criticise Morrill, who draws attention to this deficiency in his paper, but simply to show that a model of this sort can be thought through and added to on the basis of common sense alone and without any special training in quantitative techniques.

By running through the steps for various time periods Morrill is able to compare the predicted expansion for those periods with the expansion that actually occurred and to compare the final distributions in each case. The fit obtained was quite a reasonable one, using a variety of criteria for comparison, but the research does not end here. The study could be continued (assuming the research resources were available) by varying the rules or adding other rules until the predictions obtained approached much closer to reality. When the closest possible fit with reality is obtained we may begin to feel, still with some caution, that we are acquiring a fuller understanding of the principles at work in this situation. We may feel this because the ability to make an accurate prediction about a set of events is one indication that the events are understood.

There is, however, an important reservation to be made here. Making an accurate prediction based either on repeated observation of an event or, as in this case, on combining a number of abstracted principles into a model does not necessarily mean that a complete understanding has been achieved. Classical astronomers could predict the time at which the sun rose and set to within a few minutes. This did not mean that they understood why this occurred and why the times varied with the seasons. In the case of the Morrill diffusion model it is possible that other important principles are at work which are not incorporated into the rules and the effects of which may to some extent cancel out in this particular situation so that a good prediction is still achieved. The suspicion that important omissions of this kind have been made will be reduced as repeated experiments elsewhere give equally good predictions, but it would be imprudent even then to assume that we fully understood the processes of ghetto expansion. Socio-economic processes of this kind are so complex that there are bound to be important factors that are just not amenable to measurement and prediction. We can predict fairly successfully on the basis of repeated observation but it would be unwise to believe because of this that we fully comprehend the causal connection between events. Observing a correlation is not the same thing as understanding the causation.

Models of the type attempted by Morrill can be devised to simulate any spatial diffusion process. One could simulate the spread of information about a new farming technique (although in this case, as in others involving the spread of information, it is easier to think in terms of an era before the means of mass communication were invented). Alternatively one could simulate the spread of a particular type of plant into a new area, or the diffusion of foot and mouth disease. It may be profitable to spend some time thinking about the main factors operating in each of these situations—the nature of the source of propagation, the means of transmission, the likelihood of acceptance, and so on—and to suggest simple rules that might help to make a model to reproduce them. In this way one is concentrating on the essential features of some spatial process and this constitutes a big advance on the approach that is content to make maps of the distribution of phenomena at various points in time and to leave it at that.

Notes and references

[1] A recent and comprehensive review of geographical models is CHORLEY, R. J., and HAGGETT, P. *Models in Geography*, Methuen, 1967.

For the human geographer much of the material from this book is published in more manageable form in CHORLEY, R. J., and HAGGETT, P. *Socio-economic Models in Geography*, University Paperbacks, 1967.

[2] For a useful review and typology of geographical models see CHORLEY, R. J. 'Geography and analogue theory', *Ann. Assoc. Am. Geogr.* (1964) 127–37.

[3] See, for example, the review in HAGGETT, P. *Locational Analysis in Human Geography*, Arnold, 1965, pp. 35–40. Also OLSSON, G. *Distance and Human Interaction*, Regional Science Research Institute, Philadelphia, 1965; ISARD, W., *et al. Methods of Regional Analysis*, M.I.T. Press 1960, chap. 11; and HAGERSTRAND, T. 'Migration and area: survey of a sample of Swedish migration fields and hypothetical considerations of their genesis', *Lund Studies in Geography*, B, 13, 1957, pp. 27–158.

[4] Department of Town and Country Planning, University of Manchester, *Regional Shopping Centres in North-West England*, vol. 1, 1964, vol. 2, 1966.

[5] A number of possible sources are suggested by Gould. A recent introductory text is DUCKWORTH, E. *A Guide to Operational Research*, University Paperbacks, 1965.

[6] For another example of this technique see HAGERSTRAND, T. 'A Monte Carlo approach to diffusion', *Archives Européenes de Sociologie* (1965) 43–67.

An historical review of the gravity and potential concepts of human interaction*

Gerald A. P. Carrothers†

In recent years increasing attention has been paid by social scientists and city planners to the so-called gravity and potential concepts of human interaction. The reasons for this interest are not hard to discover. On the one hand, theorists are continually striving to discover fundamental relationships to help explain the structure of urban and metropolitan areas. On the other hand, practical planners are faced with the necessity of quantifying urban theories and of providing specific answers to problems of urban development. The gravity and potential concepts seem to have promise in both connections. They provide a basis upon which to develop theories of urban structure at the same time that they provide a basis with which data may be applied to aid in solving such specific problems as market analysis for shopping centre location, population and migration forecasting, traffic flow analysis, and allocation of land for residential, business, industrial and other uses. The purpose of this paper is to present, in a single convenient source, a brief review of the concepts as developed to date, together with a bibliography of source materials written in English.[1]

The basic concept of interaction

In general terms, the gravity concept of human interaction postulates that an attracting force of interaction between two areas of human activity is created by the population masses of the two areas, and a friction against interaction is caused by the intervening space over which the interaction must take place. That is, interaction between the two centres of population concentration varies directly with some function of the population size of the two centres and inversely with some function of the distance between them. In mathematical terms, one way in which the relationship may be expressed is as follows:

$$(1) \qquad I_{ij} = \frac{f(P_i, P_j)}{f(D_{ij})}$$

* Modified version of a paper presented at a joint meeting of the American Institute of Planners and the Regional Science Association in Providence, Rhode Island, 7 May 1956. The paper has been stimulated by the active discussion of gravity models at the several meetings of the Regional Science Association. The author is grateful to Walter Isard and to Benjamin H. Stevens for critical comment.

† Reprinted from *Journal of the American Institute of Planners* 22 (Spring 1956), 94–102, by permission of the publishers.

where I_{ij} = interaction between centre i and centre j;

P_i, P_j = population of areas i and j, respectively; and

D_{ij} = distance between centre i and centre j.

Stated in this way, the hypothesis is based upon the reasoning that: (1) to produce interaction, individuals must be in communication, directly or indirectly, with one another; (2) an individual, as a unit of a large group, may be considered to generate the same influence of interaction as any other individual; (3) the probable frequency of interaction generated by an individual at a given location is inversely proportional to the difficulty of reaching, or communicating with, that location; and (4) the friction against this transportation or communication is directly proportional to the intervening physical distance between the individual and the given location.

Early formulations of the concept

Probably the earliest known explicit formulation of the gravity concept of human interaction was made by H. C. Carey [16]‡ during the first half of the nineteenth century. He reasoned that social and physical phenomena are based on the same fundamental law, formulated as follows:

> Man, the molecule of society, is the subject of Social Science. . . . The great law of *Molecular Gravitation* [is] the indispensable condition of the existence of the being known as man. . . . The greater the number collected in a given space the greater is the attractive force that is there exerted. . . . Gravitation is here, as everywhere, in the *direct* ratio of the mass, and the *inverse* one of distance.[2]

After Carey's original statement of the concept it was apparently neglected and, until quite recently, reappeared only in partial form. An early partial formulation was made by E. G. Ravenstein [48] in 1885. Ravenstein was concerned with explaining migration and presented empirical evidence suggesting that migratory movement tends to be toward cities of large population and that the volume of movement decreases with distance between the source of migration and the 'centre of absorption'. The relationship may be described mathematically:

$$(2) \qquad {}_iM_j = \frac{f(P_i)}{D_{ij}}$$

where ${}_iM_j$ = migration from source j to centre of absorption i;

$f(P_i)$ = some function of the population of i; and

D_{ij} = distance between source j and centre i.

‡ Numbers set thus refer to the Bibliography, see pp. 237–241.

There was apparently no further development of the concepts until the late 1920s when E. C. Young [76] made a somewhat similar attempt to measure migration. Young hypothesised that the relative volume of migration to a given destination from each of several source areas varies directly with the 'force of attraction' of the destination and inversely with the square of the distance between the source and the destination. That is:

$$(3) \qquad \qquad {}_iM_j = k \, \frac{Z_i}{D_{ij}{}^2}$$

where Z_i = the force of attraction of destination i; and
$\quad\ \ k$ = a constant of proportionality.

At about the same time, W. J. Reilly [49] [50] postulated his 'Law of Retail Gravitation' which approaches the gravity concept from a somewhat different direction. According to this formulation, a city will attract retail trade from an individual in its surrounding territory in direct proportion to the population size of the retail centre and in inverse proportion to the square of his distance away from the centre. For any two cities competing for retail trade, the point of equilibrium on the line joining them, where competitive influence is equal, will be described by the equation:[3]

$$(4) \qquad \qquad \frac{P_i}{d_{xi}{}^2} = \frac{P_j}{d_{xj}{}^2}$$

where P_i, P_j = population of cities i and j, respectively;
$\qquad\ \ x$ = point of equilibrium on the line joining i and j;
$\quad\ d_{xi}$ = distance from city i to point x;
$\quad\ d_{xj}$ = distance from city j to point x; and
$\quad\ D_{ij}$ = $d_{xi} + d_{xj}$.

In the 1930s, an early sociological application of the concept was made by H. S. Bossard [12] [13], who examined the function of distance as a factor in marriage selection. Bossard found, from empirical tests in Philadelphia, that the number of marriages decreased as the distance between the pre-marriage residences of the principals increased.[4]

Formalisation of the concepts

In the early 1940s the gravity concept of human interaction was generalised by J. Q. Stewart [53 to 60] and by G. K. Zipf [77 to 83]. A return was made to the original formulation in terms of Newtonian physics, as first set forth by Carey, namely that the 'force' of interaction between two concentrations of population, acting along a line joining their centres, is directly proportional to the product of the populations of the two centres and inversely proportional to the square of the distance between them. That is, mathematically:[5]

$$(5) \qquad F_{ij} = \frac{P_i P_j}{D_{ij}^2}$$

where $F_{ij} =$ the force of interaction between concentrations i and j.

Following the analogy from physics, the 'energy' of interaction between the two centres, E_{ij}, which results from this force, would be:

$$(6) \qquad E_{ij} = k\,\frac{P_i P_j}{D_{ij}}$$

where $E_{ij} =$ energy of interaction between i and j; and
$\qquad k =$ a constant of proportionality, equivalent to the gravitational constant of physics.

Thus, the energy of interaction between any two centres of population increases as the product of the two populations increases, and falls off as the distance between the two centres increases. The total energy of interaction of a given region i would be the sum of the energy of interaction of i with each of the n other regions into which a given universe may be divided. That is:

$$E_i = k\left(\frac{P_i P_1}{D_{i1}} + \frac{P_i P_2}{D_{i2}} + \cdots + \frac{P_i P_j}{D_{ij}} + \cdots + \frac{P_i P_n}{D_{in}}\right)$$

or, more formally:

$$(7) \qquad E_i = k \sum_{j=1}^{n} \frac{P_i P_j}{D_{ij}}$$

Zipf, Stewart, and others[6] have tested and applied this formulation of the gravity concept empirically, measuring the energy of interaction between pairs of cities by a variety of characteristics such as telephone calls, bus passenger movements, newspaper circulation, and the like.

Stewart extended the physical analogy to include the concept of 'potential of population', which may be thought of as a measure indicating the intensity of the possibility of interaction. At a given location i, the potential influence, or possibility of interaction, with respect to an individual at i, which is generated by the population of any given area j, will be greater as the population of j is larger and will be less as the distance between i and j increases. As derived from physics, the equation which shows the population potential at i of the population of area j takes the form:[7]

$$(8) \qquad {}_iV_j = k\frac{P_j}{D_{ij}}$$

where ${}_iV_j$ = potential at i of the population of area j.

The total possibility of interaction between an individual at i and the population of all other areas in the particular universe under consideration (i.e., the total population potential at i) would be:

$$(9) \qquad {}_iV = k\sum_{j=1}^{n}\frac{P_j}{D_{ij}}$$

where ${}_iV$ = total population potential at i.

In calculating the total potential at a given location, it is necessary to include also a measure of the potential of the population of the given location with respect to an individual at that location, in order to account for the internal cohesive force of the location. In the above formulation, this is implied when $j = 1, 2, \ldots, i, \ldots, n$ (i.e., the total number of regions in the universe under consideration). In practice, the distance of the given area from itself (D_{ij}) has been taken as the average of the distance from the centre of the area to its periphery.[8]

Mapping measures of gravity and potential

In application, the gravity and potential concepts lend themselves to being mapped. In much the same way as a topographic map records lines of equal physical height, a map may be constructed to show 'contours' of equal potential. In a given area under study, total potential may be calculated at a series of points and plotted on a map of the area. Interpolation between these points produces lines of equal potential at desired intervals. From such maps, areas of different potential are readily discernible and interrelations between areas are easily visualised. Stewart [54] [58] [59] and others[9] have plotted such maps for the United States and other regions of the world. A similar mapping device consists of plotting contours of equal percentage above or below a given potential datum.[10]

J. D. Carroll [17] describes a technique by which a somewhat different aspect of the concepts is mapped. Carroll was concerned with describing the area over which urban centres have influence. As measures of influence, he used numbers of telephone calls and volume of highway traffic. Starting with assumptions of (1) a flat terrain, (2) urban influence proportional to city size, and (3) constant rate of change in the decline of influence with distance, Carroll erected at each urban centre a vertical axis, or 'pole', equal in height to the population size. Since influence is assumed to extend in all directions, with each of these poles will be associated a surface forming a 'tent' which corresponds, in plan, to the area of influence of the centre. Each tent is made up of elements which are described by the basic equation:

$$(10) \qquad\qquad {}_jU_i = k\,\frac{P_i}{D_{ij}{}^\alpha}$$

where ${}_jU_i$ = urban influence of centre i upon any point j; and
α = a constant exponent.

The plan view of the lines of intersection between the tents of the various centres will constitute a map of the areas of influence of the centres. Carroll carried out this process for twenty-one major cities in southern Michigan. He determined a value of 2·8 for the exponent of distance from empirical tests of telephone messages and intercity travel which he then used in a modification of Reilly's equation (4) to determine the points of intersection of the various pairs of tents. For each pair of centres two points were thus obtained on the boundary line where its influence on each centre would be theoretically equal. Through these two points Carroll constructed a circle which he took to be the area of influence of the smaller centre.[11] The pattern of theoretical boundaries of urban influence for the twenty-one centres was not unlike a set of trade area boundaries determined independently from field studies by the Michigan Highway Department [43].

A map of market areas in the United States for various types of manufactured goods has been prepared by the Curtis Publishing Company, using the formulation made originally by Reilly and developed by Converse.[12]

Modification of the distance factor

The distance factor in the gravity and potential concepts has been a source of much debate. Empirical evidence developed by Price [47], Carroll [17], Iklé [35] and others suggests that the impact of distance is not uniform and that its relationship in the basic equations (6) and (8) is not a simple inverse one, but one in which distance is raised to some power other than unity. Various exponents have been used as a result of empirical testing, ranging from one-half to over three.[13] T. R. Anderson [3] has suggested that the exponent is itself a variable, inversely related to the size of population. For instance, of two centres j and m of unequal population size $(P_j > P_m)$ at equal distances from a third centre i, $(D_{ij} = D_{im})$ the potential exerted by the smaller centre m at i would be more significantly reduced by the intervening distance than would the potential exerted by the larger centre j at i. Thus:

$$(11) \qquad {}_iV_j = k \frac{P_j}{D_{ij}{}^\alpha}$$

where $\alpha = f(1/P_j)$.

However, I would suggest that the evidence may also be interpreted in a somewhat different way: namely, that the exponent may be a variable function related inversely to distance itself, rather than to population. In this case, the interpretation would be that friction per unit of distance against interaction caused by short distances is disproportionately greater than friction per unit of distance caused by longer distances. For instance, friction against movement within an urban area is generally greater than that caused by an equal distance in the less densely developed space between two such areas. Or, again, an extra unit of distance added to a long movement is of less importance than an extra unit added to a short movement. Thus, in equation (11) the exponent of distance becomes $\alpha = f(1/D_{ij})$.

This latter interpretation would seem to the writer to be more logical for two reasons. First, since density of interaction is greater in centres of large population, friction would tend to be greater and the exponent might more logically be expected to vary *directly* with population size, rather than inversely. Secondly, any discrepancy in impact as population size varies, which cannot be accounted for by difference in size alone, would be better accounted for by modifying the population factor explicitly in the numerator, rather than implicitly through the distance factor in the denominator.

In reporting investigations of the relation of distance to migration, D. O. Price [47] has suggested that the function of distance is affected by the particular direction from the destination in which the measures are made, and that the distance factor of equation (8) varies accordingly.

Modification of the population factor

In calculating population potentials an energy of interaction for various countries and for various kinds of activity within a country, Stewart [52] [59] found that frequently an area would have a pull, or influence, either greater or less than would be expected from the simple formulations of the concepts. He concluded that population under one set of circumstances is not necessarily of the same importance as under other circumstances, contrary to the assumptions implied in his original formulation where a value of unity was assigned to the element in the equation equivalent to molecular weight in the physical analogy (thus eliminating molecular weight from the equation). By assigning values other than one to these weights, he sought to account for differences in degree of influence which result from different characteristics of the populations. When this is done, the basic energy equation (6) becomes:

$$(12) \qquad E_{ij} = k \frac{\mu_i P_i \cdot \mu_j P_j}{D_{ij}}$$

where μ_i = molecular weight of an individual in i; and
$\quad\ \ \mu_j$ = molecular weight of an individual in j.

Stewart interprets molecular weight in this context as a measure of the individual's capacity for sociological interaction. In one study [59] he assigned values of 1, 0·8, and 2 to the molecular weights of population in the North, the Deep South and the Far West regions of the United States, respectively. These weights were found to be consistent with various sets of empirical data, such as the flow of bank checks into New York from various areas of the country. This implies that an individual in the Far West has twice the capacity to interact as an individual in the North, while an individual in the South has four-fifths this capacity to interact, thus affecting the potentials created by the total populations in these areas.

This formulation corresponds to Dodd's 'interactance hypothesis' [27] in which he introduces variables other than those of population numbers and distance into the original formulation, by making them multipliers of the basic variables, in order to account for differentials in sex, income, education, and other characteristics.[14] The basic energy equation thus becomes:

$$(13) \qquad E_{ij} = k \frac{(\Sigma\phi_i)P_i \cdot (\Sigma\psi_j)P_j}{D_{ij}}$$

where $\Sigma\phi_i$ = weighting factors for population P_i; and
$\quad\ \ \Sigma\psi_j$ = weighting factors for population P_j.

But the application of simple indexes to the population factor in the equation may not be enough to account for observed differences in the influence of population in different circumstances. For instance, a larger population in one area than in another may of itself result in an influence for the first area larger proportionately than can be accounted for by the modification of population size by a simple multiplier. This may be the case, for instance, where agglomeration economies are present. Anderson

[3] [5] suggests the possibility of raising the numerator of the basic equation to some power other than one. But this still implies that populations of different kinds have equal influence, and it would seem more logical to the writer to raise the *individual* population elements to some power other than one, and not necessarily the same power (nor necessarily a constant power).

When the various modifications of the distance and population factors that have been suggested so far are added to the basic energy equation (6), it becomes:

$$(14) \qquad E_{ij} = k \frac{(\Sigma\phi_i)P_i^{\beta} \cdot (\Sigma\psi_j)P_j^{\gamma}}{D_{ij}^{\alpha}}$$

Adaptations of the basic concepts

The adjustments of the basic concepts described in the previous sections open the way for introducing different kinds of key variables in place of population and distance, in the formulation of the gravity and potential relationships.

S. A. Stouffer [6] has suggested such an adaptation in connection with measuring population mobility. He suggests that there is no necessary relationship between distance and mobility, but that the number of persons going a given distance is directly proportional to the number of opportunities *at* that distance and inversely proportional to the number of *intervening* opportunities. That is, the function of distance is not necessarily continuous in the formulation. Mathematically, the relation may be expressed:

$$(15) \qquad \frac{\Delta y}{\Delta s} = \frac{\alpha \cdot \Delta x}{x \cdot \Delta s}$$

where Δy = number of persons moving from origin to a circular band of width Δs;

x = cumulated number of opportunities between the origin and destination s;

Δx = number of opportunities within the band of width Δs; and

α = a constant.

In testing the hypothesis, Stouffer encountered problems of measuring 'opportunities', and Anderson [3] has pointed out the element of circularity involved in Stouffer's use of total in-migrants as a measure of opportunities.[15]

For purposes of developing models for projecting national and regional product, W. Isard and G. Freutel [39] consider income to be a critical variable and suggest the use of an 'income potential' measure, in which regional (or national) income is substituted for the population factor. They also suggest that the friction against interaction caused by distance is not so much a function of the intervening physical space, but rather a function of the cost of traversing this space. They therefore utilise a measure of 'effective' or 'economic' distance, in which physical distance is modified by transport cost. The basic potential equation (8) thus becomes:

$$(16) \qquad {}_iW = \sum_{j=1}^{n} K_{ij} \frac{Y_j}{D_{ij}^{\alpha}}$$

where ${}_iW$ = income potential at i;

Y_j = income of region j;

α = a constant exponent; and

K_{ij} = a parameter which differs from one pair of regions to another and which is some function of transport cost between each pair of regions.

Carroll [17], Anderson [5], and others have suggested that a time-cost measure of distance would be appropriate in many circumstances. This would appear to be particularly pertinent with respect to intra-metropolitan interaction where time of communication is obviously a critical factor.

In applying the gravitation principle to traffic analysis, A. Voorhees [69] uses time of travel as a measure of distance, classifying movement by mode of travel to account for differences in rates. At the same time, he suggests classifying trips by nature of destination (e.g. shopping area), measuring the size of the attracting influence of the destination in terms such as floor area devoted to sale of apparel.

C. D. Harris [34] has extended the potential concept to include a measure of 'market potential', which he defines as 'the summation of markets accessible to a point divided by their distances from that point'. He measures the markets in terms of retail sales and distance in terms of transport costs. Harris calculated generalised formulas for estimating transport costs between any two points in the United States and obtained measures of the market potential at selected points through dividing the total retail sales occurring in distance bands radiating concentrically from these points by the cost of reaching each band from the point under consideration. Thus:

$$(17) \qquad {}_iR = \sum_{j=1}^{n} \frac{S_j}{C_{ij}}$$

where $_iR$ = market potential at i;

S_j = volume of retail sales in region j; and

C_{ij} = transport cost from i to j.

Dunn [30] has pointed out that this procedure implicitly constitutes raising the distance factor in the basic equation (9) to a variable exponent since transport costs are a product of distance and rate, and the rate is a function of distance.

Harris [34] has also calculated 'manufacturing potential', measured by volume of employment, and 'farm potential', measured by numbers of tractors, in both cases for the United States. He has plotted maps of these various potential measures, which are comparable to the maps of population potential developed by Stewart.[16]

Anderson [5] has generalised the potential concept in such a way that the numerator may be identified as any given resource (including population) the distribution of which may be useful in describing the variations in intensity of potential of interaction which may occur among areas. In the exponent to which he raises the distance factor, Anderson includes a measure of the impact of technological innovation which will, in general, tend to decrease the energy consumed in traversing distance. His formulation may be expressed mathematically as follows:

$$(18) \qquad\qquad _iH = k \sum_{j=1}^{n} \frac{X_j}{D_{ij}{}^{\alpha}}$$

where $_iH$ = potential at i created by resource X in region j;

X_j = measure of a given resource in region j; and

α = a constant exponent.

Conclusions

As has been pointed out, the gravity and potential concepts of human interaction were developed originally from analogy to Newtonian physics of matter. The behaviour of molecules, individually, is not normally predictable, but in large numbers their behaviour is predictable on the basis of mathematical probability. Similarly, while it may not be possible to describe the actions and reactions of the individual human in mathematical terms, it is quite conceivable that interactions of groups of people may be described this way. This possibility is suggested by the phenomenon, observable in all the social sciences and in city planning, that people behave differently in groups than they do as individuals.[17] But it is important to keep in mind that, although the use of analogy in developing a concept may be attractive, it may defeat its purpose if strict and inflexible adherence is insisted upon. In this case, a fundamental difficulty arises from the different nature of the two basic units of measure involved: the individual human being can make decisions with respect to his actions, while the individual molecule (presumably) cannot. This does not imply that interaction of humans in large numbers cannot be described mathematically, but it does mean that the threshold where the power of individual decision-making critically affects the results must be determined before the concepts can be broadly applied in practice.

The various gravity concepts of interaction are only a very few of the many theoretical concepts being applied to urban and metropolitan structure. Even though the present state of development of the gravity concepts is inadequate, nothing in them is inherently inconsistent with other theoretical formulations.[18] A great deal of empirical investigation is needed (and is currently in process[19]) before the theories can be directly applied to problems of urban and metropolitan development.

Selected bibliography

1. ABRAMS, R. H. 'Residential propinquity as a factor in marriage selection: fifty year trends in Philadelphia', *Am. sociol. Rev.*, 8:3 (6/43) 288–94.

2. ANDERSON, THEODORE R. 'Characteristics of metropolitan subregions associated with intermetropolitan migration, 1935 to 1940, unpublished Ph.D. dissertation, University of Wisconsin, 1953.

3. ANDERSON, THEODORE R. 'Intermetropolitan migration: a comparison of the hypotheses of Zipf and Stouffer', *Am. sociol. Rev.*, 20:3 (6/55) 287–91.

4. ANDERSON, THEODORE R. 'Intermetropolitan migration: a correlation analysis', *Am. J. Sociol.*, 61:5 (3/56) 459–62.

5. ANDERSON, THEODORE R. 'Potential models and spatial distribution of population', *Papers and Proceedings of the Regional Science Association*, 2 (1956).

6. APPLEBAUM, WILLIAM, and SPEARS, RICHARD F. 'How to measure a trading area', *Chain Store Age*, January 1951.

7. APPLEBAUM, WILLIAM, 'A technique for constructing a population and urban land-use map', *Econ. Geogr.*, 28:3 (7/52) 240–3.

8. BEVIS, HOWARD W. 'Forecasting zonal traffic volumes', *Traffic Quarterly*, 10:2 (4/56) 207–22.

9. BOGUE, D. J. *The Structure of the Metropolitan Community, A Study of Dominance and Subdominance*. Ann Arbor, University of Michigan 1949.

10. BOGUE, D. J. 'Nodal versus homogeneous regions, and statistical techniques for measuring the influence of each', paper read before the International Statistical Institute Conference, Rio de Janeiro, 27 June 1955.

11. BOLAND, JOHN P. 'On the number and sizes of radio stations in relation to the populations of their cities', *Sociometry*, 11:1–2 (2–5/48) 111–16.

12. BOSSARD, J. H. S. 'Residential propinquity as a factor in marriage selection', *Am. J. Sociol.*, 38:2 (9/32) 219–44.

13. BOSSARD, J. H. S. *Marriage and the Child*, Philadelphia, University of Pennsylvania Press, 1940, chap. 4.

14. BRIGHT, MARGARET, and THOMAS, DOROTHY S. 'Interstate migration and intervening opportunities', *Am. sociol. Rev.*, 6:6 (12/41) 773–83.

15. BRUSH, JOHN E. 'The hierarchy of central places in Southwestern Wisconsin', *Geogr. Rev.*, 43:3 (7/53) 380–402.

16. CAREY, H. C. *Principles of Social Science*, Philadelphia, Lippincott, 1858–59.

17. CARROLL, J. DOUGLAS, 'Spatial interaction and the urban-metropolitan description', *Papers and Proceedings of the Regional Science Association*, I (1955); Also in *Traffic Quarterly*, 9:2 (4/55) 149–61.

18. CAVANAUGH, JOSEPH A. 'Formulation, analysis and testing of the interactance hypothesis', *Am. sociol. Rev.*, 15:6 (12/50) 763–66.

19. CHANDLER, W. R. 'The relationship of distance to the occurrence of pedestrian accidents', *Sociometry*, 11:1–2 (2–5/48) 108–10.

20. CLARK, PHILIP J., and EVANS, F. C. 'Distance to nearest neighbor as a measure of spatial relationships in populations', *Ecology*, 35:4 (10/54) 445–53.

21. CONVERSE, P. D. 'New laws of retail gravitation', *Journal of Marketing* 14:3 (11/49) 379–84.

22. CONVERSE, P. D. *A Study of Retail Trade Areas in East Central Illinois*, University of Illinois, Bureau of Economic and Business Research, Business Studies 2, 1943.

23. CONVERSE, P. D. *Retail Trade Areas in Illinois*, University of Illinois, Business Studies 4, 1946.

24. DAVIE, M. R., and REEVES, R. J. 'Propinquity of residence before marriage', *Am. J. Sociol.*, 44:4 (1/39) 510–17.

25. DAY, D. W. 'The mathematical determination of theoretical retail trading areas', unpublished Ph.D. dissertation, State University of Iowa, 1951.

26. Detroit Metropolitan Area Traffic Study, *Report: Part 1, Data Summary and Interpretation*. Detroit, July 1955.

27. DODD, STUART C. 'The interactance hypothesis: a gravity model fitting physical masses and human groups', *Am. sociol. Rev.*, 15:2 (4/50) 245–56.

28. DODD, STUART C. 'Testing message diffusion in controlled experiments: charting the distance and time factors in the interactance hypothesis', *Am. sociol. Rev.*, 18:4 (8/53) 410–16.

29. DODD, STUART C. 'Diffusion is predictable: testing probability models for laws of interaction', *Am. sociol. Rev.*, 20:4 (7/55) 393–401.

30. DUNN, EDGAR S. 'The market potential concept and the analysis of location', *Papers and Proceedings of the Regional Science Association*, 2 (1956).

31. FOLGER, JOHN, 'Some aspects of migration in the Tennessee Valley', *Am. sociol. Rev.*, 18:3 (6/53) 253–60.

32. GARRISON, WILLIAM L. 'Estimates of the parameters of spatial interaction', *Papers and Proceedings of the Regional Science Association*, 2 (1956).

33. GREEN, HOWARD L. 'The geographic use of point-to-point telephone-call data', *Ann. Ass. Am. Geogr.*, 43:2 (6/53) 169–70.

34. HARRIS, C. D. 'The market as a factor in the localization of industry in the United States', *Ann. Ass. Am. Geogr.*, 44:4 (12/54) 315–48.

35. IKLÉ, F. C. 'Sociological relationship of traffic to population and distance', *Traffic Quarterly*, 8:2 (4/54) 123–36.

36. ISARD, WALTER, 'Distance inputs and the space-economy', *The Quarterly Journal of Economics*. Part I: The Conceptual Framework, 65: (5/51) 181–91. Part II: The Locational Equilibrium of the Firm, 65 (8/51) 373–99.

37. ISARD, WALTER, 'Current developments in regional analysis', *Weltwirtschaftliches Archiv*, 69:1 (1952) 81–91.

38. ISARD, WALTER, 'Location theory and trade theory: short-run analysis', *Quart. J. Econ.*, 68 (5/54) 305–20.

39. ISARD, WALTER, and FREUTEL, GUY, 'Regional and national product projections and their interrelations', in *Long-Range Economic Projection, Studies in Income and Wealth*, Volume 16, by the Conference on Research in Income and Wealth. Princeton: Princeton University Press, for the National Bureau of Economic Research, 1954.

40. ISARD, WALTER, and PECK, MERTON J. 'Location theory and international and interregional trade theory', *Quart. J. Econ.*, 68 (2/54) 97–114.

41. ISBELL, ELEANOR C. 'Internal migration in Sweden and intervening opportunities', *Am. sociol. Rev.*, 9:6 (12/44) 627–39.

42. MCKEAN, KATE, *Manual of Social Science: Being a Condensation of the 'Principles of Social Science' of H. C. Carey*, Philadelphia, Henry Carey Baird 1870.

43. MCMONAGLE, J. C. *A Method of Rural Road Classification*, Report to the Annual Meeting of the Highway Research Board by the Michigan State Highway Planning and Traffic Division, January 1950.

44. MAYER, HAROLD M. 'Urban geography', in Preston E. James and Clarence F. Jones, eds., *American Geography, Inventory and Prospect*, Syracuse University Press, for the Association of American Geographers, 1954.

45. MAYER, HAROLD M. 'Urban nodality and the economic base', *J. Am. Inst. Planners*, 20:3 (Summer/54) 117–21.

46. MYLROIE, WILLA, 'Evaluation of Intercity-travel desire', in *Factors Influencing Travel Patterns*. Washington: Highway Research Board, Bulletin number 119, 1956.

47. PRICE, D. O. 'Distance and direction as vectors of internal migration, 1935–40', *Social Forces*, 27:1 (10/48) 48–53.

48. RAVENSTEIN, E. G. 'The laws of migration', *J. Roy. stat. Soc.*, 48 (6/1885) 167–235 and 52 (6/1889) 241–305.

49. REILLY, W. J. *Methods for the Study of Retail Relationships*. University of Texas, Bureau of Business Research, Research Monograph 4, University of Texas Bull. 2994, Nov. 1929.

50. REILLY, W. J. *The Law of Retail Gravitation*, New York, Reilly, 1931.

51. REYNOLDS, ROBERT B. 'A test of the law of retail gravitation', *Journal of Marketing*, 17:3 (1/53) 273–77.

52. ROETHER, RICHARD W. 'Population potential in metropolitan areas', unpublished M.C.P. thesis, M.I.T., 1949.

53. STEWART, J. Q. 'An inverse distance variation for certain social influences', *Science*, 93:2404 (1/41) 89–90.

54. STEWART, J. Q. 'Empirical mathematical rules concerning the distribution and equilibrium of population', *Geogr. Rev.*, 37:3 (7/47) 461–85.

55. STEWART, J. Q. 'Suggested principles of "social physics"', *Science*, 106:2747 (8/47) 179–80.

56. STEWART, J. Q. 'Demographic gravitation: evidence and applications', *Sociometry*, 11:1–2 (2–5/48) 31–58.

57. STEWART, J. Q. 'Concerning social physics', *Scientific American*, 178:5 (5/48) 20–3.

58. STEWART, J. Q. 'The development of social physics', *Am. J. Phys.*, 18:5 (5/50) 239–53.

59. STEWART, J. Q. 'Potential of population and its relationship to marketing', in Reavis Cox and Wroe Alderson, eds., *Theory in Marketing*, Chicago, Richard D. Irwin, 1950.

60. STEWART, J. Q. 'A basis for social physics', *Impact of Science on Society*, 3:2 (Summer/52) 110–33.

61. STOUFFER, SAMUEL A. 'Intervening opportunities: a theory relating mobility and distance', *Am. sociol. Rev.*, 5:6 (12/40) 845–57.

62. STRODTBECK, FRED, 'Equal opportunity intervals: a contribution to the method of intervening opportunity analysis', *Am. sociol. Rev.*, 14:4 (8/49) 490–97.

63. STRODTBECK, FRED, 'Population, distance and migration from Kentucky', *Sociometry*, 13:2 (5/50) 123–30.

64. STROHKARCK, F., and PHELPS, K. 'The mechanics of constructing a market area map', *Journal of Marketing*, 12:4 (4/48) 493–96.

65. ULLMAN, EDWARD L., and ISARD, WALTER, *Toward a More Analytical Economic Geography: The Analysis of Flow Phenomena*. Cambridge, Mass. Harvard University, Office of Naval Research Contract N5 ORI-07633, Report No. 1, June 1951.

66. ULLMAN, EDWARD L. and others, *Maps of State-to State Rail Freight Movement for 13 States of the United States in 1948*. Cambridge, Mass., Harvard University Office of Naval Research Contract N5 ORI-07633, Report No. 3, June 1951.

67. ULLMAN, EDWARD L. *Advances in Mapping Human Phenomena*. Cambridge, Mass., Harvard University, Office of Naval Research Contract N5 ORI-07633, Report No. 5, June 1951.

68. ULLMAN, EDWARD L. 'Human geography and area research', *Ann. Ass. Am. Geogr.*, 43:1 (3/53) 54–66.

69. ULLMAN, EDWARD L. 'Transportation geography', in Preston E. James and Clarence F. Jones, eds., *American Geography, Inventory and Prospect*, Syracuse University Press for the Association of American Geographers, 1954.

70. VINING, RUTLEDGE, 'The region as an economic entity and certain variations to be observed in the study of systems of regions', *Am. econ. Rev.*, 39:3 (5/49) 89–119.

71. VINING, RUTLEDGE, 'Delimitation of economic areas: statistical conceptions in the study of the spatial structure of an economic system', *J. Am. stat. Ass.*, 48:261 (3/53) 44–64.

72. VINING, RUTLEDGE, 'A description of certain spatial aspects of an economic system', *Economic Development and Cultural Change*, 3:2 (1/55) 147–95.

73. VOORHEES, ALAN M. *A General Theory of Traffic Movement*. The 1955 Past Presidents' Award Paper, Institute of Traffic Engineers, New Haven, Connecticut.

74. VOORHEES, ALAN M., SHARPE, G. B., and STEGMAIER, J. T. *Shopping Habits and Travel Patterns*, Washington, Highway Research Board, Special Report 11-B, 1955.

75. WYNN, F. H. 'Intracity traffic movements', in *Factors Influencing Travel Patterns*, Washington, Highway Research Board, Bull. 119, 1956.

76. YOUNG, E. C. *The Movement of Farm Population*. Cornell Agricultural Experiment Station, Bull. 426, 1924.

77. ZIPF, G. K. *National Unity and Disunity*. Bloomington, Indiana, Principia Press, 1941.

78. ZIPF, G. K. 'The unity of nature, least-action and natural social science', *Sociometry*, 5:1 (2/42) 48–62.

79. ZIPF, G. K. 'The P_1P_2/D hypothesis: on the intercity movement of persons', *Am. sociol. Rev.*, 11:6 (12/46) 677–86.

80. ZIPF, G. K. 'Some determinants of the circulation of information', *Am. J. Psychol.*, 59:3 (7/46) 401–21.

81. ZIPF, G. K. 'The P_1P_2/D hypothesis: the case of railway express', *J. Psychol.*, 22 (7/46) 3–8.

82. ZIPF, G. K. 'The hypothesis of the "minimum equation" as a unifying social principle: with attempted synthesis', *Am. sociol. Rev.*, 12:6 (12/47) 627–50.

83. ZIPF, G. K. *Human Behavior and the Principle of Least Effort*. Cambridge, Mass., Addison-Wesley Press, 1949.

Notes

1 For general discussion of the gravity and potential concepts, see, for example: BRUSH [15]; ISARD [36] [37]; MAYER [44] [45]; STEWART [58] [60]; ULLMAN [68] [69]; and VINING [70] [72].

2 Quotation taken from MCKEAN [42], pp. 37–8. It is interesting to note that this formulation is described by equation (5) and has not changed basically in the past one hundred years.

3 For subsequent tests and application of Reilly's formulation, see: CONVERSE [21–23]; DAY [25]; REYNOLDS [51]; STROHKARCK and PHELPS [64]; and VOORHEES *et al.* [74].

4 For further tests of Bossard's application, see: ABRAMS [1] and DAVIE and REEVES [24].

5 Note that Reilly's equation (4) can be put into this form.

6 For tests of Zipf's and Stewart's formulation, see, for example: ANDERSON [3]; BOLAND [11]; CAVANAUGH [18]; CHANDLER [19]; FOLGER [31]; and STRODTBECK [63].

[7] Conversely, the potential at j of the population of area i would be:

$$_jV_i = k\,\frac{P_i}{D_{ji}}$$

[8] See, for example, STEWART [54].

[9] For example, see ROETHER [52].

[10] See HARRIS [34]; and DUNN [30].

[11] The line of intersection between two such surfaces would not, in fact, be a circle, unless the surface of the larger 'tent' were horizontal where the smaller 'tent' penetrates it. Also, it is not expected that the boundary of equal influence would be a clearcut line, but rather a somewhat indefinite band. However, the line of intersection as determined above may be considered to represent the centre of this band and thus constitute a reasonable approximation of the boundary.

[12] See STROHKARCK and PHELPS [64]. For a further example of the application of the concepts in mapping trading areas, see APPLEBAUM [7]. For studies of mapping other aspects of the concepts, see ULLMAN and others [66] [67].

[13] As mentioned, Zipf and Stewart use unity and Reilly uses two. ISARD and PECK [40] have derived a value of 1·7 empirically. CARROLL [17] reports empirically determined exponents of over three. VOORHEES [69] finds values of one-half to three for various kinds of interaction.

[14] For tests of Dodd's hypothesis, see CAVANAUGH [18].

[15] For other tests of Stouffer's hypothesis, see, for example: BRIGHT and THOMAS [14]; FOLGER [31]; ISBELL [41]; and STRODTBECK [58] [59].

[16] For further application of Harris's approach, see DUNN [30].

[17] Cf. the 'fallacy of composition' as applied to economics by SAMUELSON, P.A. *Economics: An Introductory Analysis*, 3rd edn., McGraw-Hill, 1955, pp. 9–19, 237, *et al.*

[18] For instance, it should be perfectly feasible to construct potential measures for a set of hypothetical (or real) regions as developed by Christaller and Lösch.

[19] To cite only a very few examples of but one application of the concepts, the analysis of traffic flows, see current work by: the Detroit Metropolitan Area Traffic Study [26]; the Chicago Area Transportation Study; the Philadelphia Urban Traffic and Transportation Board; the Automotive Safety Foundation, e.g. [69]; the Bureau of Highway Traffic, Yale University, e.g. [71]; the University of Washington, e.g. [46].

Man against his environment: a game theoretic framework*

Peter R. Gould

Without cataloguing the many and various definitions of human geography by professional geographers over the past few decades, it is safe to say that most have included the words *man and environment*. Traditionally, geographers have had a deep intellectual curiosity and concern for the face of the earth and the way it provides, in a larger sense, a home for mankind. Much of what we see upon the surface of the earth is the work of man, and is the result of a variety of decisions that men have made as individuals or groups. Unfortunately, we have all too often lacked, or failed to consider, conceptual frameworks of theory in which to examine man's relationship to his environment, the manner in which he weighs the alternatives presented, and the rationality of his choices once they have been made. Underlining a belief that such theoretical structures are desirable, and that they sometimes enable us to see old and oft-examined things with new eyes, this paper attempts to draw the attention of geographers to the Theory of Games as a conceptual framework and tool of research in human geography.[1] Upon its initial and formal appearance in 1944,[2] a reviewer stated: 'Posterity may regard this ... as one of the major scientific achievements of the first half of the twentieth century', and although the social sciences have been relatively slow in considering the Theory of Games, compared to the widespread application of all forms of decision theory throughout engineering, business, and statistics, its increasing use in our sister disciplines of economics, anthropology, and sociology indicates a sure trend, fulfilling the extravagant praise heaped upon it at an earlier date.

The Theory of Games, despite its immediate connotation of amusements of a frivolous kind, is an imposing structure dealing, in essence, with the question of making rational decisions in the face of uncertain conditions by choosing certain strategies to outwit an opponent, or, at the very least, to maintain a position superior to others. Of course, we do not have to think in terms of two opponents sitting over a chessboard; we may, as geographers, think in terms of competition for locations whose value depends upon the locational choices of others;[3] or, perhaps more usefully, in terms of man choosing certain strategies to overcome or

* Reprinted from *Annals of the Association of American Geographers* 53 (1963), 290–97, by permission of the publishers.

outwit his environment. A good example of the latter is a Jamaican fishing village,[4] where the captains of the fishing canoes can set all their fishing pots close to the shore, all of them out to sea, or set a proportion in each area. Those canoes setting pots close to the shore have few pot losses, but the quality of the fish is poor so that the market price is low, particularly when the deep-water pots have a good day and drive the price of poor fish down still further. On the other hand, those who set their pots out to sea catch much better fish, but every now and then a current runs in an unpredictable fashion, battering the pots and sinking the floats, so that pot losses are higher. Thus, the village has three choices, to set all the pots in, all the pots out, or some in and some out, while the environment has two strategies, current or no-current. Game Theory has successfully predicted the best choice of strategies and the proportion each should be used, a proportion very close to that arrived at by the villagers over a long period of trial and error.

Man continually finds himself in situations where a number of different choices or strategies may be available to wrest a living from his environment. Indeed, without soaring to those stratospheric heights of philosophical, or even metaphysical, discussion, to which all discourse in the social and physical sciences ultimately leads, let it be said that to be man rather than animal is, in part, to be able to recognise a variety of alternatives, and in a *rational* manner, reasoning from those little rocks of knowledge that stick up above the vast sea of uncertainty, choose strategies to win the basic struggle for survival. The perception that alternatives exist, and the recognition that their specific value, or utility, for a given time and place may depend upon an unpredictable environment, about which man has only highly probabilistic notions based upon past experience, is clearly central to any discussion of man–environment relationships within a game theoretic framework. Thus, growing concomitantly with, and, indeed, embedded in, the Theory of Games, is a theory of utility intuitively raised, axiomatically treated, and experimentally tested in the real world.[5]

The barren middle zone of Ghana (Fig. 1), a belt which, for environmental and historical reasons, has a very low population density, has one of the severest agricultural climates in West Africa,[6] with heavy precipitation followed by the extreme aridity of the Harmattan, which sweeps south from the Sahara. A further problem is that the high degree of variability of the precipitation makes it difficult for the farmers to plan effectively.[7]

Let us assume that the farmers of Jantilla, a small village in western Ghana, may use the land to grow the following crops, cach with different degrees of resistance to dry conditions, as their main staple food: yams, cassava, maize, millet, and hill rice.[8] In Game Theory terms the cultivation of these crops represents five strategies. In the same terms, and to simplify this initial example, let us make the somewhat unrealistic assumption that the environment has only two strategies; dry years and wet

Fig. 1. The barren middle zone of Ghana of low population density and extreme variability of rainfall

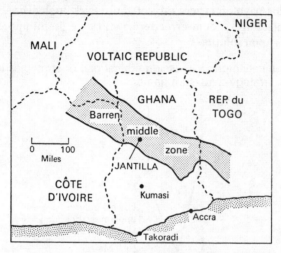

years. These strategies may be put into matrix form (Fig. 2), called the payoff matrix, and represent a two-person-five-strategy-zero-sum game, in which the values in the boxes represent the average yields of the crops

Fig. 2. Payoff matrix for two-persons-five-strategy-zero-sum game; crop choices against moisture choices

			ENVIRONMENT MOISTURE CHOICES	
			Wet years	Dry years
		Yams	82	11
FARMERS		Maize	61	49
OF	CROP CHOICE	Cassava	12	38
JANTILLA		Millet	43	32
		Hill rice	30	71

under varying conditions, perhaps in calorific or other nutritional terms. For example, if the farmers of Jantilla choose to grow only yams, they will obtain a yield of eighty-two under wet year conditions, but the yield will drop to eleven if the environment does its worst. It should be noted that the values in the boxes have been chosen simply to provide an example of Game Theory, but this, in turn, emphasises the close relationship of these methods to direct field work, for only in this way can we obtain these critical subcensus data. In a very real sense, our tools are outrunning our efforts to gather the necessary materials. We might also note, parenthetically, that extreme accuracy of data, while always desirable, is not essential in order to use Game Theory as a tool, since it can be shown that payoff matrices subjected to a fairly high degree of random shock by injecting random error terms still give useful approximations and insights upon solution.[9]

Fig. 3. Graphical solution to assign critical pair of strategies in two-person-five-strategy-zero-sum game

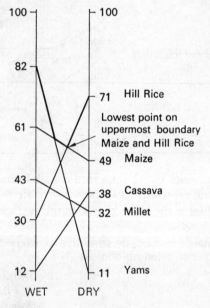

A payoff matrix in which one opponent has only two strategies can always be reduced to a two-by-two game which is the solution for the complete game, in this case a five-by-two. We may, if time is no object, and we like dull, tedious work, take every pair of rows in turn and solve them for the maximum payoff to the farmers; but, fortunately, we also have a graphical solution which will point to the critical pair at once (Fig. 3). If we draw two scales from zero to one hundred, plot the values of each of the farmers' strategies on alternate axes, and connect the points, then the lowest point on the uppermost boundary will indicate which crops the farmers should grow to maximise their chances of filling their bellies.[10] Now we can take this pair of strategies, maize and hill rice (Fig. 4), and by calculating the difference between each pair of values and assigning it, regardless of sign, to the alternate strategy, we can find the proportion each strategy should be used. Thus, maize should be grown 77·4 per cent of the time and hill rice 22·6 per cent of the time, and if this is done the farmers can assure themselves the maximum return or payoff over the long run of fifty-four.

These proportions immediately raise the question as to how the solution should be interpreted. Should the farmers plant maize 77·4 per cent of the years and hill rice for the remaining 22·6 per cent, mixing the years in a random fashion;[11] or, should they plant these proportions each year? As Game Theory provides a conceptual framework for problems where choices are made repeatedly, rather than those involving choices of the unique, once-in-history variety, the cold-blooded answer is that

Fig. 4. Solution of two-by-two payoff matrix to achieve most efficient choice of crop proportions

	Wet Years	Dry Years
Maize	61	49
Hill Rice	30	71

$$12 = 61 - 49 \qquad \frac{41}{12+41} = 77·4\%$$

$$41 = 30 - 71 \qquad \frac{12}{12+41} = 22·6\%$$

over the long haul it makes no difference. However, when men have experienced famine and have looked into the glazed eyes of their swollen-bellied children, the long run view becomes somewhat meaningless. Thus, we may conclude that the farmers will hold strongly to the short-term view and will plant the proportions *each year* since the truly catastrophic case of hill rice and wet year could not then occur.

It is interesting to note, simply as an aside, that solving this two-by-two matrix vertically tells us that over the long run we may expect dry years 58·5 per cent of the time (Fig. 5), if we assume the environment to be a totally vindictive opposing player trying to minimise the farmers' returns.

The solution of this little game raises some interesting questions for the geographer. Does the land-use pattern approach the ideal? And if not, why not? If the land-use pattern does not approach the ideal, does this imply a conscious departure on the part of the people, or does their less-than-ideal use of the land reflect only the best estimate they can make with the knowledge available to them, rather than any degree of irrationality? Do the farmers display rational behaviour in our western

Fig. 5. Vertical solution of two-by-two payoff matrix to yield proportion of dry years expected

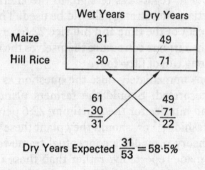

	Wet Years	Dry Years
Maize	61	49
Hill Rice	30	71

$$\begin{array}{c} 61 \\ -30 \\ \hline 31 \end{array} \qquad \begin{array}{c} 49 \\ -71 \\ \hline 22 \end{array}$$

Dry Years Expected $\dfrac{31}{53} = 58.5\%$

Fig. 6. Areas of cattle production and main route to traditional cattle markets

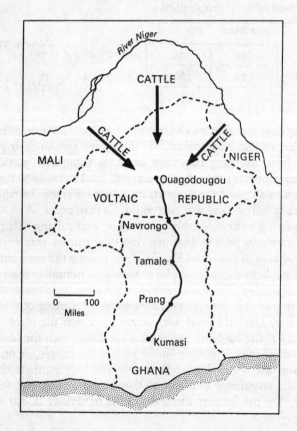

sense of the term despite all the warnings of the anthropologists about the illusory concept of economic man in Africa? If one were in an advisory position, would this help to make decisions regarding the improvement of agricultural practices? If the solution exceeds the basic calorific requirements of the people, is it worth gambling and decreasing the proportion of one or both crops to achieve a better variety of foods—if this is desired by the people? How far can they gamble and decrease these proportions if inexpensive, but efficient, storage facilities are available, either to hold the surpluses of one year to allay the belt-tightening 'hungry season' of the next, or to sell in the markets of the south when prices are high? Thus, the usefulness of the tool is not so much the solving of the basic problem, but the host of questions it raises for further research.

A further example from Ghana will make this clear (Fig. 6). For centuries the people living south of the great Niger arc have raised cattle and have driven them along the old cattle trails to the markets of Ghana.[12] The driving of cattle is a chancy business because, while man can overcome cattle diseases such as rinderpest with modern veterinary medicines, he cannot yet predict the very dry years in this area of high rainfall variability through which the cattle have to be driven to market. Let us assume that the northern cattle traders of the Voltaic Republic, Mali, and Niger have the choice of selling their cattle in five markets: Ouagadougou, Navrongo, Tamale, Prang, and Kumasi. Each market thus represents a strategy and the traders may choose any one, or a mixture, of these in which to sell their animals. Let us further assume that Nature, or the environment, also has five strategies ranging from years with intensely dry conditions to unusually wet years. Thus, the strategies available to the cattle traders and the environment form a two-person-five-by-five-zero-sum game and may be represented by a five-by-five matrix which indicates, for example, the average price of an animal in various markets under different conditions (Fig. 7). The matrix indi-

Fig. 7. Payoff matrix in two-person-five-by-five-zero-sum game; market choices against available moisture choices

		ENVIRONMENT AVAILABLE MOISTURE CHOICES				
		Very wet	Above average	Average	Below average	Intense drought
	Ouagadougou	15	20	30	40	50
	Navrongo	20	15	15	20	5
MARKETS	Tamale	40	30	20	15	10
	Prang	60	50	40	20	15
	Kumasi	80	70	40	25	10

Fig. 8. Solution by iteration of payoff matrix

CATTLE TRADERS MARKETS

ENVIRONMENT AVAILABLE MOISTURE CHOICES

										1	2	3	4		59	60	Total
Ouagadougou	15	20	30	40	50					15	65	115*	165*		2,060	2,110*	32
Navrongo	20	15	15	20	5					20	25	30	35		870	875	0
Tamale	40	30	20	15	10					40	50	60	70		2,045	2,055	0
Prang	60	50	40	20	15					60	75	90	105		1,875	1,890	0
Kumasi	80	70	40	25	10					80*	90*	100	110		2,065	2,075	28
	15*	20	30	40	50*												
	95	90	70	65	60*												
	175	160	110	90	70*												
	.	.	.	.	.												
	.	.	.	.	.												
	.	.	etc.	.	.												
	2,190	2,250	1,880	1,845	1,830												

Ouagadougou 32 $\dfrac{32}{60} = 53.4\%$

Kumasi 28 $\dfrac{28}{60} = 46.6\%$

cates that a trader may gamble upon the season being a very wet one, in which case he would drive all his animals to Kumasi; but, if he guessed wrong, and the season was a less than average one, cattle would die or lose a great deal of weight on the way and he would get much less in Kumasi than if he had sold them in another market such as Ouagadougou.[13] This, of course, is a deliberate simplification, for we are not taking into account the possibility of varying demands, the question of alternative local supplies at some of the markets, nor the probability of Ghanaian consumers substituting one source of protein for another, for example, fresh fish from the coast or dried Niger perch.[14] It might be possible to gather data to fill payoff matrices for other suppliers, but the situation would become much more difficult since we would be in the realm of non-zero-sum games that are, both conceptually and computationally, much more complex.[15]

Given the above strategies, what are the best markets the cattle traders can choose, and what are the best proportions?—'best' in the sense that over the long run the traders selling certain proportions of their cattle in these markets will get the maximum payoff. The solution of a five-by-five matrix in a zero-sum game is not as easy as the case where one opponent has two, or even three, choices. We do have, however, ways of choosing the strategies and *estimating* the proportions that should be used, the estimation being based upon a relatively simple iteration* which converges upon the solution and which may be carried to any degree of required accuracy (Fig. 8). In the above example, the iteration has been carried out sixty times, and by counting the number of asterisks in each row of a market, which mark the maximum figure in each column of the

* The procedure used each move by the traders and the weather to decide which strategy to choose is complicated to explain but relatively simple once grasped. The traders move first and, because the weather has not yet moved and they have to select something, they select Ouagadougou as a market. This gives them a return, depending upon the weather, of 15, 20, 30, 40 or 50. This row is set out below the basic 5 × 5 matrix. The weather sees that he can minimise the traders' return by choosing 'Very Wet' (a return of only 15 to the traders). The 'Very Wet' values are therefore set out as column 1 to the right of the basic matrix. On the basis of this choice, Kumasi offers the best return (80) to the traders and for their second move (to simulate the second year) they choose this market. The returns for Kumasi (80, 70, 40, 25 or 10) are added to the traders returns from Ouagadougou the previous year and this gives a total of 95, 90, 70, 65, and 60 (set out as row 2 below the matrix). The weather sees that row 'Intense drought' minimises man's cumulative return and chooses this strategy which, added to column 1, gives the values in column 2. Again Kumasi is the traders' best choice, followed by 'Intense drought' again for the weather. This procedure goes on for 60 iterations at the end of which the traders have chosen Ouagadougou 32 times and Kumasi 28. On average, therefore, assuming that the weather acts in a totally vindictive fashion, the traders cannot do worse than sell 53·4 per cent of their cattle at Ouagadougou and drive the rest through to Kumasi.—Editor.

Fig. 9. Proportional sales and flows of cattle prior to road improvements and trucking

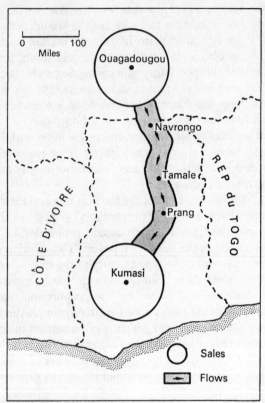

estimating process, we can calculate that the traders should sell thirty-two sixtieths, or 53·4 per cent, of their cattle in Ouagadougou and then drive the remainder right through Navrongo, Tamale, and Prang to the Kumasi market (Fig. 9).

Fig. 10. New payoff matrix indicating price changes in markets as a result of new road link between Tamale and Navrongo

		ENVIRONMENT AVAILABLE MOISTURE CHOICES				
		Very wet	Above average	Average	Below average	Intense drought
	Ouagadougou	15	20	30	40	50
	Navrongo	20	15	15	20	5
MARKETS	Tamale	80	80	70	70	80
	Prang	100	100	90	80	70
	Kumasi	130	130	120	90	60

Fig. 11. Solution by iteration of new payoff matrix

MARKETS	ENVIRONMENT AVAILABLE MOISTURE CHOICES					1	2	3	4	Total
Ouagadougou	15	20	30	40	50	50	100	150	190	0
Navrongo	20	15	15	20	5	5	10	15	35	0
Tamale	80	80	70	80	80	80*	160*	240*	310*	100
Prang	100	100	90	80	70	70	140	210	290	40
Kumasi	130	130	120	90	60	60	120	180	270	20
	130	130	120	90	60*					
	210	210	190	160	140*					
					etc					

$$\text{Tamale } \frac{100}{160} = 62\!\cdot\!5\%$$

$$\text{Prang } \frac{40}{160} = 25\!\cdot\!0\%$$

$$\text{Kumasi } \frac{20}{160} = 12\!\cdot\!5\%$$

Let us pose the question, now, of what might happen if a really strong transportation link were forged between Tamale and Navrongo, such as the remaking and tarring of a road, so that upon arrival at the Voltaic–Ghanaian border cattle would no longer have to make their way on the hoof, but could be driven in trucks to the southern markets arriving in much better condition even in the very driest of seasons (Fig. 10). The payoff matrix would obviously change, and we might expect very much higher prices to prevail in Tamale, Prang, and Kumasi for the fat, sleek animals, rather than the bags-of-bones that often stumbled into these markets in former years. Again, the payoff matrix can be solved using the iterative method 160 times on this occasion (Fig. 11), to produce completely different choices and proportions from the previous example. Now it is no longer worthwhile for the traders to sell cattle in the Ouaga-

Fig. 12. Proportional sales and flows of cattle after road improvements and trucking

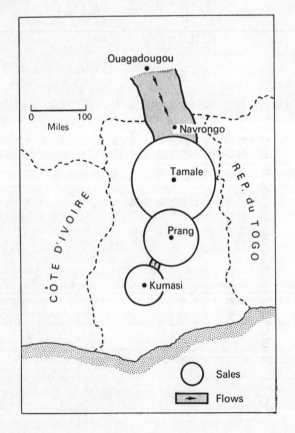

dougou or Navrongo markets, but sell instead 62·5 per cent in Tamale, 25 per cent in Prang, and 12·5 per cent in Kumasi. Thus, an improved road link, a visible sign on the landscape of a technological improvement, changes man's perception and evaluation of the same choices available to him before, and as a result changes the patterns of flows and sales (Fig. 12). Now the flow has increased over the northern portion of the route, and it has become desirable to sell portions of the herds in the Tamale and Prang markets, the increases at these markets coming from former sales at Ouagadougou and Kumasi. Again, solving the payoff matrix points up some interesting questions for the geographer. First, it raises the whole question of estimating the effects of improving a transportation link—what will the flows be before and after? Can we obtain payoff values from one part of West Africa and use them to estimate changes of flows in other parts? Secondly, the question, again: how close does the behaviour of the cattle traders approach that required to obtain the maximum payoff over the long run? Thirdly, what would be the effect of increasing the speed of communication so that cattle traders who started early in the season could inform others on the trail to the north about the conditions they find? And, finally, we should note the way an improved transportation link in effect extends the influence of one or more markets over others as the effect of distance is broken down allowing the demands of one centre to impinge upon another.

By taking two examples from the traditional economy of Ghana, this paper has tried to point out the possible utility of the Theory of Games as a tool of research and as a conceptual framework in human and economic geography. That such frameworks are needed is evident, for without these broad conceptual constructions in which to place our facts and observations it becomes an almost impossible task to raise and tackle, in a meaningful and lasting fashion, questions of man's equilibrium with his environment, his perceptions and judgments about it, and the rules by which he reacts at different points in time and space. The work of man is all around us upon the face of our earth, and is the result of men perceiving a variety of alternatives, subsequently limiting the range of choices according to their idea of what is useful and good, and *deciding* upon certain strategies to gain those ends. Thus, the whole body of decision theory, of which the Theory of Games is but one part, has an increasingly important rôle to play. Perhaps, in the same way that information theory has illuminated old problems of central-place structure, linear-programming solutions have helped our understanding of shifting flows and boundaries, and the theory of queues is throwing light upon problems ranging from those of the Ice Age to those of livestock production, the Theory of Games may also have a rôle to play.

SOME PREDICTIVE MODELS

Notes and references

[1] References to Game Theory in geographic literature are almost non-existent. What few references there are usually appear as peripheral points to a larger discussion on linear-programming solutions, for example: GARRISON, WILLIAM L. 'Spatial structure of the economy II', *Ann. Ass. Am. Geogr.* 49:4 (1959) 480–1. It should be noted parenthetically that much of the mathematics used in Game Theory is the same as that used in linear programming, and one of the hopeful things about the new ways of looking at old problems is that a common mathematics underlies many of the same theoretical structures. In terms of efficiency, a key made from a little modern algebra may often open many doors.
[2] The basic work, now revised, is NEUMANN, JOHN VON, and MORGENSTERN, OSKAR, *Theory of Games and Economic Behavior*, Princeton University Press, 1953. Excellent introductions are WILLIAMS, J. D. *The Complete Stratygyst*, McGraw-Hill, 1954; RAPOPORT, ANATOL, *Fights, Games and Decisions*, Ann Arbor, University of Michigan Press, 1961; while a complete critique and survey is LUCE, R. DUNCAN and RAIFFA, HOWARD, *Games and Decisions*, New York, Wiley, 1958.
[3] GARRISON, W. L. *Ann. Ass. Am. Geog.* 49 (1959) 480–1, reviewing Tjalling C. Koopmans and Martin Beckmann, 'Assignment problems and the location of economic activities', *Econometrica* 25 (1957) 53–76.
[4] DAVENPORT, WILLIAM, *Jamaican Fishing: a Game Theory analysis*, Yale University Publications in Anthropology, 59 (1960); an excellent case study drawn from detailed anthropological field work which provided the basis for assigning actual monetary values to the various choices presented to the village as a whole.
[5] The barbarous treatment of utility theory by those who fail, or refuse, to see the difference between a man declaring a preference because of the supposedly existing greater utility, rather than assigning a higher utility to a man's preference after it has been declared, did much damage at one time in the field of economics. The latter must always be kept in mind to avoid confusion; see LUCE and RAIFFA, *op. cit.*, p. 22.
[6] MANSHARD, WALTER, 'Land use patterns and agricultural migration in central Ghana', *Tijdschrift voor Economishe en Sociale Geografie* (Sept. 1961), 225.
[7] WALKER, H. O. *Weather and Climate of Ghana*, Ghana Meteorological Department, Departmental note 5 (Accra 1957, p. 37, map (mimeographed)).
[8] MANSHARD, 'Land use patterns . . .', pp. 226–9. See also POLEMAN, THOMAS, *The Food Economies of Urban Middle Africa*, Stanford, Food Research Institute, 1961.
[9] In linear-programming terms this would follow from the notion that the boundary conditions would have to change quite drastically, in most cases, in order for there to be a change in the mini-max point which would alter, in turn, the choice of strategies (see Fig. 3).
[10] This is simply the graphical solution to the basic linear-programming problem. The values, and the resulting slopes, have been deliberately exaggerated for the purposes of illustration.
[11] For a discussion of the necessity of a random mix of strategies see BRAITHWAITE, R. B. *Scientific Explanation: a study of the function of theory, probability and law in science*, Cambridge University Press, 1955, pp. 236–9.

[12] GOULD, PETER R. *The Development of the Transportation Problems in Ghana*, Evanston, Northwestern University Studies in Geography 5, 1961, p. 137.

[13] It has been suggested by Professor William Garrison that this problem might be readily handled in a practical sense by a standard linear-programming approach; a suggestion that would confirm Luce's and Raiffa's evocative comment on the Theory of Games that '...one can often discover a natural linear programming problem lurking in the background', *op. cit.*, p. 18.

[14] GARLICK, PETER, 'The French trade de nouveau', *Economic Bulletin* of the Department of Economics, University of Ghana (mimeographed), p. 19.

[15] Zero-sum games are so called because upon choosing a particular strategy one competitor's gain (+) becomes the opponent's loss (−), the gain and loss summing to zero. Non-zero-sum games are those cases where an alteration in strategic choice *may* raise or lower the payoff for both players. Two-person-non-zero-sum games can be handled using the notion of imaginary side payments. *N*-person-non-zero-sum games may best be described as computationally miserable.

The Negro ghetto: problems and alternatives*
Richard L. Morrill

'Ghettos', as we must realistically term the segregated areas occupied by Negroes and other minority groups, are common features of American urban life. The vast majority of Negroes, Japanese, Puerto Ricans, and Mexican-Americans are forced by a variety of pressures to reside in restricted areas, in which they themselves are dominant. So general is this phenomenon that not one of the hundred largest urban areas can be said to be without ghettos.[1]

Inferiority in almost every conceivable material respect is the mark of the ghetto. But also, to the minority person, the ghetto implies a rejection, a stamp of inferiority, which stifles ambition and initiative. The very fact of residential segregation reinforces other forms of discrimination by preventing the normal contacts through which prejudice may be gradually overcome. Yet because the home and the neighbourhood are so personal and intimate, housing will be the last and most difficult step in the struggle for equal rights.

The purpose here is to trace the origin of the ghetto and the forces that perpetuate it and to evaluate proposals for controlling it. The Negro community of Seattle, Washington, is used in illustration of a simple model of ghetto expansion as a diffusion process into the surrounding white area.

From the beginning of the nineteenth century the newest immigrants were accustomed to spend some time in slum ghettos of New York Philadelphia, or Boston.[2] But as their incomes grew and their English improved they moved out into the American mainstream, making way for the next group. During the nineteenth century the American Negro population, in this country from the beginning but accustomed to servitude, remained predominantly southern and rural. Relatively few moved to the North, and those who did move lived in small clusters about the cities. The Negro ghetto did not exist.[3] Even in southern cities the Negroes, largely in the service of whites, lived side by side with the white majority. Rather suddenly, with the social upheaval and employment opportunities of World War I, Negro discontent grew, and large-scale migration began from the rural south to the urban north, to Philadelphia, New York, Chicago, and St Louis, and beyond.

The influx was far larger than the cities could absorb without prejudice. The vision of a flood of Negroes, uneducated and unskilled, was

* Reprinted from *Geographical Review* 55 (1965) 339–61, by permission of the publishers.

frightening both to the whites and to the old-time Negro residents. As the poorest and newest migrants, the Negroes were forced to double up in the slums that had already been created on the periphery of business and industrial districts. The pattern has never been broken. Just as one group was becoming settled, another would follow, placing ever greater pressure on the limited area of settlement, and forcing expansion into neighbouring areas, being emptied from fear of inundation. Only in a few cities, such as Minneapolis–St Paul and Providence and other New England cities, has the migration been so small *and* so gradual that the Negro could be accepted into most sections as an individual.

America has experienced four gigantic streams of migration: the European immigration, which up to 1920 must have brought thirty million or more; the westward movement, in which from 1900 to the present close to ten million persons have participated; the movement from the farms

Table 1: Major destinations of net 3,000,000 Negroes moving north, 1940–1960

New York	635,000	Washington, D.C.	201,000
Chicago	445,000	San Francisco	130,000
Los Angeles	260,000	Cleveland	120,000
Detroit	260,000	St. Louis	118,000
Philadelphia	255,000	Baltimore	115,000

to the cities, which since 1900 has attracted some thirty million; and the migration of Negroes to the North and West, which has amounted since World War I to about five million, including some three million between 1940 and 1960 (Table 1). The pace has not abated. Contributing also to the ghetto population have been 900,000 Puerto Ricans, who came between 1940 and 1960, largely to New York City; about 1,500,000 Mexicans, descendants of migrants to the farms and cities of the Southwest; and smaller numbers of Chinese, Japanese, and others.[4] Economic opportunity has been the prime motivation for all these migrant groups, but for the Negro there was the additional hope of less discrimination.

The rapidity and magnitude of the Negro stream not only have increased the intensity and size of ghettos in the North but no doubt have also accelerated the white 'flight to the suburbs' and have strongly affected the economic, political, and social life of the central cities.[5] In the South, too, Negroes have participated in the new and rapid urbanisation, which has been accompanied by increased ghettoisation and more rigid segregation.

As a result of these migrations, the present urban minority population consists, in the North and West, of 7·5 million Negroes and 4 million others, together 12·5 per cent of the total regional urban population; in the South, of 6·5 million Negroes, 20 per cent; in total, of 18 million, 14 per cent.[6] The proportion is increasing in the North, decreasing in the South. Minority populations in large American cities are presented in Table 2.

Table 2: Minority populations of major urbanised areas, United States, 1960

City	Minority population	Total population	Minority %
1. New York City	2,271,000	14,115,000	16
Negro	1,545,000		
Puerto Rican	671,000		
2. Los Angeles	1,233,000	6,489,000	19
Negro	465,000		
Mexican	629,000		
Asian	120,000		
3. Chicago	1,032,000	5,959,000	17
4. Philadelphia	655,000	3,635,000	18
5. Detroit	560,000	3,538,000	16
6. San Francisco	519,000	2,430,000	21
7. Washington, D.C.	468,000	1,808,000	26
8. Baltimore	346,000	1,419,000	24
9. Houston	314,000	1,140,000	28
10. San Antonio	303,000	642,000	47
11. St Louis	287,000	1,668,000	17
12. Cleveland-Lorain	279,000	1,928,000	15
13. New Orleans	265,000	845,000	31
14. Dallas-Fort Worth	252,000	1,435,000	18
15. Atlanta	207,000	768,000	27
16. Birmingham	201,000	521,000	38
17. Memphis	200,000	545,000	37

Sources: Census of Population, 1960: vol. 1, chap. C, General Social and Economic Characteristics; vol. 2, Subject Reports: Nonwhite Population by Race.

The nature of the ghetto

If we study the minority population in various cities, we can discern real differences in income, education, occupational structure, and quality of homes.[7] For example, median family income of Negroes ranges from $2600 in Jackson, Mississippi, to $5500 in Seattle; and as a proportion of median white family income, from 46 per cent to 80 per cent respectively. The United States median family income for Negroes in urban areas is only $3700, as compared with $6400 for whites, but it is more than double the figure for Negroes still living in rural areas, $1750. It is not hard, therefore, to understand the motivation for Negro migration to the northern cities, where striking progress has really been made.

But the stronger impression is of those general characteristics which are repeated over and over. The ghetto system is dual: not only are Negroes excluded from white areas, but whites are largely absent from Negro areas. Areas entirely or almost exclusively white or nonwhite are the rule, areas of mixture the exception. The ghettos, irrespective of regional differences, are always sharply inferior to white areas; home ownership is less and the houses are older, less valuable, more crowded, and more likely to be substandard.[8] More than 30 per cent of Negro urban housing is dilapidated or without indoor plumbing, as compared with less than 15 per cent for whites. The ghetto is almost always in a zone peripheral to the central business district, often containing formerly elegant houses intermingled with commercial and light industrial uses. As poor, unskilled labour, Negroes settled near the warehouses and the railroads, sometimes in shacktowns, and gradually took over the older central houses being abandoned by the most recently segregated groups —for example, the Italians and the Jews—as their rise in economic status enabled them to move farther out. More than one ghetto may appear on different sides of the business district, perhaps separated by ridges of wealthy, exclusive houses or apartments.

The Negro differs fundamentally from these earlier groups, and from the Mexicans and Puerto Ricans as well. As soon as economic and educational improvements permit, the lighter-skinned members of the other groups may escape the ghetto, but black skin constitutes a qualitative difference in the minds of whites, and even the wealthy Negro rarely finds it possible to leave the ghetto. Colour takes precedence over the normal determinants of our associations.[9]

In the southern city Negroes have always constituted a large proportion of the population and have traditionally occupied sections or wedges, extending from the centre of the city out into the open country. Indeed, around some cities, such as Charleston, South Carolina, the outer suburban zone is largely Negro. Figure 1 depicts the ghetto pattern for selected cities.

The impact of the ghetto on the life of its residents is partly well known, partly hidden. The white person driving through is struck by the poverty, the substandard housing, the mixture of uses, and the dirt; he is likely to feel that these conditions are due to the innate character of the Negro. The underlying fact is, of course, that Negroes on the average are much poorer, owing partly to far inferior educational opportunities in most areas, but more to systematic discrimination in employment, which is only now beginning to be broken. Besides pure poverty, pressure of the influx into most northern cities itself induces deterioration: formerly elegant houses, abandoned by whites, have had ·to be divided and redivided to accommodate the newcomers, maintenance is almost impossible, much ownership is by absentee whites. Public services, such as street maintenance and garbage collection, and amenities,

Fig. 1. A group of representative ghettos. The dashed-line boundary on the Boston map indicates the inner urbanised area. Source: 1960 census data

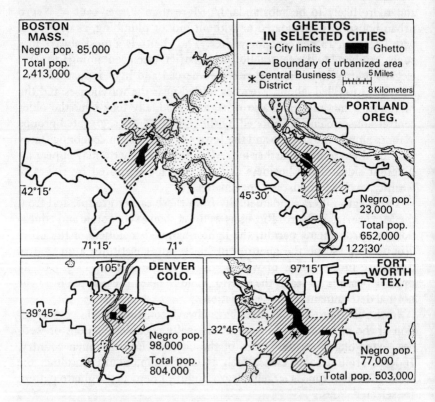

such as parks and playgrounds, are often neglected. Residential segregation means *de facto* school segregation. Unemployment is high, at least double the white average, and delinquency and crime are the almost inevitable result. A feeling of inferiority and hopelessness comes to pervade the ghetto. Most important is the enormous waste of human resources in the failure to utilise Negroes to reasonable capacity. The real cost of maintaining the ghetto system is fantastic. In direct costs the city spends much more in crime prevention, welfare payments, and so forth than it can collect.[10] The ghetto is the key to the Negro problem.

What are the forces that operate to maintain the ghetto system? Four kinds of barriers hinder change: prejudice of whites against Negroes; characteristics of the Negroes; discrimination by the real estate industry and associated financial institutions; and legal and governmental barriers. Naked prejudice is disclaimed by a majority of Americans today. Today's prejudice is not an outright dislike; it is, rather, a subtle fear, consisting of many elements. The typical white American may now welcome the chance to meet a Negro, but he is afraid that if a Negro moves into his neighbourhood it will break up and soon be all Negro. Of course, on a national average there are not as many Negroes as that—only one or two families to a block—but the fear exists because that is the way the ghetto has grown. A greater fear is of loss in social status if Negroes move in. This reflects the culture-bred notion that Negroes are inherently of lower standing. Some persons are terrified at the unlikely prospect of intermarriage. Finally, people are basically afraid of, or uncertain about, people who are different, especially in any obvious physical way. These fears combine into powerful controls to maintain segregation: refusal to sell to Negroes, so as not to offend the neighbours; and the tendency to move out as soon as a Negro enters, in order not to lose status by association.

2 The Negro himself contributes, however unwillingly, to ghettoisation. It is difficult to be a minority as a group, but more difficult still to be a minority alone. Consequently the desire to escape the ghetto and move freely in the larger society is tempered by a realisation of the problems in store for the 'pioneer' and hesitancy to cut neighbourhood ties with his own kind. Few people have such courage. In most cities, even if there were no housing discrimination, the ghetto would still persist, simply because a large proportion of Negroes could not afford, or would be afraid, to leave. Most Negroes achieve status and acceptance only within the Negro community. Usually Negroes who leave the ghetto prefer Negro neighbours; the risk is that this number, however small, is enough to initiate the conversion to full-scale ghetto.[11]

The Negro today suffers from his past. The lack of initiative and the family instability resulting from generations of enforced or inculcated subservience and denial of normal family formation are still present and are a barrier to white acceptance. The far lower levels of Negro income and education, no matter how much they are due to direct neglect and discrimination by the white majority, are nevertheless a strong force to maintain the ghetto. Studies show that whites will accept Negroes of equivalent income, education, and occupation.[12]

263

The strongest force, however, in maintaining the ghetto may well be real estate institutions: the real estate broker and sources of financing. It has always been, and continues to be, the clearcut official, and absolute policy of the associations of real estate brokers that 'a realtor should never be instrumental in introducing into a neighbourhood a character of property or occupancy, members of any race or nationality, or any individuals whose presence will clearly be detrimental to property values in that neighbourhood'.[13] Many studies have attempted to resolve this problem. In the long run, property values and rents exhibit little if any change in the transition from white to Negro occupancy.[14] Sale prices may fall temporarily under panic selling, a phenomenon called the 'self-fulfilling prophecy'—believing that values will fall, the owner panics and sells, and thus depresses market values.[15]

The real estate industry opposes with all its resources not only all laws but any device, such as cooperative apartments or open-occupancy advertising, to further integration. Real estate and home-building industries base this policy on the desirability of neighbourhood homogeneity and compatibility. Perhaps underlying the collective action is the fear of the individual real estate broker that if he introduces a Negro into a white area he will be penalised by withdrawal of business. There is, then, a real business risk to the individual broker in a policy of integration, if none to the industry as a whole. Segregation is maintained by refusal of real estate brokers even to show, let alone sell, houses to Negroes in white areas. Countless devices are used: quoting excessive prices, saying the house is already sold, demanding unfair down payments, removing 'For sale' signs, not keeping appointments, and so on. Even if the Negro finds someone willing to sell him a house in a white area, financing may remain a barrier. Although his income may be sufficient, the bank or savings institution often refuses to provide financing from a fear of Negro income instability, and of retaliatory withdrawal of deposits by whites. If financing is offered, the terms may be prohibitive. Similar circumstances may also result when a white attempts to buy a house—for *his* residence—in a heavily minority area.

Through the years many legal procedures have been used to maintain segregation. Early in the century races were zoned to certain areas, but these laws were abolished by the courts in 1917. The restrictive covenant, in which the transfer of property contained a promise not to sell to minorities, became the vehicle and stood as legal until 1948, since when more subtle and extralegal restrictions have been used.

Until 1949 the federal government was a strong supporter of residential segregation, since the Federal Housing Administration required racial homogeneity in housing it financed or insured. As late as 1963, when the President by Executive order forbade discrimination in FHA-financed housing, the old philosophy still prevailed in most areas. Finally, many states, and not just those in the South, still encourage separation. Even in the few states with laws against discrimination in housing, the combined forces for maintaining segregation have proved by far the stronger.

The process of ghetto expansion

The Negro community in the North has grown so rapidly in the last forty years, almost doubling in every decade, that even the subdivision of houses cannot accommodate the newcomers. How does the ghetto expand? Along its edge the white area is also fairly old and perhaps deteriorating. Many whites would be considering a move to the suburbs even if the ghetto were not there, and fears of deterioration of schools and services, and the feeling that all the other whites will move out, reinforce their inclination to move. Individual owners, especially in blocks adjoining the ghetto, may become anxious to sell. Pressure of Negro buyers and fleeing white residents, who see the solid ghetto a block or two away, combine to scare off potential white purchasers; the owner's resistance gradually weakens; and the transfer is made.

The rôle of proximity is crucial. On adjacent blocks the only buyers will be Negroes, but five or six blocks away white buyers will still be the rule. In a typical ghetto fringe in Philadelphia the proportion of white buyers climbed from less than 4 per cent adjacent to the ghetto itself to 100 per cent five to seven blocks away.[16] Figure 2 illustrates the great concentration of initial entry of new street fronts in a band of two or three blocks around a ghetto. The 'break' zone contains 5 per cent or fewer Negroes, but 60 per cent of the purchases are by Negroes. Typically, a white on the edge does not mind one or two Negroes on the block or across the street, but if a Negro moves next door the white is likely to move out. He is replaced by a Negro, and the evacuation-replacement process continues until the block has been solidly transferred from white to Negro residence. Expansion of the ghetto is thus a block-by-block total transition.

In this process the real estate agent is also operative. If the demand for Negro housing can be met in the area adjacent to the ghetto, pressure to move elsewhere in the city will diminish. The real estate industry thus strongly supports the gradual transition along the periphery. After the initial break the real estate broker encourages whites to sell. The transition is often orderly, but the unscrupulous dealer sometimes encourages panic selling at deflated prices, purchasing the properties himself and

Fig. 2. Distribution of Negro purchases on the edge of the ghetto, showing initial entry of street fronts, 1955. Adapted from diagram in Rapkin and Grigsby, *The Demand for Housing in Racially Mixed Areas* (see note 11), p. 76

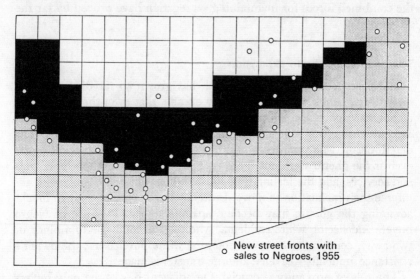

o New street fronts with sales to Negroes, 1955

		Number of white purchases	Percent of total purchases	Percent of area negro
	Area 1	8	3·9	32
	Area 2	26	4·3	16
	Area 3	65	40·6	5
	Area 4	72	98·7	1
	Area 5	112	100·0	< 1

reselling them to Negroes for windfall profits. The probability of finding a white seller is high in the blocks adjacent to the ghetto but falls off rapidly at greater distances, as whites try to maintain familiar neighbourhood patterns and conceive this to be possible if the Negro proportion can be kept small. The process of transition is destructive to both groups, separately and together. Whites are in a sense 'forced' to sell, move, and see their neighbourhoods disband, and Negroes are forced to remain isolated; and total transition reinforces prejudice and hinders healthy contact.

Spread of the Negro ghetto can be described as a *spatial diffusion* process, in which Negro migrants gradually penetrate the surrounding white area. From some origin, a block-by-block substitution or diffusion of a new condition—that is, Negro for white occupancy—takes place. The Negro is the active agent; he can move easily within the ghetto and can, though with difficulty, 'pioneer' outside it. The white is passive, an agent of resistance or inertia. Resistance against escape of Negroes from the ghetto takes two forms: rebuff of attempts to buy; and diminishing willingness to sell with increasing distance from areas or blocks that already have Negroes. On the average the Negro will have to try more than once to consummate a sale, or, conversely, the owner will have to be approached by more than one buyer. Once the block is broken, however, resistance falls markedly, and transition begins. Although a complete model would take into account that a few whites continue to purchase in transition areas, the rate is insufficient, the net flow clearcut and the transition inevitable.

The proposed diffusion model is of the probabilistic simulation type.[17] It is probabilistic rather than deterministic for several reasons. We do not have sufficient definite information concerning the motivations for specific house-to-house moves of particular persons, but only general ideas concerning the likelihood of movement and how far. We are not dealing with a large aggregate of migrants, but with only a few individuals in a short period of time in a small area. If we had a thousand migrants, we could safely predict how many would move how far, but at the micro-level a probabilistic approach is required to evaluate individual decisions in the face of a complex of possible choices. Rather than determine that a specific migrant moves from one particular house to another, we find the probability of a typical migrant's move from a block to any and all other blocks, and we use random numbers to decide which destination, among the many possible, he chooses. We thus obtain a spatial pattern of moves, which spreads settlement into new blocks and intensifies it in old blocks.

The model is simulated rather than 'real' because it does not purport to predict individual behaviour of actual people, but to simulate or pretend moves for typical households. Simulation is a valuable technique in science and technology, in which a model is constructed to depict artificially certain *major* features of some real process.

The simulation of diffusion model is important in biology, in rural and general sociology, and in communications, and has been used in geography.[18] It is an ideal vehicle for the characteristics of ghetto expansion —a process of growth in time, concerning behaviour of small groups in small areas in small units of time, in which a powerful element of uncertainty remains, even though the general parameters of the model tend to channel the results. This randomness is evident in the real situation, since we observe that the ghetto, like a rumour or an innovation, does not progress evenly and smoothly in all directions but exhibits an uneven edge and moves at different rates in different directions, here advancing from block to block, there jumping over an obstacle.

We do not expect the simulated patterns to match precisely the actual patterns. We do want the model to generate a pattern of expansion that corresponds in its characteristics to the real pattern, and we can satisfy ourselves of the correspondence by visual and statistical tests. The purpose and hope are to discover and illustrate the nature of the ghetto expansion process, in full knowledge that the detail of the ultimate step is omitted—how the actual individual decides between his specific alternatives. The omission is justified, because we know that the combined effect of many individual decisions can often be described by a random process. The real test here is whether the spread, over a period of time, has the right extent, intensity, solidity or lack of it, and so on.

The model

A model of ghetto expansion must incorporate several elements: natural increase of the Negro population; Negro immigration into the ghetto; the nature of the resistance to Negro out-migration and its relation to distance; land values and housing characteristics; and the population size limits of destination blocks.

Beginning with the residential pattern at a particular time (in the Seattle example, 1940), migration and the spread of Negro settlement are simulated for ten two-year periods through 1960. The steps are as follows.

A. Taking into account natural increase for each period of the Negro population resident in the Seattle ghetto, at the observed rate of 5 per cent every two years.

B. Assigning immigrants who enter the study area from outside at the observed mean rate of 10 per cent every two years of the Negro population at the beginning of a period. These are assigned by random numbers, the probability that an area will be chosen being proportional to its present Negro population. Presumably, immigrants entering the area will find it easier to live, at least temporarily, and will find opportunities in houses or apartments or with friends, in approximate reflection of the number of Negro units available. After initial residence in the ghetto, the model allows these immigrants to participate in further migration.

C. Assigning internal migrants, at the rate of 20 per cent of the Negro households (including natural increase and immigration) of each block every two years, in the following manner:

1. Each would-be migrant behaves according to a migration probability field (Fig. 3) superimposed over his block. This migration probability field can be shifted about so that each would-be migrant can in turn be regarded as located at the position indicated by X. The

Fig. 3 (left) The migration probability field

Fig. 4 (upper right). Negro residents at start of period

Fig. 5 (centre). Distribution of immigrants. Tally marks indicate entry into appropriate blocks

Fig. 6 (lower right). Movement of migrants from three sample blocks. Large figures, resident Negroes; italic figures, number of migrants; broken lines, contact only; solid lines, actual moves

Fig. 3

1	2	3	4	5	6	7	8	9
10	11	12	13	14–15	16	17	18	19
20	21	22	23	24–25	26	27	28	29
30	31	32	33–34	35–37	38–39	40	41	42
43	44–45	46–47	48–50	X	51–53	54–55	56–57	58
59	60	61	62–63	64–66	67–68	69	70	71
72	73	74	75	76–77	78	79	80	81
82	83	84	85	86–87	88	89	90	91
92	93	94	95	96	97	98	99	00

Fig. 4

		2	2		
1	5	10	10	5	1
5	10	15	15	15	4

Fig. 5

	1-2	3-4			
5	6-10 „	11-20 „	21-30	31-35	36
37-41	42-51 „	52-66 „	67-81 ,	82-96 „	97-00

Fig. 6

numbers in the blocks show where the migrant is to move, depending on which number is selected for him in the manner described below. Blocks adjoining position X have three numbers (for example, 48–50); more distant blocks have two numbers (for example, 54–55); and the most distant have one number (for example, 98). Since 100 numbers are used, the total number of these numbers used in any one block may be regarded as the probability, expressed as a percentage, that any one migrant will move there. Thus a movable probability field, or information field, such as this states the probabilities of a migrant for moving any distance in any direction from his original block. Probability fields are often derived, as this one was, from empirical observations of migration distances. That is, if we look at a large number of moves, their lengths follow a simple frequency distribution, in which the probability of moving declines as distance from the home block increases. Such probabilities reflect the obvious fact of decreasing likelihood of knowing about opportunities at greater and greater distances from home. Thus the probability is higher that a prospective migrant will move to adjacent blocks than to more distant ones. The probability field provides a mechanism for incorporating this empirical knowledge in a model.

2. Randomly selected numbers, as many as there are migrants, are used to choose specific destinations, according to these probabilities, as will be illustrated below. The probability field as such makes it as likely for a Negro family to move into a white area as to move within the ghetto. A method is needed to take into account the differential resistance of Negro areas, and of different kinds or qualities of white areas, to Negro migration. Modification of the probability field is accomplished by the following procedures.

(a) If a random number indicates a block that already contains Negroes, the move is made immediately (no resistance). (b) If a random number indicates a block with no Negroes, the fact of contact is registered, but no move is made. (c) If, however, additional numbers indicate the same block contacted in (b), in the same or the next two-year period, and from whatever location, then the move is made. This provides a means for the gradual penetration of new areas, after some persistence by Negroes and resistance by whites. Under such a rule, the majority of Negro contacts into white areas will not be followed by other contacts soon enough, and no migration takes place. In the actual study area chosen, it was found that resistance to Negro entry was great to the west, requiring that a move be allowed there only after three contacts, if the simulated rate of expansion was to match the observed rate. This is an area of apartments and high-value houses. To the north and east, during this period, resistance varied. At times initial contacts ended in successful moves and transition was rapid; at other times a second contact was required. These facts were incorporated into the operation of this phase of the model.

D. There is a limit (based on zoning and lot size) to the number of families that may live on a block. Thus when the population, after natural increase and immigration, temporarily exceeds this limit, the surplus must be moved according to the procedures above, Obviously, in the internal-migration phase no moves are allowed to blocks that are already filled. The entire process is repeated for the next and subsequent time periods.

Hypothetical example of the model

Immigration (A and B). Let us assume at the start that the total Negro population—that is, the number of families—including natural increase is one hundred, distributed spatially as in Fig. 4. Here the numbers indicate the number of families in each block. Ten immigrant families (10 per cent) enter from outside. The probability of their moving to any of the blocks is proportional to the block's population and here, then, is the same in percentage as the population is in number. In order that we may use random numbers to obtain a location for each immigrant family, the probabilities are first accumulated as whole integers, from 1 to 100, as illustrated in Fig. 5. That is, each original family is assigned a number. Thus the third block from the left in the second row has two of the one hundred families, identified by the numbers 1 and 2, and therefore has a 2 per cent chance of being chosen as a destination by an immigrant family. The range of integral numbers 1–2 corresponds to these chances. The bottom lefthand block has a 5 per cent probability, as the five numbers 37–41 for the families now living there indicate. If, then, the random number 1 or 2, representing an immigrant family, comes up, that family will move to the third block in the second row. For the ten immigrant families we need ten random numbers. Assume that from a table of random numbers we obtain, for example, the numbers 91, 62, 17, 08, 82, 51, 47, 77, 11, and 56. The first number, 91, falls in the range of probabilities for the next to the last block in the bottom row. We place an immigrant family in that block. The second number, 62, places an immigrant family in the third block from the left in the bottom row. This process is continued until all ten random numbers are used. The final distribution of immigrant families is shown by the small tally marks in various blocks in Fig. 5. The population of blocks after this immigration is shown in Fig. 6. Here the large numerals indicate the number of families now in the blocks. It should be made clear that the migrants could not have been assigned exactly proportional to population, because there are not enough whole migrants to go around. The first two blocks, for example, would each have required two-tenths of a migrant. In the probabilistic model, however, this difficulty does not exist.

Local migration (C). Twenty per cent of the Negro families of each block rounded off to the nearer whole number, are now taken as potential migrants. The rounding off yields a total of nineteen families who will try to migrate from the blocks as indicated by the italic numerals in Fig. 6. To illustrate, let us consider migration from the three blocks identified by a, b, and c in the bottom row. Random numbers are now needed to match against the migration probability field, Fig. 3. Let the random numbers now obtained from the table of random numbers be 49, 75, 14, 50, 36, 68, 26, 12, and 33. The first migrant from a is represented by the random number 49. This provides a location one block to the left of the migrant's origin, X, to d. The second migrant's random number, 75, provides a location two blocks down and one to the left, which is beyond the study area. We interpret this as moot, as though he were replaced by another migrant from outside the area. The third migrant's number, 14, provides a location three blocks up, location f. Since this block has no Negroes, this is only a contact, and no move is made at the time. This is indicated by a dashed line. Now let us proceed to migration from block b. The first migrant's number, 50, provides a location one block to the left, in block a, and the move is made. The second migrant's number, 36, provides a location one block up, in block e, and the move is made. The third migrant's number, 68, provides a location beyond the area. From block c the first migrant's number is 26, a location two blocks up and one to the right. This is an area with no Negroes, and only a contact path is shown. The second migrant's number, 12, provides a location three blocks up and two to the left. This location coincides with the contact made earlier by the third migrant from block a, and the move is made. The third migrant's number, 33, provides a location one block up and one to the left, or block e again, and the move is made. The net result of all this migration is the opening of one new block to settlement, the reinforcement of three blocks, and two lost contacts.

Northward expansion of the ghetto in Seattle

The ghetto in Seattle, with only 25,000 residents, is of course smaller than those in the large metropolises, and it may seem less of a threat to the surrounding area.[19] Nevertheless, the nature of expansion does not differ from one ghetto to another, though the size of the ghetto and the rate of expansion may vary.

The expansion of the Seattle ghetto is shown on Fig. 7, on which the study area is indicated. From 1940 to 1960 the Negro population in the study area more than quadrupled, from 347 families to 1520. Except for a few blocks just north and east of the 1940 Negro area, expansion was into middle-class single-family houses. To the west, where expansion

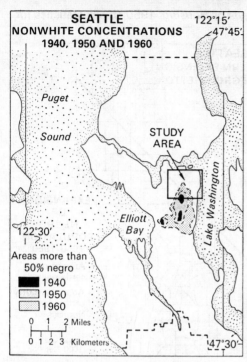

SEATTLE
NONWHITE CONCENTRATIONS
1940, 1950 AND 1960

122°15'
47°45'

Puget

Sound

STUDY
AREA

Elliott
Bay

Lake Washington

122°30'

Areas more than
50% negro

1940
1950
1960

0   1   2 Miles

0 1 2 3 Kilometers

47°30'

Fig. 7 (left). The ghetto
area of Seattle. Source:
Census data for the
relevant years

Fig. 8 (below). Blocks
predominantly Negro in
the northern part of
Seattle's ghetto. Source:
Census of Housing, 1960
(block statistics for Seattle).

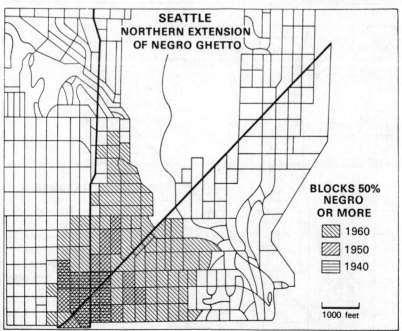

SEATTLE
NORTHERN EXTENSION
OF NEGRO GHETTO

BLOCKS 50%
NEGRO
OR MORE

1960
1950
1940

1000 feet

Figs. 9 and 10. Source: *Census of Housing,* 1950 (block statistics for Seattle.)

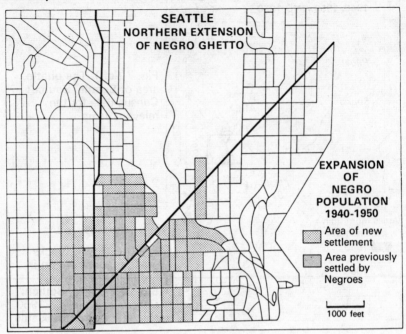

SEATTLE
NORTHERN EXTENSION
OF NEGRO GHETTO

EXPANSION
OF
NEGRO
POPULATION
1940-1950

Area of new settlement

Area previously settled by Negroes

1000 feet

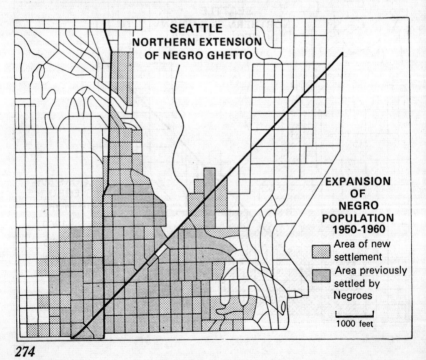

SEATTLE
NORTHERN EXTENSION
OF NEGRO GHETTO

EXPANSION
OF
NEGRO
POPULATION
1950-1960

Area of new settlement

Area previously settled by Negroes

1000 feet

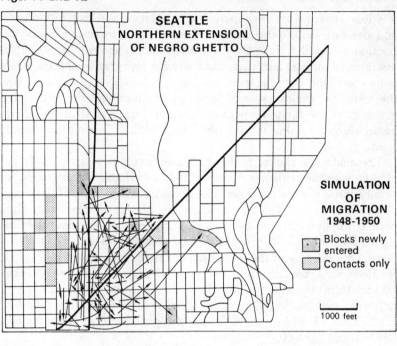

SEATTLE
NORTHERN EXTENSION
OF NEGRO GHETTO

SIMULATION
OF
MIGRATION
1948-1950

Blocks newly
entered

Contacts only

1000 feet

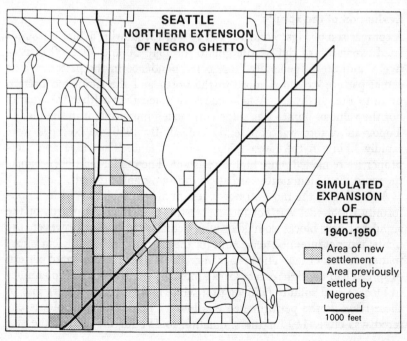

SEATTLE
NORTHERN EXTENSION
OF NEGRO GHETTO

SIMULATED
EXPANSION
OF
GHETTO
1940-1950

Area of new
settlement

Area previously
settled by
Negroes

1000 feet

was least, apartments offer increasing resistance, and to the northwest and along the lake to the east houses reach rather expensive levels. Expansion was easiest along the major south–north and southwest–northeast arterial streets, and northward along a topographic trough where houses and land were the least valuable. The solidity of the ghetto core, the relatively shallow zone of initial penetration, and the consequent extension of the ghetto proper are shown on Figs. 8 to 10. As the ghetto became larger and thus more threatening, transition became more nearly solid.

The model was applied to the study area for ten two-year periods, beginning with the actual conditions of 1940 and simulating migration for twenty years. For each two-year period the natural increase of the Negro population was added to the resident population at the beginning of the period. Immigrants were assigned as in the model. Migrants were assigned according to the probability field (Fig. 3) and the rules of resistance. One example of the simulation of migration is shown on Fig. 11, for 1948–50. Typically, out of 147 potential migrants, 131 were successful and 16 made contacts, but only 8 of the movers pioneered successfully into new blocks. The results of the simulation are illustrated by Figs. 12 and 13, which summarise the changes within two larger periods, 1940–50 and 1950–60.

Evaluation of the results

A comparison of Figs. 9 and 12, and 10 and 13, showing actual and simulated expansion of the Seattle ghetto for 1940–50 and 1950–60 respectively, indicates a generally close correspondence in the patterns. The actual pattern extended more to the north and the simulated pattern more to the northwest. A field check revealed that neither the quality nor the value of homes was sufficiently taken into account in the model. Topography, too, was apparently crucial. By 1960 the Negroes were rapidly filling in the lower-lying, nonview land. The ridge and view properties remained more highly resistant. The model did not recognise the rapid movement northward along the topographic trough.

According to the most stringent test of absolute block-by-block conformity the model was not too successful. Less than two-thirds of the simulated new blocks coincided with actual new blocks. However, the model was not intended to account for the exact pattern. Sufficient information does not exist. The proper test was whether the simulated pattern of spread had the right extent (area), intensity (number of Negro families in blocks), and solidity (allowing for white and Negro enclaves), and in these respects the performance was better. The number of blocks entered was close, 140 for the simulation to 151 for the actual; the size

Figs. 13 and 14

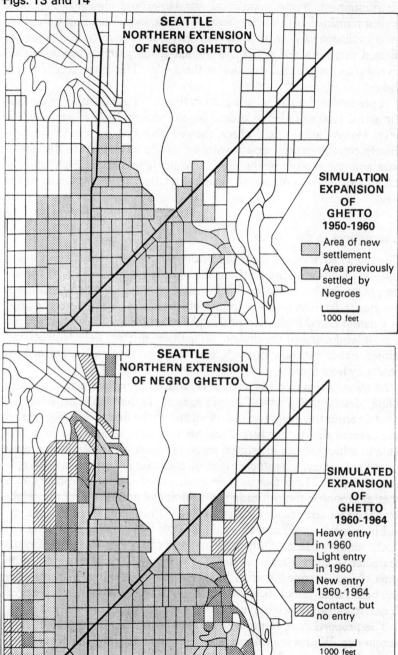

SEATTLE
NORTHERN EXTENSION
OF NEGRO GHETTO

SIMULATION
EXPANSION
OF
GHETTO
1950-1960

Area of new
settlement

Area previously
settled by
Negroes

1000 feet

SEATTLE
NORTHERN EXTENSION
OF NEGRO GHETTO

SIMULATED
EXPANSION
OF
GHETTO
1960-1964

Heavy entry
in 1960

Light entry
in 1960

New entry
1960-1964

Contact, but
no entry

1000 feet

distribution of Negro population was close; and similar numbers of whites remained within the ghetto (with the model tending toward too great exclusion of whites). This similarity, rather than conformance, indicated that both the actual and the simulated patterns *could have occurred* according to the operation of the model. This is the crucial test of theory.

A predictive simulation, as a pattern that could occur, using as the base the actual 1960 situation, was done for the periods 1960–62 and 1962–64 (Fig. 14). A limited field check showed that this pattern is approximately correct, except, again, with too much movement to the northwest and not enough to the north. No prediction from 1964 has been attempted, because of risk of misinterpretation by the residents of the area.

Alternatives to the ghetto

The model attempted merely to identify the process of ghetto expansion and thus helps only indirectly in the evaluation of measures to control the ghetto. We know that such a diffusion process is common in nature— the growth from an origin or origins of something new or different within a parent body. Reduction of this phenomenon would seem to require a great weakening of the distinction between groups, here Negroes and whites, either naturally through new conceptions of each other or artificially by legal means.

In ghetto expansion the process is reduced to replacement of passive white 'deserters' by active Negro migrants. Is there an alternative that would permit the integration of minorities in the overall housing market and prevent the further spread and consolidation of ghettos? Is it possible to achieve stable interracial areas, in which white purchasers, even after Negro entry, are sufficiently numerous to maintain a balance acceptable to both? Three factors have been found crucial: proximity to a ghetto; proportions of white and nonwhite; and preparation of the neighbourhood for acceptance of Negro entry.[20] Proximity to a ghetto almost forbids a stable interracial situation. Fear of inundation either panics or steels white residents. Only wealthy areas can maintain any interracial character in such a location, since few, if any, Negroes can afford to enter. Negroes entering areas remote from the ghetto are more easily accepted (after initial difficulties), because the great body of Negroes does not 'threaten' neighbourhood structures.

The proportion of Negroes in an area is critical for continued white purchasing. Whites are willing to accept 5 per cent to 25 per cent (with a mean of 10 per cent) Negro occupancy for a long time before beginning abandonment—depending on such factors as the characteristics of the Negroes moving in, the proximity of the ghetto, and the open-mindedness of the resident white population. On the other hand, although the Negro is accustomed to minority status, he usually prefers a larger proportion of his own group nearby than the critical 10 per cent. Thus a fundamental dilemma arises, and there are in fact few interracial neighbourhoods. For cities with low Negro ratios, say less than 10 per cent, the long-run possibilities are encouraging, especially with the rise of Negro education and income, increased enforcement of nondiscrimination laws, and the more liberal views of youth today. For urban areas with high Negro ratios, such as Philadelphia, with 20 per cent (40 per cent in the city proper), it is difficult to imagine an alternative to the ghetto. The same conclusion holds for southern cities. No spatial arrangement, given present levels of prejudice, will permit so large a proportion of Negroes to be spread throughout the city without serious white reaction.

Private interracial projects have begun integration and have been successful and stable, if few in number.[21] From these experiments it has been learned that white buyers in such developments are not unusually liberal but are a normal cross section. Also, the spatial arrangement that permits the largest stable proportion of nonwhites has been found to be a cluster pattern—small, compact colonies of a few houses—rather than dispersed isolates.[22] This makes possible easy contact within the minority group, but also good opportunity for interaction with the white group, while minimising the frequency of direct neighbours, which few whites are as yet able to accept.

Integrated residential living will become more acceptable as Negroes achieve equality in education and employment, but housing integration will probably lag years or decades behind. At most we may expect an arrest of the extension of existing ghettos, their internal upgrading, and prevention of new ones. Experience certainly indicates a long wait for goodwill to achieve even internal improvement; hence a real reduction in ghettoisation implies a governmental, not a voluntary, regulation of the urban land and housing market—that is, enforced open-housing ordinances. Everything short of that has already been tried.

The suggested model of diffusion-expansion still describes the dominant ghettoisation pattern. In the future we may be able to recognise an alternative 'colonisation' model, in which small clusters of Negroes or other minorities break out of the ghetto and spread throughout the urban area under the fostering or protection of government.

Notes and references

1 Census Tracts Reports, 1960, *Ser. PHC (1)*, selected cities. Subject Reports (*Census of Population*, 1960, vol. 2), 1960, *Ser. PC (2)*: *Nonwhite Population by Race: State of Birth*, U.S. Bureau of Census, various dates.

2 HANDLIN, OSCAR, *The Newcomers*, New York Metropolitan Region Study, vol. 3, Cambridge, Mass., 1959.

3 ABRAMS, CHARLES, *Forbidden Neighbors*, New York, 1955, p. 19.

4 *Ibid.*, pp. 29–43.

5 MCENTIRE, DAVIS, *Residence and Race*, final and comprehensive report to the Commission on Race and Housing, Berkeley, 1960, pp. 88–104.

6 *Nonwhite Population by Race*, see n. 1 above.

7 Census Tract Reports, see n. 1 above.

8 MCENTIRE, *op. cit.*, pp. 148–56.

9 ABRAMS, *op. cit.*, p. 73.

10 ALSTON, JOHN C. *Cost of a Slum Area*, Wilberforce State College, Wilberforce, Ohio, 1948.

11 RAPKIN, CHESTER, and GRIGSBY, WILLIAM G. *The Demand for Housing in Racially Mixed Areas*, special report to the Commission on Race and Housing, Berkeley 1950, pp. 27–30.

12 GLAZER, NATHAN, and MCENTIRE, DAVIS, eds. *Studies in Housing and Minority Groups*, special research report to the Commission on Race and Housing, Berkeley 1960, pp. 5–11.

13 MCENTIRE, *op. cit.* (n. 5 above), p. 245.

14 LAURENTI, LUIGI M. *Property Values and Race: studies in 7 cities*, special research report to the Commission on Race and Housing, Berkeley 1960. [HOYT, HOMER] *The Structure and Growth of Residential Neighborhoods in American Cities*, Federal Housing Association, Washington, D.C., 1939; RODWIN, LLOYD, 'The theory of residential growth and structure', *Appraisal Journ.* 18 (1950) 295–317.

15 WOLF, ELEANOR P. 'The invasion-succession sequence as a self-fulfilling prophecy', *J. Social Issues* 13 (1957) 7–20.

16 RAPKIN and GRIGSBY, *op. cit.*, pp. 56–8.

17 MEYER, HERBERT A., ed. Symposium on Monte Carlo Methods, held at the University of Florida . . . 16–17 March 1954, New York and London, 1956; ROGERS, EVERETT M. *Diffusion of Innovations*, New York, 1962; SCOVILLE, WARREN C. 'Minority migrations and the diffusion of technology', *J. econ. Hist.* 11 (1951) 347–60.

18 HAGERSTRAND, TORSTEN, 'On Monte Carlo simulation of diffusion', *Quantitative Geography*, ed. W. L. Garrison and D. F. Marble, 1967.

PITTS, FORREST R. 'Problems in computer simulation of diffusion', *Papers and Proc. Regional Science Ass.* 11 (1963) 111–19.

19 SCHMID, CALVIN F., and MCVEY, WAYNE W., jnr. *Growth and Distribution of Minority Races in Seattle, Washington* [Seattle], 1964; WATSON, WALTER B., and BARTH, E. A. T. *Summary of Recent Research Concerning Minority Housing in Seattle*, Institute for Social Research, Dept. of Sociology, University of Washington, 1962; FEI, JOHN C. 'Rent differentiation related to segregated housing markets for racial groups with special reference to Seattle', unpublished Master's thesis, University of Washington, 1949.

[20] GRIER, EUNICE, and GRIER, GEORGE, *Privately Developed Interracial Housing: an analysis of experience*, special report to the Commission on Race and Housing, Berkeley, 1960, pp. 29–30.

[21] *Ibid.*, p. 8.

[22] AMDUR, REUEL S. 'An exploratory study of 19 Negro families in the Seattle area who were first Negro residents in white neighborhoods, of their white neighbors and of the integration process, together with a proposed program to promote integration in Seattle', unpublished Master's thesis in social work, University of Washington, 1962; ROSE, ARNOLD M. and others, 'Neighborhood reactions to isolated Negro residents: an alternative to invasion and succession', *Am. sociol. Rev.* 18 (1953) 497–507; NORTHWOOD, L. K., and BARTH, E. A. T. *Neighborhoods in Transition: the new American pioneers and their neighbors*, University of Washington, School of Social Work, Seattle, pp. 27–8.

Suggested practical exercise

Gravity model

(*Note*. This exercise can be carried out only if the class live in a village or small town so that fairly frequent journeys are necessary to various other larger towns to use the shopping facilities and services of these towns.)

List all the towns within, say, fifty miles that are larger than the home town or village. Using the simple gravity formula:

$$\frac{P_i}{D_i}$$

where P_i = the population of the ith distant town

D_i = straight line distance in miles to the ith distant town

calculate a value for each town. This represents the predicted comparative likelihood that each of the towns will be visited.

Keep a record (perhaps over a month or so) of all journeys made by members of the class, and all members of their households, to each of the towns for which calculations have been made. Compare the distribution of these journeys between the towns with the distribution predicted by the gravity model. (This can perhaps most easily be done by calculating the percentage gained by each town: (i) of the total predicted likelihood and, (ii) of the total number of actual journeys.)

Probably the pair of percentages applying to each town will differ considerably. This would not be surprising as the model used is a very crude one. Try to refine it, bearing in mind the following considerations:

1. Is population, as such, a good index of the attractiveness of a distant town? If not, could information in the Census of Distribution be used to make a better index of attraction to replace P_i?

2. Does D_i adequately represent the 'friction of distance', that is, the force that leads us to make shorter, rather than longer, journeys? Is it sensible to use straight line distances, or miles as a unit of distance? Should the distance value, however expressed, be raised to a power?

On the basis of considerations *1.* and *2.*, and any others that may present themselves, experiment with the simple gravity model until it begins to produce a predicted distribution of journeys that is more closely in accord with the distribution of journeys which actually took place. If a model is produced that gives a reasonable fit with reality, how likely is it that it would 'work' in similar situations elsewhere? And why might is not?

Finally, use the data on the attractiveness of centres, and the distances to them, to satisfy the model contained in the paper by *Huff* in Section 4. In what ways does the Huff model differ from the model developed in this exercise?

Epilogue
A redefinition and some concepts

The development of the 'locationalist' school

The material contained in this book viewed collectively, constitutes a clear statement that human geography has taken a step in a new direction. The outcome of such a step is unknown and it is perfectly within the rights of any well-informed geographer to put up reasoned arguments which would question the wisdom of this step. It is, equally obviously, not within anyone's rights to reject recent trends without a fairly detailed understanding of what is going on. Ignoring recent work and hoping that it will go away is an affront to intellectual integrity and betrays an outlook better left to ostriches.

To provide a well-balanced view, reference should have been made to methodological contributions by researchers who have carried out quantitative and theory-building work and who have been convinced that this approach is suspect, or even misguided, for the study of human geography. But this viewpoint, which no doubt exists, is almost unrepresented in recent literature. The few studies that have questioned the value of recent trends seem mostly to have been written by geographers who have not themselves researched using new methods and they are, to this extent, not valid. Perhaps ten or fifteen years is too short a period for a reasoned critical reaction to have occurred. The alternative view, perhaps a more attractive one, is that human geography really has achieved a significant step forward. If this is so, the ponderous process of reorienting syllabuses below university level ought soon to begin in earnest. In this process those who teach the subject at school have a most important part to play because their special expertise includes a knowledge of the extent to which work of a given level of complexity can be comprehended at various age levels. They also have a clearer idea than academic researchers of the type of work that is likely to stimulate those studying geography in the secondary school system.

By commenting on the various contributions, some attempt has been made to 'interpret' recent trends. Briefly, the trends represent a move to a more careful concern for measurement, for scientific methodology, and for an understanding of process as well as of pattern. These have all been dealt with at length in earlier sections and, as has been pointed out, they are trends which our discipline shares with various related social sciences. If, as they apply in human geography, these trends had to be characterised with a one-word label (so that they could enter into fair competition with, for example, the 'determinist' and 'regionalist' schools of thought) this word could well be 'locationalist'. A concern with the patterns made by phenomena on the earth has for long been central to the geographer's interest. But only recently, it seems, has the spatial pattern made by some phenomena been recognised as the normal point of entry for research work. Only recently has such systematic attention been given to the problem of measuring and interpreting distributions. In short, only recently have the implications of spatial pattern and location been so clearly recognised as the geographer's particular province. It may soon, perhaps, be appropriate to define human geography as *the science of the location and spatial distribution of man and his works*.[1]

The use of spatial concepts

One other aspect of recent developments should be singled out for examination. This is the increasing concern with certain ideas, or concepts, which provide a framework round which geographical work can be organised, much as a modern high building is organised round its steel framework. These ideas, since they are useful in a wide range of situations involving location and spatial distribution, might well be termed *spatial concepts*.[2] The four which have been singled out for brief examination are very diverse in nature and differ widely in their possible application. They do, however, share two vital features. These common features may not become immediately apparent as each concept is considered so they will be discussed at the end. It should be stressed, and indeed it will become obvious, that this brief review of ideas is inadequate for any purpose except to provoke discussion. No attempt is made to provide an inclusive list of concepts or to make any very thorough examination of those that have been selected. The view is intended to provide a guideline towards a mode of study that might relieve some of the tedium inherent in the rote learning of a number of poorly related geographical facts.

1. Gradient

The idea of gradient or slope, when applied to a hill, is well understood by everyone. From a very early stage in geographical training we learn that the most accurate way to show a gradient on a map is by means of contours. In the case of a hill these are lines joining points that share a common value on a scale which measures height above sea level. We get some idea of the steepness of the slope, and the way this steepness varies, by examining the spacing and pattern of the contours.

This is too useful a device to be used solely in relation to height. Scales exist to measure other variables, for example, the density of population. Obtaining suitable data is always a problem but it should be possible to get population density figures for the census divisions of a nearby city and then to construct a rough relief model of these values. This could be done quite quickly by taking a map of the city, erecting a pillar of wood to a height proportional to the density value of each urban division, and then draping some material over the pillars. The peaks and valleys of the *population density surface* will be immediately apparent and those parts of the city where high density housing gives place rapidly to low density (perhaps because there is a railway or river in between) will be easily picked out. Normally in 'western European' cities, including those in previously colonial territories, the population density gradient falls with increasing distance from the city centre. It may fall more steeply in some cities than others or, within the same city, it may fall at a different rate along sectors well served by transport routes to the centre than in sectors not well served. In fact research could be carried to a very advanced level on this problem of the population density gradient of cities.[3]

Surfaces of this type exist, within any city, for such variables as the amount of rent that houses, shops or land are worth, the amount of traffic flowing at important intersections, the proportion of the population working in offices and so on. While the construction of these surfaces may be hampered by the difficulty of obtaining the necessary data, it is as well to remember that they exist and that the surface pattern and gradient of most of them can at least be guessed at.

Other examples of gradient have already been referred to in this book. Figure 3 in the paper by *Huff* in Section 4 depicts a probability surface around a trading centre. In this case the contours join points from which there is an equal probability of going to the centre to shop. In the paper by *Berry and Garrison* in the same section there is a discussion of the gradient likely to be formed by a rank/size curve of city size. The shape of this gradient, and the extent to which it flattens out at various values, is an important indicator of the success of central place theory as a predictor of the comparative size of cities in a region or country. Gradients, in short, crop up in a wide variety of geographical analyses and to restrict their use to the depiction of physical phenomena is to under-use a very productive idea.

2. Network

Most people are aware that a network consists of a number of places, people or things bound together by links of some sort. The existence of underground railway networks, family networks, or electricity powerline networks is known to everyone. The human geographer, at various times, may well be interested in analysing these networks and a great variety of others, including the obvious example of a road network dealt with in *Garrison's* paper in Section 3.

Communication networks exist because in the normal course of events certain things, such as ideas, goods and people, tend not to remain in one place. Ideas are generated at certain localised points (say, an agricultural research institute) and flow outwards. Goods are produced at a limited number of points (factories) and are distributed to a very much larger number of points (houses). People normally have a certain fixed point (their home), from which they travel regularly to other locations. The network used, and the nature of the flow, is clearly different in each case. Ideas tend to flow only one way and they normally use some electronic means of transport (radio or television) or some rapidly transportable written form (newspapers or books). Goods also normally flow one way and they use special compartments in trains, road vehicles, ships or aeroplanes. People use different compartments in these same vehicles, or use their private vehicles, and they almost always flow two ways because they usually return to the point from which they started. The efficiency with which all these flows take place is an important index of the degree of economic development of a region or state. Over the shorter term a temporary or partial breakdown in one of the many networks serving the country is likely to lead to serious or at least irritating consequences. To realise this one need only think of the state of telephone communications after a heavy snowstorm or railway communications during a 'go slow'. Clearly networks are vitally important and because they always have a spatial dimension they are of particular interest to geographers. If the concept of a network is introduced at an early stage of training, using very simple examples, the task of understanding progressively more difficult techniques of network analysis becomes that much easier.

A clear distinction can be drawn, at all levels of study, between the existence of a network and the intensity of its use. In the family situation, a network exists because kin relationships are known. A second cousin in some distant country is known to be part of the family network although we may never have met him. Similarly our family network 'link' with favourite Uncle George is formally as strong as that with frosty Aunt Lavinia because they are both equally distant relatives. But perhaps the flow of letters, presents and visits is much stronger in the case of the former than of the latter. In other words the mere existence of the network is a different thing from the intensity of the use we make of it. Precisely the same distinction applies to any other communication network, whether its function is to carry ideas, goods or people.

It is a relatively simple matter in most cases to determine the degree of interaction taking place along a network and it is often interesting to compare the actual amount of flow with the maximum possible flow. This sort of study has enormous practical significance because when a network link begins to approach saturation, in other words when the actual flow is approaching 100 per cent of the possible flow, important decisions have to be made about how to add extra capacity to the link (or to other parts of the network) or possibly how to reduce the flow in some way. This situation can arise in countless forms, for example in the planning and development of a motorway network, an electricity power grid, a broadcasting network or a telephone system. These problems will all have to be faced by network analysts of one type or another and the human geographer, because of his interest in spatial distributions and the interactions they produce, should be equipped to contribute to their solution. To ensure that this contribution could be made it would be necessary for geographers to have thought in terms of networks for as long a period of their training as possible and to be thoroughly familiar with the techniques of analysis which may be applied to them.

3. Least cost location

Almost any feature that man builds on the earth, for example a factory, an airport, or a new housing estate, is located with a view to the important consideration of minimising the cost of its operation. To decide upon a wise location many cost factors will have to be taken into account and some attempt will have to be made to predict the way in which these costs, and their relative importance, will change over the life of the feature in question. It is possible to point to exceptions to these general remarks. A war memorial, for example, may be located in a very costly position at a central point in a city or perhaps on top of a large mountain, but economic considerations are normally secondary in this type of situation. For most purposes it is sensible to locate buildings used for production, living, or transportation in such a way that the principle of 'least cost' is observed.

Very often, especially in the case of the location of industry, the cost of transporting materials and products plays a large part in the total cost structure and the minimisation of transport costs may be a vital consideration. If this is so, the geographer should be able to cooperate with the economist in choosing a location which has the particular quality that, as far as can be predicted, the cost of moving the necessary materials to and from it is minimised. Analysis of this problem constitutes part of what is normally termed 'economic geography'[4] at college and university level, but there is no reason why some of the principles involved should not be introduced much earlier.

Imagine a situation where we wish to address a group of people who are standing in a circle and we wish to 'economise' on our vocal chords by speaking as softly as possible. We will take up a position in the centre of the circle, assuming for a moment that we can project our voice with equal strength in all directions simultaneously. The central position will suit our purpose best because it is the position that minimises the total distance our voice needs to travel to reach every listener. It is a 'least cost location'. Similarly there is a least cost location when playing a singles match of Badminton. Normally it is near the centre of the court because there is a more or less equal chance of our opponent returning the shuttle to any part of the court. The situation is not quite as simple as in the previous example because the position we take up depends to some extent on the shot we played last, our knowledge of the opponent's game, and the relative speeds with which we can move forwards, backwards, and sideways.

The difference between these simple examples and the problem of finding the least cost location for a steel works or an aluminium smelting works is essentially a difference only in the degree of complexity of the factors involved. Industrial plants need certain inputs of raw or semi-finished materials and they need to send their products to the market or the next stage of manufacture. So clearly part of the calculations which will have to be made to find a least cost location will relate to the cost of transporting things. Calculations will also have to be made concerning other factors such as the supply of labour, the cost of suitable sites for factories, the inducements or controls operated by the government, and the industrial traditions of the area. Study of these principles of industrial location could begin at an early stage with some simple common sense examples and could progress to increasing orders of complexity. This would lead to a situation where students instinctively thought in terms of analysing and explaining a given distribution of industry rather than simply of describing it. But to reach this stage the emphasis would need to rest firmly on a study of the principles, which operate more or less universally, and not on any specific distribution of industry they may have produced in a particular region at a particular point in time.

It could be a useful exercise to think through the main factors that might be operating when the choice of a least cost location has to be made for a new wholesaling market for vegetables in a large city, a new bypass round a town, or a new urban shopping centre. Each of these examples would have a different structure of locational costs, that is to say, the relative importance of land, labour, transport, and building costs would vary, as would the rate of return, either public or private, expected from the investment involved. Unless considerations of this sort are well understood we shall find that while we can *map* the distribution of features in the landscape around us, our *explanations* of them will necessarily be superficial.

4. Cumulative causation

This is a process which operates, very powerfully, in a large number of situations which are of interest to geographers. Briefly, the phrase means that once a process has started to happen then it tends to happen with increasing rapidity until some quite large force intervenes to stop or moderate it. This effect is often known in general speech as a 'snowball' effect and this provides as good an example as any. As the snowball begins to run downhill more snow gets attached and it becomes bigger. But the rate at which it gets bigger increases because this rate is related to the size of the circumference of the snowball and this is itself getting bigger. Thus until some major change occurs in the situation, like reaching the bottom of the hill, a cumulative growth occurs. A moment's thought will suggest other examples of the same idea. Money left in a deposit account grows in a cumulative or compound manner. A new idea spreads at an increasing rate if everyone who hears it tells it to two other people.

For the geographer, this principle of cumulative causation is an invaluable key to the better understanding of a number of processes which give rise to changes in spatial distributions. For example, urban growth is often cumulative in nature. As was pointed out in the section on Central Place Theory, once a town is established it tends to attract new activities partly because it is a centre of population. Newly developed activities tend to be functionally related to the existing activities and so they latch on. The idea that more opportunities for jobs will occur in a big town than in a small one gives people incentive to migrate to a big city, especially in a period of general movement from agricultural to industrial or service jobs. At a certain stage the city becomes so large that every potential migrant feels there must be a niche for him somewhere. In the case of a large city, say London, the process of cumulative growth seems very difficult to stop or even to control. As a result, a whole range of planning restrictions may well be added to the natural operation of market forces (which cause the cost of land, goods, houses and transport to rise) in order to prevent the city stifling itself.

Another example of cumulative causation is presented by the differences in the rate at which regions enjoy economic growth, or suffer economic decline.[5] Whether measured in terms of population change, industrial production, income per head or in some other way, regions exhibit unequal growth records. This can lead, in extreme cases like the north-east of England or South Wales in the 1930s, to economic stagnation, very high rates of unemployment, and to immense hardship and poverty. The reasons for this are very complex. But running through most situations of this sort is the principle of cumulative causation. Once a region begins to lose the market for one of its principle products (for example, coal in the case of South Wales between the wars) a train of consequences ensues. It becomes difficult to attract fresh investment to modernise the means of production. This increases costs, as the machinery becomes outdated, and causes an acceleration in the rate at which markets are lost. The general slowing of activity, and the contraction in the number of jobs available, causes school leavers and other young people to migrate from the region which thus loses the vigorous manpower and new ideas that this group provides. Partly because of the loss of people, the rate income of the local government authorities begins to decline and this means that the provision of social necessities like new housing, and of civic amenities like new swimming baths, becomes much more difficult. The region acquires an 'image' as an area in decline and this may effectively arrest any movement that may take place of people, capital and ideas into the region. Meanwhile the exact reverse of this process may have been occurring elsewhere in the country (say, in London and the West Midlands in the case of Great Britain) so that the economic and social inequalities between regions may rapidly and cumulatively become very great.

Although in the long term it is inevitable, and perhaps even desirable, that some regions should absorb an increasing share of the productive capacity in a country like Britain, it is certainly not desirable that this process should entail hardship, heavy migration between regions or glaring inequalities of wealth, social provision, or employment opportunity. Some means has to be found to adjust and control the great long term processes that, left unchecked, can lead again to the situation that Britain experienced during the 1930s when all these phenomena were clearly evident. The means of control of the distribution of jobs, and thus people, have been many and varied and they have been operated, although with varying degrees of enthusiasm, by all governments since the second world war. They have been directed towards preventing the worst results of a process of cumulative causation which may look 'natural' in the short term but which has been seen to lead to great social evil if left uncontrolled.

As was made clear earlier, this review of concepts has been highly selective. Equally important ideas such as *social polarisation*, which leads to social and ethnic differentiation within cities, have been omitted. Other concepts, such as the interpretation of cities and regions as *dynamic systems* and the way in which phenomena of various types spread over space by processes of *diffusion*, have been dealt with to some extent elsewhere in the book. But more important than the inadequacy of the review is the consideration of the two features which, as was stated earlier, these concepts have in common. These are, first, *the universality of their application* and, second, their characteristic of *progressively increasing complexity*. These will be considered in turn.

Each of the ideas that has been isolated gives valuable clues to the explanation of the changing spatial distribution of features that confront the human geographer. They are able to do this because each word or phrase sums up some universally operating aspect of the total process of man's interaction with his social and physical environment. People everywhere are concerned to save money by wise choice of crops or wise location of factories. People everywhere form part of various networks. Similarly, people everywhere spread ideas and have a natural inclination to live and work with similar, rather than with different, people. The exceptions to these general tendencies are perhaps the exceptions that prove the rules. Each of these fundamental tendencies is summed up in one or other of the concepts outlined and each can, at an appropriate stage of study, be built into a model of some kind.

Methodologically, a form of geographical study which included, from a very early stage, some emphasis on concepts of this type would go some way towards meeting a criticism made of present forms of study in Section 1. This criticism relates to the sense of progression and discovery that should be felt as one proceeds deeper into a subject and which, it was argued, was conspicuously missing from much purely regional work. Each of the concepts mentioned shares the characteristic that it can be made intelligible at the level of complexity required to suit the reader. Thus examples of the working of each concept could be found for those in the first year of secondary education. The same concepts, much elaborated, are likely to appear in doctoral theses. The processes of refinement development, and of discovery of aspects of increasing complexity, that occur between these two stages seem to be much more educationally valid than the long process of accretion of fact which is a more accurate characterisation of much geographical study at the moment.

This is emphatically not to argue that facts are unimportant. One cannot deal with concepts in a factual vaccum. But explanations arise out of the *selection*, *arrangement*, and *interpretation* of those facts and

ANALYTICAL HUMAN GEOGRAPHY

events that seem to be most meaningful in giving a clue to the operation of repeating processes and to the way these processes give rise to repeating spatial patterns. Whether this process of distillation can be effectively carried out if it is undertaken with a particular *region* in mind, rather than a particular *concept or set of concepts*, is perhaps the central question posed by this book.

Notes and references

[1] No great claim for originality is made here. Various others have recently advanced similar definitions. See in particular the opening sentence of YEATES, M. *An Introduction to Quantitative Analysis in Economic Geography*, McGraw-Hill, 1968.

[2] The idea of suggesting the organisation of study round a number of key geographical concepts arose out of a discussion with John Everson, whose contribution towards more enlightened teaching of geography in schools is already considerable.

[3] See, for example, BERRY, B. J. L. 'Urban population densities: structure and change', *Geogr. Rev.* (1963) 389–405, and an earlier paper, CLARK, C. 'Urban population densities', *J. Roy. statis. Soc.*, A, 1951, 490–6.

[4] A recent excellent text on economic geography is CHISHOLM, M. *Geography and Economics*, Bell, 1966 (see especially chap. 3 for problems of industrial location).

[5] For a clear and full discussion of the principle of cumulative causation and its effects on regional growth processes see MYRDAL, G. *Economic Theory and Underdeveloped Regions*, University Paperbacks, 1957 (especially Chapters 1 to 4).

Index of Authors